INNOVATIVE INFRASTRUCTURE FINANCING THROUGH VALUE CAPTURE IN INDONESIA

MAY 2021

Coordinating Ministry for Economic Affairs
Republic of Indonesia

ADB

© 2021 Asian Development Bank
6 ADB Avenue, Mandaluyong City, 1550 Metro Manila, Philippines
Tel +63 2 8632 4444; Fax +63 2 8636 2444
www.adb.org

Some rights reserved. Published in 2021.

ISBN 978-92-9262-852-9 (print); 978-92-9262-853-6 (electronic); 978-92-9262-854-3 (ebook)
Publication Stock No. SPR200093-2
DOI: http://dx.doi.org/10.22617/SPR200093-2

Corrigenda to ADB publications may be found at http://www.adb.org/publications/corrigenda.

Notes:
In this publication, "$" refers to United States dollars, "Rp" refers to Indonesian rupiah, unless otherwise stated.

ADB recognizes "Hong Kong" as Hong Kong, China.

Cover design by Rhommell Rico.

Photo credits (clockwise from left): South Central Business district in Jakarta by AsiaTravel/Shutterstock.com; Jakarta MRT Bundaran HI Station by Shalstock/Shutterstock.com; View of Ampera bridge in Palembang by wide in creative/Shutterstock.com; Jakarta LRT by Joko SL/Shutterstock.com.

Contents

Tables and Figures

Tables

Appendix Tables

Figures

Appendix Figures

Appendixes

Foreword

As noted in the Asian Development Bank report, *Meeting Asia's Infrastructure Needs*, the Asia and Pacific region needs to invest around $1.7 trillion annually in infrastructure until 2030 if it is to maintain robust growth, eradicate poverty, and respond to climate change. The main challenge, however, is the infrastructure investment gap—that is, the difference between investment needs and current investment levels. Closing this gap requires freeing up financial resources through public finance reforms, relying much more on private sector financing, and exploring innovative sources of financing.

An important example of the latter is land value capture (LVC), or more generally, value capture financing. The basic idea is that the positive externalities generated by infrastructure investment are monetized and used to finance infrastructure projects. To help ADB's developing member countries pursue this option, ADB published in 2019 a report, *Sustaining Transit Investment in Asia's Cities*, to serve as a primer on the potential of LVC in financing investments in urban transit infrastructure following global best practices. The report described specifically how megacities in Southeast Asia, such as Bangkok, Jakarta, and Manila could replicate the positive experience with LVCs using land value improvements associated with public mass transit investments.

The present report, *Innovative Infrastructure Financing through Value Capture in Indonesia*, represents a natural progression in ADB's knowledge work on infrastructure finance based on value capture. Its objective is to support the Government of Indonesia in its efforts to build a national framework for value capture. It provides an in-depth analysis of Indonesia's existing policy and regulatory framework in terms of its ability to support this innovative concept and finds that the existing regulatory and taxation frameworks have substantial, but not the complete, components required for successful implementation. It therefore develops a road map of short-term and medium-term action plans for realizing the full potential of value capture.

Infrastructure financing based on value capture provides a new way forward that triggers a virtuous value cycle of value creation and value funding to guarantee repayment and reinvestment of capital, thereby enabling further infrastructure development. With the COVID-19 pandemic constraining the availability of public finances—the main source of funding for infrastructure—exploiting the full potential of tools such as value capture financing has therefore become even more urgent. Cities in emerging economies, such as Jakarta, Makassar, and Palembang in Indonesia, have much to gain from implementing this concept, especially in these unprecedented times.

We hope that this report serves as an important policy tool to support the Government of Indonesia in the preparation of a national-level value capture framework. The report is the outcome of extensive consultations with government stakeholders who provided valuable feedback and insights. ADB will continue to provide technical assistance to help its developing member countries in identifying new and effective financing mechanisms in making cities more livable—one of the key operational priorities of ADB Strategy 2030.

Bambang Susantono
Vice-President for Knowledge Management and Sustainable Development
Asian Development Bank

Acknowledgments

This report was prepared at the request of the Coordinating Ministry for Economic Affairs (CMEA) to support the Government of Indonesia in building a land value capture (LVC) framework that ensures the maximization of the social, economic, and environmental value of infrastructure investments.

The report was financed by the Asian Development Bank (ADB) under Knowledge and Support Technical Assistance 9441: Asia Infrastructure Insights. The groundwork was carried out by the Economic Research and Regional Cooperation Department (ERCD) under the supervision of Rana Hasan, Director of Economic Analysis and Operational Support Division in ERCD and Said Zaidansyah, Deputy Country Director of the Indonesia Resident Mission (IRM), in close coordination with Winfried Wicklein, Country Director of IRM. Kathleen Farrin, Economist, and Matthias Helble, Senior Economist, were the focal persons for this report. Orlee Velarde of ERCD provided technical support and led the production of the report together with Cahyadi Indrananto of IRM. Joanne Gerber edited the manuscript extensively to ensure coherence and consistency. Rhommell Rico designed the cover and typeset the publication.

PT PricewaterhouseCoopers Indonesia Advisory (PwC) led the drafting of the report, which included intensive research, consultations, and documentation. The contributors from PwC were Julian Smith, Euan Low, Faris Saffan, Rudi Setiaji, Gene Maxcell, Jardin Bahar, Regina Wong, Dika Fiisabillillah, Eloisa Fe Lusotan, and Maria Veronica. The contributors of PwC dedicate this report to the memory of Dika Fiisabillillah.

Special thanks are due to the officials from CMEA, namely, Wahyu Utomo, Deputy Minister of Regional Development and Spatial Planning; Bastary Pandji Indra, former Assistant to Deputy Minister for Acceleration and Utilization of Development; Suroto, Assistant to Deputy Minister for Acceleration and Utilization of Development; Yudi Adhi Purnama, Head of Development Utilization Division; Rury Fuadhilah, Subdivision Head of Development Utilization Policy Analysis; and Fachri Firdaus, Economic Analyst. They provided feedback and inputs during the report drafting process and together with ADB, also facilitated the planning of in-country workshops. The active participation of the representatives from government offices from different regions during the in-country workshops and discussion meetings is highly appreciated.

Yasuyuki Sawada
Chief Economist and Director General
Asian Development Bank

Abbreviations

Term	Definition
ADB	Asian Development Bank
APBD	Anggaran Pendapatan Belanja Daerah (Regional Revenue and Expenditure Budget)
APBN	Anggaran Pendapatan Belanja Negara (State Revenue and Expenditure Budget)
ATR/BPN	Kementerian Agraria dan Tata Ruang/Badan Pertanahan Nasional (Ministry of Agrarian Affairs and Spatial Planning/National Land Agency)
BAPPEDA	Badan Perencanaan Pengembangan Daerah (Regional Agency for Planning and Development)
BAPPENAS	Badan Perencanaan Pembangunan Nasional (Ministry of National Development Planning/ National Development Planning Agency)
BCDA	Bases Conversion and Development Authority (Philippines)
BLUD	badan layanan umum daerah (local public service agency)
BMN/D	property of the state/region
BOT	Build–Operate–Transfer
BPHTB	bea perolehan hak atas tanah dan bangunan (duty on the acquisition of land and building rights)
CAGR	compound annual growth rate
CAPEX	capital expenditure
CMEA	Coordinating Ministry for Economic Affairs
CMMIA	Coordinating Ministry for Maritime and Investment Affairs
DINFRA	Dana Investasi Infrastruktur (Infrastructure Investment Fund)
DKI	Daerah Khusus Ibukota (Special Capital Region)
DMC	developing member country
ECBA	economic cost–benefit analysis
FAR	floor area ratio (also "KLB")
FSI	floor space index
FSR	floor space ratio
GDP	gross domestic product
GFA	gross floor area
GRDP	gross regional domestic product
HGB	hak guna bangunan (right to build)
HGU	hak guna usaha (right to cultivate)
IMF	International Monetary Fund
IUKI	Izin Usaha Kawasan Industri (Industrial Estate Business Permit)
KKOP	kawasan keselamatan operasi penerbangan (aviation operations safety zone)
KLB	koefisien lantai bangunan (floor area ratio, also "FAR")
KLHS	kajian lingkungan hidup strategis (strategic environmental assessment)
LRT	Light Rail Transit
LVC	land value capture
MOF	Ministry of Finance
MOHA	Ministry of Home Affairs
MRT	Mass Rapid Transit (Jakarta)
MTR	Mass Transit Railway (Hong Kong, China)
NIB	nomor induk berusaha (single business number)
NJKB	nilai jual kendaraan bermotor (motor vehicle sales value)
NJOP	nilai jual objek pajak (sales value of a taxable object)

OECD	Organisation for Economic Co-operation and Development
OJK	Otoritas Jasa Keuangan (Financial Services Authority)
OPEX	operational expenditure
PILOT	payment in lieu of taxes
PNBP	nontax state revenue
PTSL	Pendaftaran Tanah Sistematis Lengkap (Complete Systematic Land Register)
RDPT	*reksadana penyertaan terbatas* (limited participation mutual fund)
RDTR	*rencana detil tata ruang* (detailed spatial plan)
ROE	regional-owned enterprise
RPJMN	Rencana Pembangunan Jangka Menengah Nasional (National Medium-Term Development Plan)
RTBL	urban design guidelines
RTRW	*rencana tata ruang dan wilayah* (regional spatial plan)
SDG	Sustainable Development Goal
SKBG	*sertifikat kepemilikan bangunan gedung* (building ownership certificate)
SLF	*sertifikat laik fungsi* (function-worthiness certificate)
SOE	state-owned enterprise
TEP	tax equivalent payment
TIF	tax increment financing
TOD	transit-oriented development
UDGL	urban design guidelines
UN	United Nations
VGF	viability gap funding

Legal Abbreviations

Term	Definition[1]
Law 39/2008	Law No. 39 of 2008 on State Ministries
Law 2/2018	Law No. 2 of 2018 on the Second Amendment of Law No. 17 of 2014 on the People's Consultative Assembly, House of Representatives, Regional Representative Council, and Regional House of Representatives
Law 17/2003	Law No. 17 of 2003 on State Finance
Law 1/2004	Law No. 1 of 2004 on the State Treasury
Law 15/2004	Law No. 15 of 2004 on the State Financial Management and Accountability Audit
Law 20/2019	Law No. 20 of 2019 on the State Budget for Fiscal Year 2020
Law 9/2018	Law No. 9 of 2018 on Nontax State Revenues
Law 33/2004	Law No. 33 of 2004 on Fiscal Balance between the Central and Regional Governments
Law 23/2014	Law No. 23 of 2014 on Regional Government (as last amended by Law No. 9 of 2015 on the Second Amendment of Law No. 23 of 2014 on Regional Government)
Law 17/2014	Law No. 17 of 2014 on People's Consultative Assembly
Law 28/2002	Law No. 28 of 2002 on Building

---

[1]   The details of these laws and regulations are given and explained in Appendix 5.

Term	Definition[1]
Law 28/2009	Law No. 28 of 2009 on Local Tax and Retribution
Law 5/1960	Law No. 5 of 1960 on Basic Agrarian Law
Law 2/2012	Law No. 2 of 2012 on Land Procurement in the Public Interest
Law 20/2011	Law No. 20 of 2011 on Strata Title Buildings
Law 25/2007	Law No. 25 of 2007 on Capital Investment
Law 26/2007	Law No. 26 of 2007 on Spatial Planning
Law 29/2009	Law No. 29 of 2009 on Regional Taxes and Levies
Law 32/2009	Law No. 32 of 2009 on Environmental Protection and Management
Law 1/2011	Law No. 1 of 2011 on Housing and Settlement Areas
Law 4/1996	Law No. 4 of 1996 on Encumbrance Right over Land and Land-Related Objects
GR 24/2005	Government Regulation No. 24 of 2005 on Government Accounting Standards
GR 24/1997	Government Regulation No. 24 of 1997 on Land Registration
GR 63/2019	Government Regulation No. 63 of 2019 on Government Investment
GR 10/2011	Government Regulation No. 10 of 2011 on Procedures of Foreign Loan Procurement and Grants Receipt
GR 39/2007	Government Regulation No. 39 of 2007 on State/Regional Cash Management
GR 40/1996	Government Regulation No. 40 of 1996 on the Right to Cultivate, Right to Build, and Right of Use over Land
GR 12/2019	Government Regulation No. 12 of 2019 on Regional Financial Management
GR 27/2014	Government Regulation No. 27 of 2014 on the Management of State/ Regional Property
GR 15/2010	Government Regulation No. 15 of 2010 on Spatial Planning Implementation
GR 30/2011	Government Regulation No. 30 of 2011 on Regional Loans
GR 142/2015	Government Regulation No. 142 of 2015 on Industrial Estates
GR 72/2019	Government Regulation Number 72 of 2019 on Local Government Structure
PR 11/2015	Presidential Regulation No. 11 of 2015 on Ministry of Home Affairs
PR 71/2012	Presidential Regulation No. 71 of 2012 on the Implementation of Land Procurement in the Public Interest, as amended by Presidential Regulation No. 148 of 2015, Presidential Regulation No. 30 of 2015, Presidential Regulation No. 99 of 2014, and Presidential Regulation No. 40 of 2014
PR 38/2015	Presidential Regulation No. 38 of 2015 on Cooperation between Government and Business Entities in Infrastructure Procurement
PR 9/2016	Presidential Regulation No. 9 of 2016 on the Acceleration of the Implementation of the One Map Policy

Term	Definition[1]
BAPPENAS 4/2015	Ministry of National Development Planning/National Development Planning Agency Regulation No. 4 of 2015 on the Procedure for Cooperation between Government and Business Entities in Procurement of Infrastructure
MOE 69/2017	Minister of Environment Regulation No. 69 of 2017 on Environmental Assessment Study Guidelines
MOHA 33/2019	Minister of Home Affairs Regulation No. 33 of 2019 on Local Government Budget Development Guidelines
MOF 111/PMK.07/2012	Minister of Finance Regulation No. 111/PMK.07/2012 on Procedures for the Issuance and Accountability of Municipal Bonds, as amended by Minister of Finance Regulation No. 180/PMK.07/2015
MOAASP/NLA 17/2019	Minister of Agrarian Affairs and Spatial Planning/Head of National Land Agency Regulation No. 17 of 2019 on Location Permits
MOAASP/NLA 16/2017	Minister of Agrarian Affairs and Spatial Planning/Head of National Land Agency Regulation No. 16 of 2017 on Guidelines for Transit-Oriented Development
MOAASP/NLA 16/2018	Minister of Agrarian Affairs and Spatial Planning/Head of National Land Agency Regulation No. 16 of 2018 on the Instruction Guide, Detailed Spatial Plan and Regency/City Zoning Regulation
MOT 75/2015	Minister of Transportation Regulation No. 75 of 2015 on Traffic Impact Assessments
MPW 06/2017	Minister of Public Works Regulation No. 06/PRT/M/2007 on Building Blocks and Neighborhood Plan Guidelines
MPWH 7/2013	Minister of Public Works and Housing Regulation No. 7 of 2013 on the Implementation of Housing and Settlement Areas
MPWPH 5/2016	Minister of Public Works and Public Housing Regulation No. 5/PRT/M/2016 on Building Construction Permits, as amended by Minister of Public Works and Public Housing Regulation No. 6/PRT/M/2017
MPWPH 11/2019	Minister of Public Works and Public Housing Regulation No. 11/PRT/M/2019 on the Preliminary House Purchase Agreement System
MONDP 4/2015	Minister of National Development Planning/Head of National Development Planning Agency Regulation No. 4 of 2015 on the Procedure of Cooperation between the Government and Business Entities in Infrastructure Procurement
Governor DKI 67/2019	DKI Jakarta Governor Regulation No. 67 of 2019 on the Implementation of Transit-Oriented Areas
OJK 52/2017	Financial Services Authority Regulation No. 52/POJK.04/2017 on Infrastructure Investment Funds in the Form of Collective Investment Contracts
OJK 37/POJK.04/2014	Financial Services Authority Regulation No. 37/POJK.04/2014 on Private Funds

Foreign Exchange Rates

In this report, "$" refers to United States dollars.

The Indonesian rupiah (Rp)–United States dollar exchange rate used throughout this document is 14,070:1 (in September 2019)

Executive Summary

This report finds that value capture has significant potential for addressing several of the Government of Indonesia's key challenges:

- Building economic corridors will create jobs, social inclusion, and fiscal stability. It will entail developing transport infrastructure, not through stand-alone projects, but through projects that will be part of the creation of economic corridors that will deliver transformational urban regeneration.
- A virtuous value cycle can close the infrastructure funding gap. It can provide a progressive whole-of-government and policy framework-based approach to creating value, capturing value, and engendering confidence that a share of the incremental economic uplift will be used to repay the up-front financing of the original investments.
- Value capture can be deployed in Indonesia. The existing regulatory and taxation frameworks have been assessed and found to have substantial, but not the complete, components required for a value capture policy framework. Road maps of short-term and medium-term action plans are provided in this report for securing immediate benefits and for achieving the frameworks' full potential.

Introduction

Investment in urban and transport infrastructure generally stimulates economic productivity. However, the government is facing a funding shortfall that is constraining its ability to commit to the up-front financing of infrastructure investments. It is therefore trying to find ways to financially support the growth of economic productivity.

Urban and transport infrastructure are key components of the achievement of the United Nations (UN) Sustainable Development Goals (SDGs), especially Goal 11: Creating Sustainable Cities and Communities. To this end, this report outlines options available to the government for the preparation of a national-level value capture policy framework.

It looks at Indonesia's existing policy and regulatory framework in terms of its ability to support value capture as a basis for proactive planning for enhanced economic productivity. It is envisaged that the economic benefits will contribute to the funding of up-front investment, thus reducing the funding shortfall.

Section 1 of this report sets out the challenges, solutions, and expected outcomes.

CHALLENGES: There is a strong rationale for urban and transport infrastructure. However, four key challenges are hindering investment in the sector:

- Urbanization in Indonesia is resulting in high-density conurbations that can increase economic output, but it has caused intense traffic congestion. Public transport infrastructure helps reduce congestion, but it is too expensive to fund solely through ticketing revenue.
- The fiscal situation is marked by a funding shortfall, so there is a fundamental need to use increasing economic output to fund the country's development plans. The Indonesian government has a relatively low level of taxation relative to other countries in the region. The current low level of taxation cannot sustain the targeted level of infrastructure investment. There is a need to identify alternative approaches that could increase the funding for infrastructure projects, and thus provide improved access to larger volumes of finance.
- Appraisals of overall transport project viability normally have a very narrow focus on revenues

Figure 1: Challenges, Solutions, and Expected Outcomes

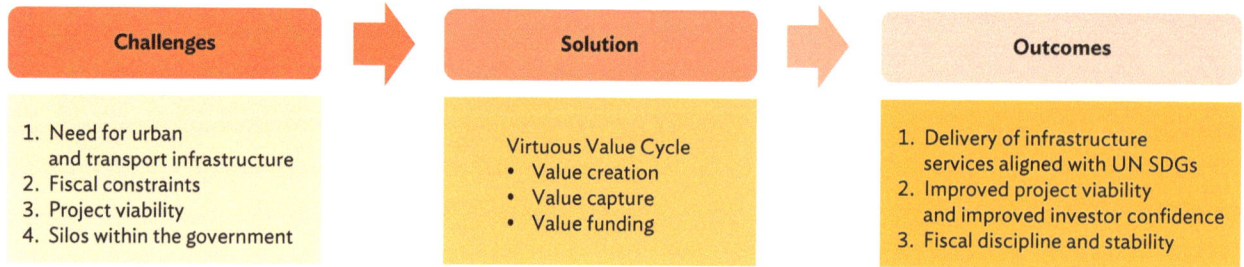

Challenges	Solution	Outcomes
1. Need for urban and transport infrastructure 2. Fiscal constraints 3. Project viability 4. Silos within the government	Virtuous Value Cycle • Value creation • Value capture • Value funding	1. Delivery of infrastructure services aligned with UN SDGs 2. Improved project viability and improved investor confidence 3. Fiscal discipline and stability

SDG = Sustainable Development Goal, UN = United Nations.
Source: Authors.

from fares and non-fare sources, time savings, and vehicle savings, while ignoring the fundamental motivation for investing in public transport infrastructure: to enable corridors for increased economic activity.

• Shortfalls in economic planning, land use planning, and infrastructure procurement will often lead to escalating project costs and program overruns.

SOLUTION: Introduce the virtuous value cycle.

Value capture provides a broad and useful perspective regarding the harnessing of economic productivity. Recognizing the difference between funding and financing is also important.

The virtuous value cycle provides a progressive whole-of-government and policy framework-based approach to creating value, capturing value, and engendering confidence that a share of the incremental economic uplift will be allocated to the repayment of the up-front financing used for the original investments. Value creation is based on the observation that public transport infrastructure enables corridors for increased economic activity.

The approach seeks only to apply value capture mechanisms to a share of the incremental economic uplift created; there is no impingement on the original tax base or on other functions that depend on that tax base.

The virtuous value cycle is based on four thematic principles and seven specific principles that can be used to appraise the readiness of Indonesia's regulatory framework for enabling value capture, and they are described in Table 1.

Figure 2: Virtuous Value Cycle: The Virtuous Value Relationship among Value Creation, Value Capture, and Value Funding

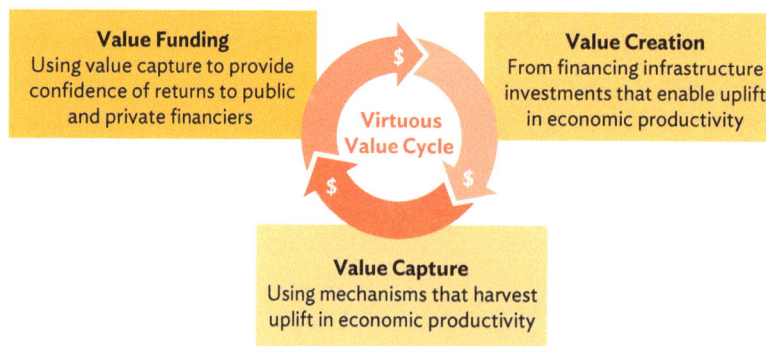

Value Funding
Using value capture to provide confidence of returns to public and private financiers

Value Creation
From financing infrastructure investments that enable uplift in economic productivity

Virtuous Value Cycle

Value Capture
Using mechanisms that harvest uplift in economic productivity

Source: Authors.

Table 1: Thematic and Specific Principles of the Virtuous Value Cycle	
Thematic Principles	**Specific Principles**
Basic Theme Land as a factor of economic productivity	1 **Economic productivity** is derived from the use of land, and serviced land creates greater value. A strategic and sustainable view of land use, based on sound land administration and management, is key to unlocking the economic potential of land.
Value Creation A more consistent, concerted approach by government to assessing and increasing the benefits of public investments	2 **A whole-of-government approach** ensures that the intended value is delivered, and that any value created is shared. This, in turn, creates a high-trust society in which a virtuous cycle of infrastructure investment improves the quality of life.
	3 **Master planning through a comprehensive economic cost-benefit analysis,** takes the United Nations Sustainable Development Goals as the starting point, and maximizes the economic, social, and environmental benefits from public investment in infrastructure.
	4 **An investment to create connectivity through the integration of urban development with transport planning** will enhance economic output and create a stable demand for economic infrastructure.
Value Capture The government capturing a portion of the incremental economic value created by public investments, activities, and policies	5 **Public action should generate public benefits.** Shifting the focus toward beneficiary funding acknowledges both the direct and indirect beneficiaries, including the government and private sector.
	6 **Value capture is only possible when value has been created.** It should not be preemptive, as this will only increase costs and make economic growth more difficult.
Value Funding Confidence regarding investments as a means of unlocking financing	7 **Value capture unlocks financing** by boosting the confidence of private investors in infrastructure projects, and enables the recycling and reinvestment of capital into further infrastructure development.

Source: Authors.

The need for a whole-of-government approach is emphasized, so that stakeholders' efforts are geared toward increasing benefits from public investments in infrastructure in order to maximize economic, social and environmental gains.

International practice has shown that where there is policy-based government commitment to and support for infrastructure asset and service delivery, there is increased private investor confidence.

A framework for assessing the current status and enablers of institutional readiness for value capture has been developed based on the seven principles of value capture.

OUTCOMES: Implementing a value capture policy framework will deliver three strategic and tangible outcomes:

- The whole-of-government approach required by value capture will be closely aligned with the planning and delivery of the UN SDGs, especially by providing a means for calculating and sharing the economic and commercial benefits across different parts of government.
- Implementing value capture principles will give a more robust approach to planning the development of economic corridors connected by public transport infrastructure, and will increase investor confidence regarding the returns on investment.
- Implementing a value capture policy framework will provide more robust economic planning for the creation of economic uplift while integrating the implementation of value capture mechanisms. The tighter control and monitoring that should arise from this approach will provide enhanced fiscal discipline and stability.

Section 2 sets out the current regulatory and institutional framework.

The Indonesian regulatory framework provides clear legal provisions, relevant to value capture implementation, that govern how the public finance budget is collected, allocated, and spent in Indonesia; and they are applicable to national and local levels of government, the latter including provinces, cities, and regencies. In general, the local governments have autonomy regarding the management of their budgets, with potential financial support from the national government.

The existing tax-and-fee regime limits the introduction of new taxes other than those already regulated. However, there are indications that a partial earmarking of tax and fee revenue is possible for transport and health within the current regulatory framework, opening the potential for further exploration.

The initial assessment of the Indonesian regulatory framework for public finance, planning for urban and transit infrastructure, land administration, and investments highlighted the fact that, while there are restrictions on the government's ability to introduce new types of taxes or fees, there is an opportunity to implement selected value capture instruments through the existing tax and fee mechanisms.

National fiscal revenue is mostly managed centrally through a "melting pot" of subsequent budgetary reallocations, which is a mechanism used by many governments worldwide. The government budget is allocated annually, and redistributed to cover all types of spending required to carry out government programs and projects, including infrastructure spending, either through direct spending (for capital and operating expenditures), indirect spending (through financial assistance and subsidies for infrastructure), or finance spending (through equity injections for infrastructure development). There is no effective process for making multiyear budgetary commitments.

Indonesia carries out economic planning at the regional level and has a well-established regulatory framework for developing urban and transport projects based on spatial planning. However, economic planning has not been carried out for the economic corridors that are to be linked by transport projects. Further, the existing spatial planning framework is not efficient at creating value for the government.

There is a well-developed regulatory framework for land management from a spatial planning perspective. However, it is weakly connected with economic planning, value creation, and value capture.

The regulatory framework for investment is broadly aligned with the principles of value capture, but caution is required to ensure that the incentives given to investors do not undermine the implementation of the planned value capture.

The implementation of value capture mechanisms in Indonesia may require the involvement and support of multiple government organizations. While decentralization provides local governments with some degree of freedom, the fact that the relevant sectors are governed by several agencies and institutions poses a challenge in terms of developing a collaborative approach.

Analysis and discussions with the relevant stakeholders have shown that a whole-of-government approach to value capture implementation would be constrained by a regulatory and institutional framework that is perceived to be too rigid, too specific, and difficult to change. Therefore, the challenge is in both building the capacity of the relevant parties and in demonstrating how to incorporate suitable value capture mechanisms into the development of business cases for large-scale infrastructure projects.

Section 3 sets out the recommended value creation framework for Indonesia.

For the effective implementation of value creation, a clear value creation framework needs to be developed, based on the building of economic infrastructure that will provide industry, commerce, and society with the key services needed to boost economic productivity. However, several crucial issues have been identified with regard to the Indonesian long-term land-use planning and regulatory framework, which will require attention going forward.

Economic theory recognizes value creation as a consistent approach that continually assesses and improves the benefits of public investments. But while value creation activities are commonplace, their implementation within a policy framework is still relatively novel. A review of international case studies on policy-based value creation has revealed four enablers of value creation: (i) land use planning and regulatory frameworks, (ii) a whole-of-government approach, (iii) economic planning, and (iv) an integrated development approach.

Value creation is achieved by financing infrastructure investments that enable growth in economic productivity.

During the assessment of the applicability of the current Indonesian framework to value creation, it was found that, while there are some obstacles to value creation, a potentially suitable entry point would be to incorporate value creation principles into the development of planning documents, and into the business cases for infrastructure projects.

Section 4 sets out the recommended value capture framework for Indonesia.

For the effective implementation of value capture, there must first be a clear identification and quantification of the positive effects on economic productivity—for instance as seen in tax revenues, gross domestic product (GDP), per capita GDP, the rate of return, employment, and other factors—that have resulted from a policy change or an infrastructure project investment. Additionally, the key beneficiaries of these economic and commercial gains must also be identified. Once these inputs are available, the value capture framework will provide a range of tools that can be used to harvest a share of the economic uplift. Value capture mechanisms have been identified (such as various categories of taxes and fees), and low-hanging fruits that could be implemented by local and national governments have also been identified.

Value capture is a mechanism whereby the government captures a portion of the incremental economic value created by the government's own investment activities and policies, and uses it as a funding source in addition to the gains from typical "government pays" and "user pays" models.

The focus is not on increasing the rate of taxation, but on increasing economic productivity, so that the volume of fiscal revenue can be increased.

Value capture is an actively planned method of improving fiscal revenue, in contrast to the current passive approach; it is a more sophisticated and layered approach that identifies the beneficiaries and quantifies the benefits, and then uses not only "government pays" and "user pays" mechanisms, but also "beneficiary pays."

Both the government and the private sector can deploy value capture mechanisms to generate broader economic, social, and environmental benefits from investments in infrastructure. International best practices have indicated that governments typically employ tax- and fee-based mechanisms, while the private sector could benefit from employing development-based mechanisms.

The Indonesian regulatory framework for public financing presents a multilayered set of tax- and fee-based instruments that are being used to capture value from both individuals and businesses. Fiscal revenue goes through the national finance system, which uses a widely recognized "melting-pot" approach before allocating fiscal resources as part of the national government's annual expenditure budgets.

This section also includes a readiness analysis regarding the potential introduction of value capture instruments through existing mechanisms.

The flow and quantities of public funds have been mapped from the source to the budgeted expenditure. The analysis shows effective taxation and the opportunities to adjust the burden of taxation in order to encourage behavioral change, such as a shift in the mode of transport from private vehicles to public transport. However, local governments rely substantially on taxes relating to the use of private vehicles, which can conflict with policies that seek to encourage a shift toward public transport, and thus may reduce local fiscal revenues.

Jakarta has a significantly greater revenue from property taxes than does Makassar, which in part reflects the fact that greater building density in the core of a city can support a denser level of economic productivity.

A detailed analysis of Indonesia's tax- and fee-based readiness for value capture is presented, together with commentary on how this can be applied or improved from a regulatory, technical, and institutional perspective. The potential for each tax category to be used as a value capture channel is also described.

An analysis of the taxes and fees recognized and collected in Indonesia has been conducted and benchmarked against international best practice to provide a gap analysis and identify where there is a potential for introducing more targeted value capture mechanisms. The gap analysis has revealed several areas where targeted taxes or fees could be introduced to recover value from beneficiaries.

There is a potential to increase the volume of property tax revenue by making the taxation system more efficient—in particular, by bringing the registered property values into alignment with real market values, and then keeping these registered values up to date.

The use of geographical information system (GIS) analysis has revealed a significant increase in market-based land value from the initial construction of MRT Jakarta (2014) to the pre-operation of the system (2017). Land values of more than Rp10 million, or $800, per square meter were observed around selected MRT stations.

Increasing the rate of the property tax per unit may not be politically preferable, as most land within a 700-meter radius of an MRT Jakarta station is used for residential housing. Moreover, increasing the unit costs will encourage gentrification through higher living costs. Thus, increasing revenues from property taxes should be through one or both of the following measures:

- increasing property taxes through updated property value assessments; and/or
- increasing transit connectivity and enabling denser urbanization to boost the total gross floor area, thus increasing the volume of tax receipts.

Section 5 sets out the recommended value funding framework.

Value funding means using policy-based value capture to build confidence in the financial returns on investment for public and private financiers. The key requirements are:

- a legal framework that gives an appropriate party or parties the mandate to develop and implement a virtuous value cycle within an economic corridor; and
- a mandate for a qualified party or parties to implement appropriate value capture mechanisms in order to recover revenue that has the potential to repay the financing used for the initial investments, for a term at least sufficient for repaying the financing used for the initial investments.

Four internationally used, policy-based value funding mechanisms are introduced and evaluated. All have the potential for deployment, but each requires further policy and regulatory development to achieve its full potential. The summary of the evaluation of Indonesia's readiness to apply these four mechanisms is presented in Table 2.

Section 6 sets out the road map toward a value creation and value capture policy.

Achieving the benefits of value capture in infrastructure financing will require the identification

Table 2: Summary of the Evaluation of Indonesia's Readiness to Apply Four Value Funding Mechanisms

Enabler	Readiness			
	Public-to-Public	Hypothecated Tax	PILOT	Concessions
Whole-of-government approach	¼	¼	¼	¼
Visionary economic master planning	¾	¾	¾	¾
Long-term land-use planning and regulatory framework	full	full	¾	full
Integrated urban and transport development	¾	½	½	¾
Value capture-oriented taxation regime	¾	¼	½	full

PILOT = payment in lieu of taxes.
Note: The proportion of shaded color in each circle shows the extent of readiness.
Source: Authors.

and appointment of a lead policy institution and a lead implementing institution. Five institutions have been identified as essential for the development of a successful value capture policy framework:

- the **Ministry of Finance**, to ensure that a mechanism is in place for channeling funds to repay up-front investments;
- the **Coordinating Ministry for Economic Affairs (CMEA)** and the **Coordinating Ministry for Maritime and Investment Affairs (CMMIA)**, which are well placed to drive the creation of an overarching policy framework, and to guide and monitor value capture implementation at the relevant ministries and agencies;
- the **Ministry of Spatial Planning**, to manage land use in a way that maximizes value creation and value capture; and
- the **Ministry of National Development Planning/National Development Planning**

Agency (BAPPENAS), to drive value capture innovation in the preparation of infrastructure investments.

The action plan in the short term (12 months) should focus on the establishment of the policy framework, capacity building, and the implementation of a pilot project. This could commence immediately, and be scheduled for full implementation within 2 years.

The lead policy institution should be selected from among the existing coordinating ministries, and the **CMEA is considered the best fit for this role**. The lead policy institution, in coordination with key stakeholders, should then prepare the legal framework for:

- providing national guidance on the fair and lawful monetization and capture of economic benefits, and on the channeling of the proceeds toward repaying infrastructure financing;

Figure 3: Short-Term Action Plan

Select lead policy institution → Prepare national LVC legal framework → Select lead implementing institution → Select specific pilot project(s)

LVC = land value capture.
Source: Authors.

- mandating a lead implementing institution to authorize and oversee the overall infrastructure project cycle with regard to value capture, a role for which **BAPPENAS is considered the best fit**; and
- coordinating with key ministries and agencies to adopt a "whole-of-government" approach.

When the national legal framework is in place, the lead implementing institution should develop a set of national value capture implementing guidelines, select a specific pilot project, and advise on the project's preparation and implementation in terms of value capture.

The action plan in the medium term (48 months) should focus on optimizing the tax and landownership framework to strengthen and broaden value capture opportunities, and on implementing large transformation programs with a view to creating economic corridors.

The lead policy institution should drive regulatory changes in the national tax framework to improve revenue collection effectiveness, such as new mandatory fees and formula adjustments in existing taxes related to property, development, and utilities, so that developers are encouraged to align their planning with the government's. It should also consider introducing tax increment financing to unlock further financing for infrastructure development.

Regulatory changes in the landownership framework should look to optimize the use of state assets, notably the ownership of apartment units constructed above state assets (SKBG), by way of allowing mixed-use development (a combination of infrastructure assets and residential or commercial areas). Other areas for exploration include:

- the right to utilize state or regional government assets as security for the benefit of financiers;
- the right to build stations and transit-oriented developments on privately owned lands; and
- air rights and underground rights, which will allow the construction of infrastructure above or below private properties.

The above regulatory changes should be reflected in national guidelines for land value capture, and then implemented. The lead implementing institution should continue to support the line ministries and local governments involved in implementing programs that drive economic growth through enhanced infrastructure connectivity.

The creation of a set of national value capture guidelines is recognized as essential for capacity building. The guidelines will need to be tailored, and the United Kingdom's "Better Business Case" methodology is proposed as a potential basis for developing these guidelines.

Improved tax collection efficiency is highlighted as a key policy that could also bring quick benefits to the government.

Figure 4: Medium-Term Action Plan

| Make regulatory changes in national tax framework | Amend laws and regulations on landownership | Implement national LVC legal framework | Implement economic development corridor projects |

LVC = land value capture.
Source: Authors.

1. Introduction: A Whole-of-Government Approach to the Funding and Financing of Urban and Transport Infrastructure

Although investments in urban and transport infrastructure generally stimulate economic productivity, the Government of Indonesia faces a funding shortfall that constrains its ability to commit to the up-front financing of infrastructure investments.

Urban and transport infrastructure are key components of achieving the United Nations (UN) Sustainable Development Goals (SDGs), especially Goal 11: creating sustainable cities and communities. To this end, this report outlines options available to the government regarding the preparation of a national-level land value capture (LVC) framework.

It appraises Indonesia's existing policy and regulatory framework with regard to supporting value capture as a holistic means of proactive planning for enhanced economic productivity, such that incremental economic benefits can contribute to the funding for up-front investments, thus reducing funding shortfalls.

This chapter, as outlined in Figure 1.1, identifies the challenges that currently exist in the financing and funding infrastructure, value capture's ability to address these challenges, and the target outcomes expected from value capture.

1.1. Challenges

There is a strong rationale for urban and transport infrastructure. However, four key challenges are hindering investment in the sector.

Challenge #1: Need for Urban and Transport Infrastructure

Urbanization in Indonesia has resulted in high-density conurbations, which can increase economic output, but also causes intense traffic congestion. Public transport infrastructure enables corridors for increased economic activity. However, public transport infrastructure is too expensive to be funded solely through passenger ticket sales.

Figure 1.1: Schematic Diagram of Chapter 1

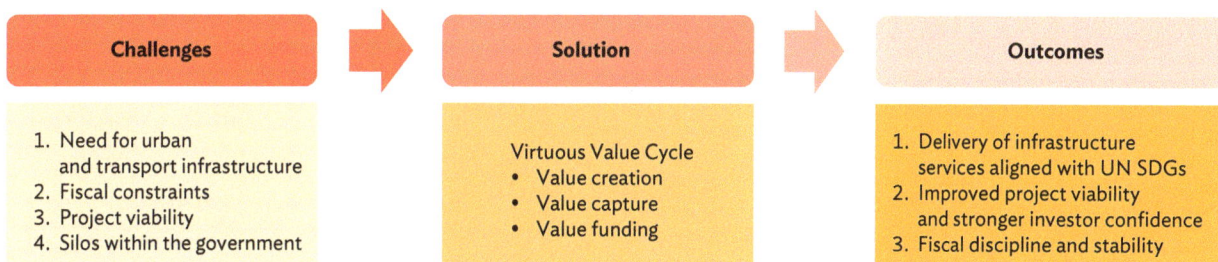

SDG = Sustainable Development Goal, UN = United Nations.
Source: Authors.

Urban infrastructure is critical for accommodating the high-density urbanization that is occurring in Indonesia's cities. High-density conurbations are desirable for the government, as they can enable the more efficient provision of public services, and can generate increased or more efficient economic output (ADB 2019a). However, higher-density conurbations in Indonesia's cities have led to intense traffic congestion, and thus to the urgent need to connect nodes of economic activity by providing public transport infrastructure systems.

Most utility-based urban infrastructure is predominantly funded by "user charges." However, public transport infrastructure systems have relatively high capital costs, and the revenue that can be obtained from ticket sales is typically barely enough to cover the operation and maintenance costs, resulting in a viability gap. City governments are under intense political pressure to resolve the funding gap by investing fiscal resources in public transport infrastructure systems to unlock the economic growth associated with urbanization.

> **Urban infrastructure** includes road networks; public transport; and flood management systems, power supplies, telecommunications, water supplies, sanitation, waste collection, etc.

Challenge #2: Fiscal Constraints

The fiscal situation in Indonesia is characterized by a funding shortfall. So, there is a fundamental need to monetize the currently increasing output to fund the country's development plans.

The government's revenue and expenditure for 2018 (actual) and 2019 (projected) are shown in Figure 1.2, which indicates a continuing funding shortfall. For 2019, the projected expenditure on infrastructure was expected to be 3.4% of gross domestic product (GDP). In contrast, the current

National Medium-Term Development Plan (RPJMN) has targeted infrastructure spending at 6.1% of GDP by 2024, which will evidently present a bigger funding challenge.

Figure 1.2: Indonesian Government Funding Shortfall, 2018–2019

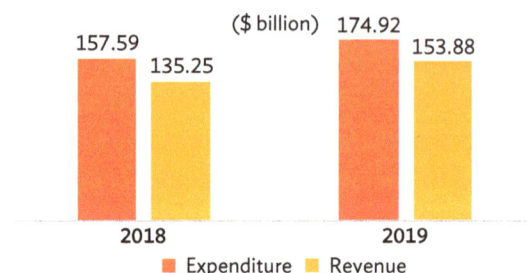

Note: In this figure, the values for 2018 are actual, and those for 2019 are projections.
Source: Government of Indonesia. National Medium-Term Development Plan, 2020–2024.

This funding shortfall means that there is a fundamental need to monetize increased economic output to fund the country's development plans.

The Indonesian government has a relatively low ratio of tax-to-GDP relative to its peers in the region, and could thus potentially afford to increase the tax burden. The current relatively low ratio of taxation cannot sustain the targeted level of infrastructure investment. There is also a need to identify alternative approaches that will increase the funding available for infrastructure projects.

The tax-to-GDP ratio is often used to measure a government's control over its economic resources. In 2017, Indonesia's tax-to-GDP ratio was 11.5%, lower than those of other middle-income Southeast Asian countries, as shown in Figure 1.3. There appears to be room for higher taxes, but fiscal revenues have already been shown to be insufficient for funding the required infrastructure investments. Therefore, the government must find alternative approaches to increasing revenue and/or attracting private sector contributions, in order to achieve a high enough income to fund the necessary infrastructure projects.

If the tax-to-GDP ratio does not improve, the projected target infrastructure spending in 2024 of Rp6,445 trillion will take up more than half of the country's revenue (BAPPENAS 2019). Thus, there is a need to borrow money for investments in infrastructure. However, to sustain fiscal discipline, Indonesia's fiscal regulations restrict the country's budget deficit to 3% of GDP, and cumulative public sector loans to 60% of GDP. Current public sector loans amount to 20% of GDP, so the public sector can only borrow around Rp1,400 trillion. That is why there is the need for alternative approaches, such as leveraging private sector financing.

Figure 1.3: Indonesia's Tax-to-GDP Ratio Compared with Those of Other Southeast Asian Countries, 2017

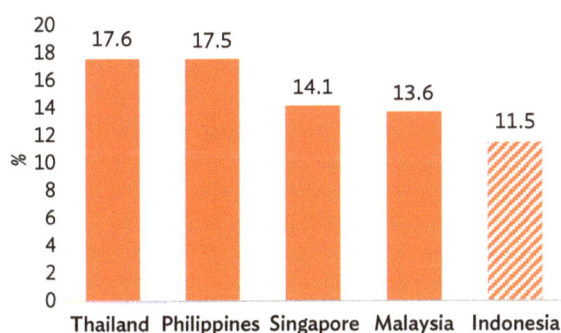

GDP = gross domestic product.
Source: Organisation for Economic Co-operation and Development (OECD). Revenue Statistics in Asian and Pacific Economies 2019 — Indonesia. https://www.oecd.org/tax/tax-policy/revenue-statistics-asia-and-pacific-indonesia.pdf.

Challenge #3: Project Viability

Appraisals of overall transport project viability normally focus narrowly on revenues from transit fares, non-fare revenues, time savings, and vehicle savings, while ignoring the fundamental motivation for investing in public transport infrastructure in the first place: to create corridors of increased economic activity.

Traditional Approach to Appraising a Project's Commercial Viability

A commercial viability assessment of a transport infrastructure project typically focuses on the revenues from transit fares, which are sensitive to the underlying demand and pricing analysis. When this type of project is put up for a public–private partnership (PPP), the government typically contributes a generous amount of viability gap funding (VGF) or subsidy payments to improve project yields and attract investors. The addition of non-fare and value capture revenues in assessments of project viability would improve project yields, without requiring the government to commit as much up-front financing or subsequent funding.

Narrow Focus in Appraising Project Economic Viability

The economic viability assessment of transport infrastructure projects is normally required to provide the government with a rationale for making fiscal contributions such as VGF or subsidies. The conventional approach is to carry out an economic cost–benefit analysis (ECBA). However, ECBAs of transport infrastructure projects focus on their direct and measurable effects, typically taking into account only fare and nonfare revenues, time savings, and vehicle savings (ADB 2017a). Infrastructure projects, especially public transport systems, provide economic uplift in other ways too, such as the following:

- Land can be used much more intensely, providing improved economic efficiency and productivity.
- Improved transport connectivity results in employers having access to a much larger labor pool, enabling them to improve their productivity and reduce frictional unemployment, while suppressing wage inflation.

Challenge #4: Silos Within the Government

Shortfalls in economic planning, land use planning, and infrastructure procurement will often lead to escalating project costs and program overruns.

Infrastructure projects are likely to span across more than one administrative boundary and be regulated by various governing bodies. Resolving these many, sometimes contradictory, regulatory requirements consumes considerable amount of time and resources. Moreover, shortfalls in planning and consultations can lead to escalating project costs and program overruns. A concerted inter-government approach to streamlining infrastructure regulations is paramount for promoting the more effective use of infrastructure funding.

1.2. Solution: The Virtuous Value Cycle

This subsection sets out the rationale for the use of a virtuous value cycle as a solution to the challenges set out in the previous section.

Definitions to Provide a Common Vocabulary

Definitions can provide a common vocabulary for this new topic, with "value capture" providing the broadest and most useful perspective on the topic. Recognizing the difference between funding and financing is also key.

The term "value capture" introduces several new concepts, and requires a correct understanding of them. Therefore, this section first sets out several definitions to facilitate a common understanding and a consistent narrative that can be shared among stakeholders in the government, as they craft a policy framework for value capture.

A range of definitions is used for "value capture" and "land value capture," but this report uses the broader view of value capture, which encompasses all the opportunities for a constructive sharing of the economic uplift that arises from public investment in economic infrastructure assets, as well as from the public services enabled by these infrastructure assets. Additional definitions are included in the Glossary.

Value Capture versus Land Value Capture

Transport for London uses the following definitions:

"Land Value Capture" is "a set of mechanisms used to monetise the increase in land values that arise in the catchment area of public infrastructure projects."

However, focusing only on increases in land values risks misses the broader economic uplift generated by urban and transit infrastructure.

This report has adopted and adapted a definition created by the Lincoln Institute of Land Policy:

"'Value Capture' is a policy-based approach that enables communities to recover and reinvest land-based value increases *and incremental economic value* that result from public investment and other government actions rooted in the notion that public action should generate public benefit."

Value capture presents an opportunity to create a virtuous cycle of economic uplift through public investment in infrastructure. However, the lack of and/or uncertainty regarding sources of funding to pay for infrastructure development has created a vicious cycle of limitations on economic productivity in developing countries such as Indonesia. These funding constraints have discouraged financing for infrastructure development, and remain a key challenge in addressing the gap for both economic and social infrastructure.

"Economic infrastructure" is infrastructure that makes business activity possible, such as communications and transportation, as well as other utilities such as power and water and sanitation.

"Social infrastructure" is infrastructure that accommodates social services: hospitals, schools and universities, prisons, housing, courts, and so on.

"Virtuous cycle" is a cycle of events in which each cycle increases the beneficial effects of the next occurrence.

"Vicious cycle" is a feedback loop in which two or more elements intensify and aggravate each other's negative effects, leading to a worsening situation.

In common English usage, "funding" and "financing" are used interchangeably. In Indonesian, both are commonly translated as *"pembiayaan"* in casual discussions. Some particularly formal discussions and reports may specify financing as *"pembiayaan"* and funding as *"pendanaan."* However, in answering the question of who pays for infrastructure that enhances economic output, an important distinction needs to be drawn, as understanding the subtle distinction between funding and financing is essential to pursuing value capture.

Funding versus Financing

Funding *(pendanaan)* is how we pay for the full costs of providing infrastructure services over the entire lifetime of a project, and cover financing and operating costs. Funding is typically sourced from taxes (in government-pays infrastructure projects), or from user charges (user-pays), or in part from beneficiaries' contributions (beneficiary-pays).

Financing *(pembiayaan)* refers to how we pay for up-front capital expenditure on infrastructure assets (e.g. from the government budget; government borrowing or private sector financing). Financing from the government budget is particularly challenging given the capital-extensive nature of building infrastructure. Hence, financing typically refers to government borrowing or private sector financing which eventually needs to be paid.

Financing, then, is the immediate challenge, considering the capital-intensive nature of infrastructure assets, while funding is longer term, as it relates to the *full life-cycle* costs of a project. Differentiating funding from financing not only sheds light on the timing of capital requirements, it also clarifies the different sources of funding and financing. Funding is typically sourced from taxes, user charges, and beneficiary contributions, while financing is typically sourced from loans provided by development banks or the private sector.

At present, funding is often thought of in terms of either government-pays or user-pays. Under these models, the burden falls on all taxpayers and direct users. Value capture requires a rethinking toward a broader and more equitable funding model that includes user-pays, government-pays, and beneficiary-pays, each in accordance with the corresponding benefits received.

It is well established that investment in infrastructure leads to improved socioeconomic outcomes.[1] There are, of course, preconditions for securing this economic uplift, including planning, taxation, procurement, implementation, and reinvestment. This report summarizes the preconditions, presenting them as principles of value creation and value capture.

The term "economic uplift" will be used in this report to refer to externality effects, spillover effects, network effects, and/or indirect effects. These may include positive socioeconomic benefits (direct or indirect) that are observed in the environment surrounding the infrastructure project, and gradually spread through networks of people, entities, and services to a wider geographical area.[a]

[a] UN Economic and Social Commission for Asia and the Pacific (ESCAP). 2019. Infrastructure Financing for Sustainable Development in Asia and the Pacific. ESCAP Financing for Development Series. No. 3. Bangkok. https://www.unescap.org/sites/default/files/publications/Infrastructure%20financing-high.pdf.

[1] There might be also negative externalities arising from infrastructure investment, such as increased noise or pollution. However, the positive externalities typically clearly outweigh the negative effects, especially in case of modern green infrastructure.

Value capture can help governments address the infrastructure gap by creating an increasingly beneficial effect that can be recovered and reinvested to further enhance economic output. However, value capture is generally only possible when benefits are created, which is the focus of this report on value creation.

A useful definition of value capture can be found in the value creation and value capture framework of the Government of the State of Victoria, Australia:

> **Value creation** is a consistent, concerted approach to assessing and increasing the benefits of public investments in infrastructure. It is about delivering enhanced public value above and beyond what would have ordinarily been achieved as a direct consequence of the relevant government investment. Some of the types of benefits that can be realized through value creation include:
>
> - economic benefits: increased growth and job opportunities, and improved workforce participation;
> - social benefits: public housing, improved access, enhanced public safety, increased recreational infrastructure (such as bike paths and parks), and improved connectivity; and
> - environmental benefits: the greening and enhancement of natural catchments in cities and towns, increased energy and/or water efficiency, sustainable buildings, climate change adaptation, and decreased greenhouse gas emissions.[a]
>
> ----
>
> [a] Government of the State of Victoria. 2016. *Victoria's Value Creation and Capture Framework: Maximising Social, Economic and Environmental Value from Infrastructure Investment.* Melbourne. https://www.vic.gov.au/sites/default/files/2019-02/Victorias-Value-Creation-Capture-Framework.pdf.

a consistent, concerted approach to assessing and increasing the benefits of public investments in infrastructure.

Virtuous Value Cycle

The virtuous value cycle provides a progressive whole-of-government and policy framework-based approach to creating value, capturing value, and providing confidence that a share of the incremental economic uplift will be allocated to the repayment of the up-front financing used for the original investments. The concept of value creation is based on the observation that public transport infrastructure enables corridors of increased economic activity.[2]

The approach seeks to apply value capture mechanisms to only a share of the incremental economic uplift created, so there is no impingement on the original tax base or on any other government activities dependent on that tax base.

The virtuous value cycle is described in Figure 1.4, which shows an iterative and continuous cycle that is based on a policy framework, specified as follows:

- Value funding uses value capture mechanisms to build confidence in the financial returns to both public and private financiers, thus encouraging further investment in infrastructure.

Figure 1.4: The Virtuous Relationship among Value Creation, Value Capture, and Value Funding

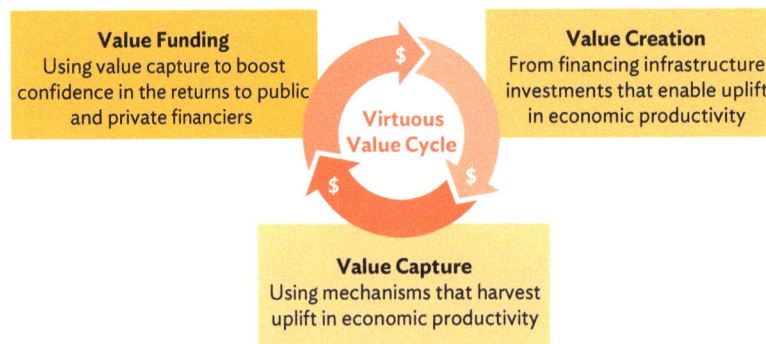

Source: Authors.

----

[2] The whole-of-government approach can be defined as a shift from isolated silos in a government to formal and informal networks among ministries and agencies to improve the government's ability to respond to more complex problems by means greater collaboration and coordination.

- Value creation takes a whole-of-government approach to planning, procuring, and investing in infrastructure that will uplift economic productivity.
- Value capture uses appropriate mechanisms to harvest the increased economic productivity, boosting the confidence of investors that secure funding will be channeled back to them as returns on their up-front investments.

The virtuous value cycle can enhance the private sector's appetite for participation in infrastructure development by increasing investor confidence in the returns from value capture and by leveraging the positive externality effects of newly developed infrastructure. For example, investment in transit projects permits the intensification of economic activity through denser urban development, which provides a more efficient space for doing business and an improved quality of life for residents. Increased economic activity, in turn, generates increased commercial and tax revenues from businesses and residents within these areas, as well as increased employment opportunities. The economic uplift could be partially harnessed to provide incentives (e.g., service fees, availability payments, or viability gap contributions) that would encourage greater private sector financing (Yoshino, Nakahigashi, and Pontines 2017).

Over the years, Japan has successfully set a high benchmark for infrastructure development. Figure 1.5 shows the key observations by Yoshino, Nakahigashi, and Pontines (2017) on how the virtuous value cycle has a positive economic effect on infrastructure investment in Japan.

Specifically, Figure 1.5 shows the estimates of the direct effect of nationwide infrastructure investment in Japan on tax revenue, and of the economic uplift (indirect effects) arising from private capital and employment, which boost outputs and translate into increased revenue. The study suggests that the rate of return to private investors would have increased by 43.8% in 1956–1960, and by 39.1% in 2006–2010, if half of the additional tax revenue anticipated from the increases in output had been used to cofinance infrastructure investment.

If captured correctly, these significant increases in the rates of return could have attracted greater private participation in infrastructure development. In practice, however, the tax revenue gains were absorbed by the government, leaving private investors and operators to rely on user charges or other direct revenue streams (Yoshino 2019).

Figure 1.5: The Economic Effects of Infrastructure Investment: the Case of Japan, 1956–2010

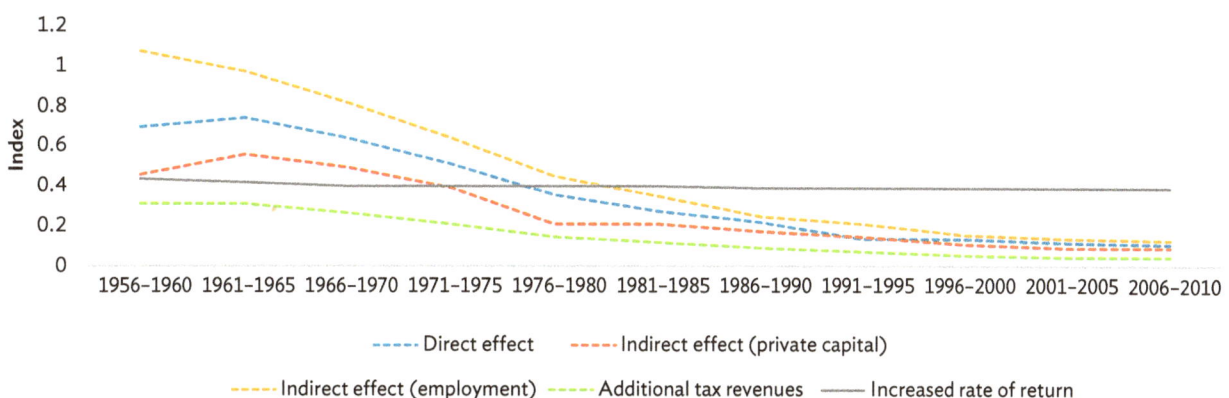

Source: N. Yoshino, M. Nakahigashi, and V. Pontines. 2017. Attract Private Financing to Infrastructure Investment by Injection of Spillover Tax Revenues. *Nomura Journal of Asian Capital Markets* 1 (2): 4–9.

Introduction to the Seven Principles of Value Creation and Value Capture

The virtuous value cycle is founded on four thematic principles and seven specific principles that can be subsequently used to appraise the readiness of Indonesia's regulatory framework for enabling value capture. The need for a whole-of-government approach is emphasized, so that the stakeholders' efforts are aligned with the goal of increasing benefits from public infrastructure investments to maximize economic, social, and environmental benefits.

International practice has shown that, where there is a policy-based government commitment to, and support for, infrastructure assets and service delivery, there is increased private investor confidence.

Value capture has taken various forms in different jurisdictions because value capture mechanisms often correspond to the regulatory framework; the levels of maturity of urban governance systems, the real estate market, and capital markets; and the extent to which private sector financing can been used. In developed countries, infrastructure financing comes more from private capital than from government funds. This is not to say that the government is not investing enough in infrastructure in those countries, but rather that the government's commitment to, and support for, infrastructure asset and service delivery is the basis for private sector investor confidence.

A review of the literature on best practices and international case studies (Appendix 4) has revealed that the fundamental rationale for value capture can be encapsulated into four thematic principles and seven specific principles of value creation and value capture, as listed in Table 1.1.

Next is a more in-depth discussion of all of the principles. Each box reflects a thematic principle; and descriptions of the specific principles that are under the rubric of the thematic principle.

Principle #1

Basic Theme—Land as a factor of economic productivity.

Economic productivity is derived from the use of land, and serviced land creates greater value. A strategic and sustainable view of land use, based on sound land administration and management, is key to unlocking the economic potential of land.

Value capture is rooted in an economic use of land that creates wider benefits that can then be captured and reinvested in new infrastructure or in maintaining existing infrastructure, to generate even greater benefits.

Table 1.1: Thematic and Specific Principles of Value Creation and Value Capture	
Thematic Principles	**Specific Principles**
Basic Theme Land as a factor of economic productivity	1 **Economic productivity** is derived from the use of land, and serviced land creates greater value. A strategic and sustainable view of land use, based on sound land administration and management, is key to unlocking the economic potential of land.
Value Creation A more consistent, concerted approach by government to assessing and increasing the benefits of public investments	2 **A whole-of-government approach** ensures that the intended value is delivered, and that any value created is shared. This, in turn, creates a high-trust society in which a virtuous circle of infrastructure investment improves the quality of life. 3 **Master planning using a comprehensive economic cost-benefit analysis,** takes the United Nations Sustainable Development Goals as the starting point, and maximizes the economic, social, and environmental benefits from public investment in infrastructure. 4 **An investment to create connectivity through the integration of urban development with transport planning** will enhance economic output and create a stable demand for economic infrastructure.
Value Capture The government capturing a portion of the incremental economic value created by public investments, activities, and policies	5 **Public action should generate public benefits.** Shifting the focus toward beneficiary funding acknowledges both the direct and indirect beneficiaries, including the government and private sector. 6 **Value capture is only possible when value has been created.** It should not be preemptive, as this will only increase costs and make economic growth more difficult.
Value Funding Confidence in revenues as a means of unlocking financing	7 **Value capture unlocks financing** by boosting the confidence of private investors in revenues from infrastructure projects, and enables the recycling and reinvestment of capital into further infrastructure development.

Source: Authors.

Land is inherently fixed and limited in quantity. As such, the use of land requires the payment of a price, referred to by Adam Smith as "rent," which in common English usage means income derived from land. Rent varies according to land use and location, with land use determining the type and intensity of economic activity, and location (vis-à-vis the markets for inputs and outputs) determining the total cost of the production and distribution of goods and services.

Serviced land is land that has been improved, for instance through drainage, transport connectivity, and connections to utilities.

According to Adam Smith, the income derived from land may be further enhanced by improving access to markets for goods and services. *Lahan budidaya* (serviced land) not only commands a higher market value, it also has the potential to create greater economic value by increasing the value of other land areas and creating new demand for other goods and services. This illustrates how economic uplift can be derived from serviced land.

However, investment in infrastructure does not guarantee enhanced economic output. For example, improved connectivity can descend into a vicious cycle if the extent of land development is uncontrolled. Issues such as congestion, rising inequality, gentrification, and urban sprawl can arise from a haphazard and reactive approach to land development.

Therefore, a virtuous cycle of value from infrastructure investment proceeds from a long-term, integrated view of land use and development, where the focus is on the inherent economic value of the land, and how this value can be enhanced through infrastructure.

Good, integrated, long-term planning that is complemented and supported by a transparent, accurate, responsive and efficient land administration and management system, has been a critical factor in Singapore's transformation from a colonial port city to a global, highly livable city and endearing home with a high quality of life, sustainable environment and competitive economy (Centre for Liveable Cities 2018).

Readers may refer to Case Study 1—Value creation story of Marina Bay, enabled by dynamic urban governance grounded in sound institutions, effective legislation, and long-term planning, Singapore, in Appendix 4.

Principle #2

Value Creation—A more consistent, concerted approach by government to assessing and increasing the benefits of public investments.

A whole-of-government approach ensures that the intended value is delivered, and that any value created is shared. This, in turn, creates a high-trust society in which a virtuous cycle of infrastructure investment improves quality of life.

Recent infrastructure procurement has been driven by the political need to respond to popular concerns about inadequate infrastructure provision. These pressures are often well founded, but they can push governments to act based on disjointed, short-term perspectives, especially when line ministries receive mandates and budgets to procure infrastructure solely for their own domains.

The line ministries function as if in silos, so challenges that are intertwined in the real world can only be addressed in a piecemeal manner. Moreover, these ministries typically rely heavily on government budgets and user charges to fund their infrastructure. Affordability is thus a primary consideration for them, and this affects the timing, type, and quality of the infrastructure procured.

One of the ways that governments have successfully accessed private sector financing and expertise is through public–private partnerships (PPPs). These partnerships are considered to be a way to tap private sector efficiency, an implicit admission that complex infrastructure is not within the government's core area of expertise.

It may be expected that the private sector is more able to identify real infrastructure market needs and then self-finance the provision of these infrastructure services. However, PPPs are typically defined by line ministries focusing on a single sector's infrastructure requirements that will deliver services directed solely at users.

The opportunity is that economic and social infrastructure can provide broader economic benefits that brings material benefits for many parties. For example, a toll road does not only bring time savings and vehicle savings, but also connects communities and nodes of economic activities.

Thus we need to go beyond the normal practices, namely:

- beyond the mandates of individual ministries or agencies, toward a concerted approach to creating and capturing not only increases in land value, but also the wider socioeconomic benefits of infrastructure delivery;
- beyond the direct users of infrastructure, to include indirect beneficiaries in the public and private sectors, to achieve an infrastructure funding mix that is more equitable, efficient, and sustainable; and
- beyond single-plot/"island" developments characteristic of uncoordinated urban development being poorly plugged into the surrounding urban infrastructure and straining public services into well-connected nodes and corridors of economic productivity that maximize the economic, social, and environmental value generated from infrastructure.

These "beyonds" can only be achieved through a whole-of-government approach, in which planning and development are enabled by the collaboration among expert officials from key agencies, such as the ministries of finance, planning, land administration, housing, and transportation, and from city governments. Encouraging collaboration is virtuous in

strengthening trust in society; building private-sector investors' confidence in the markets; and maximizing the economic, social, and environmental benefits.

> **Principle #3**
>
> Master planning, based on a comprehensive economic cost–benefit analysis, takes the United Nations (UN) Sustainable Development Goals (SDGs), nationally adapted, as the starting point, and maximizes the economic, social, and environmental benefits from public investment in infrastructure.

A master plan produced by a government should include an analysis, recommendations, and proposals for a site's population, economy, land use, and infrastructure. It must focus on identifying key growth areas and on providing the infrastructure required to support the planned economic growth. In addition, the government needs to draw up different drivers (e.g., industrial zones, housing needs, and transport corridors) to generate employment.

Such master planning requires a strategic and sustainable view of land use, as well as a robust vision of economic development. For example, Singapore has adopted a disciplined and visionary approach to master planning because of its land and natural resource constraints. Singapore's master plan, a statutory land-use plan with a horizon of 40–50 years, identifies the city-state's economic gateways, allowing the government to plan and progressively implement supporting infrastructure, while taking into account limitations such as heritage and preservation areas.

A statutory master plan with such an overarching economic vision can provide a comprehensive framework for coordinating development efforts on both public and private land, by government and private developers. It can also ensure transparent zoning (land use and density) restrictions, which influence the preparation and approval of project-specific master plans.

Apart from aligning development efforts with the strategic function that has been set for an area, economic master planning also empowers the government to invest in the economic infrastructure needed for the development of greenfield public land. Once the serviced land becomes available, the government can lease or sell parcels of it for private sector development in accordance with the applicable land-use and density restrictions that have been established.

This approach to master planning requires a comprehensive economic cost–benefit analysis of investments in infrastructure, in order to increase the confidence of both public and private developers in the gains to be made. For example, the Crossrail financing scheme in the United Kingdom (UK) was based on an in-depth business case study that estimated the benefits and beneficiaries of the planned Elizabeth railway line, thereby enabling the UK government to negotiate contributions from major businesses that had been identified as beneficiaries of the project (as they stood to gain advantages such as access to a wider labor market and an uplift in property values).

A business case which included a detailed economic cost-benefit analysis was prepared to illustrate Crossrail's transformative value to a wide range of beneficiaries as well as a plan to implement an alternative funding mechanism that would ensure that those who benefit from the project would contribute substantially to its delivery (Buck 2017).

Readers may refer to Case Study 2—Innovative funding, financing, and a value capture mechanism, contributing two-thirds of the project costs for Crossrail, United Kingdom, in Appendix 4.

An economic cost-benefit analysis ensures the rigorous identification of benefits and beneficiaries, and provides a basis for justifying how planned infrastructure will create value within the catchment area, which will be the basis for a beneficiary-pays model for funding.

Assessing broader value opportunities will help ensure that the government can make informed choices on value for money and societal benefits. By using an economic cost–benefit appraisal approach, governments can measure and manage the total impact of an undertaking, including the meeting of social, environmental, and economic obligations. Typical opportunities are illustrated in Figure 1.6.

Figure 1.6: Opportunities for Value Creation, State of Victoria, Australia

Improving Productivity and Cost Efficiency	Level crossing removals and motorway projects improve the efficiency of the movement of people and freight across Melbourne, and potentially reduce transport costs.
Improving Asset Values	Investment in infrastructure and land development can increase the value of land and business in the vicinity of the investment.
Unlocking Commercial Opportunities	Government regularly rezones land to enable higher-value use. This can be small scale or large scale (e.g., the rezoning of entire precincts), and can create commercial opportunities for urban renewal and property development.
Improving Accessibility	Investment in new transport infrastructure improves access to economic opportunities (e.g., jobs and education), and to services, housing, and recreation.
Enhancing Public Safety and Amenities	Infrastructure, public land development, and precinct projects can facilitate the creation of new public facilities (e.g., parks, bike paths, and cultural facilities), benefiting local businesses and residents. They can also increase public safety (e.g., through improved road design and reduced traffic congestion).
Protecting and Enhancing the Environment	Infrastructure and public land-development projects can facilitate environmental outcomes (e.g., climate change adaptation and resilience, biodiversity, and efficient energy and water use).
Increasing Social Capital	Delivering infrastructure (e.g., social housing) and services (e.g., health and education), or pursuing policy outcomes through procurement (e.g., trade apprenticeships to reduce youth unemployment), can reduce inequality and improve social outcomes.

Source: Government of the State of Victoria. 2016. *Victoria's Value Creation and Capture Framework: Maximising Social, Economic and Environmental Value from Infrastructure Investment* (as modified by the authors). Melbourne. https://www.vic.gov.au/sites/default/files/2019-02/Victorias-Value-Creation-Capture-Framework.pdf.

> **Principle #4**
>
> An investment to create connectivity through the integration of urban development with transport planning will enhance economic output and create a stable demand for economic infrastructure.

It is widely agreed that enhanced connectivity facilitates the movement of goods, services, and human resources; enhances the economies of scale; promotes trade and investment; creates new business opportunities; and improves regional productivity and competitiveness through expanded regional production (UN ESCAP 2014).

Creating connectivity through integrated urban and transport development means that urban planning and development should be consistent with local and regional investments in transportation infrastructure, as well as in housing, education, and health-care facilities, which are all components of a well-connected economy (ADB 2019a).

An integrated urban and transport development approach often results in high-density, compact, mixed-use urban areas served by an efficient public transportation network that reduces reliance on private vehicles. Encouraging mixed-use, high-density development can lead to sustainable urban and rural communities, easing the pressure to set aside more and more agricultural or preservation areas for urban use. In addition, measures such as providing affordable in-city housing options and developing an equitable public transportation network can democratize the city, even amid rising property values, thus reducing the impetus toward urban sprawl.

The focus on urban areas reflects the global trend toward increasing urbanization, driven by the affluence of cities, which often results in various challenges. Especially in developing countries, where cities are not prepared for inward migration from rural areas, a host of urbanization issues can arise, such as congestion in urban centers, gentrification, urban sprawl, the underserving of rural areas, and unregulated land use conversion.

High density creates more efficient land use, makes it easier to provide public services and facilities, reduces energy and infrastructure costs and maximizes the effectiveness of public transit, while minimizing the distance between the sites of day-to-day activities (Salat and Ollivier 2017).

Readers may refer to Case Study 3—Rail-based high-density development of rail + property model, Hong Kong, China in Appendix 4.

Therefore, integrated urban–rural development, a concept that links urbanization to a lack of development in rural areas, should also seek to provide equitable access to education, health-care, and transport facilities in rural areas. The objective should be to make rural areas, which are typically characterized by land suitable for the cultivation and preservation of life (agricultural land, shores, forests, etc.), sustainable and less susceptible to unregulated land use conversion.

For example, complementary facilities such as farm-to-market roads, cold chain facilities, and food processing plants, and the application of advanced technologies, could transform agricultural land into serviced land, which will enhance economic productivity. Broader benefits could include increasing incomes beyond subsistence level, and reduce wastage, thus incentivizing farmers to continue to till the land and adopt new approaches, and safeguarding national food security.

The intensification of urban land use is similarly an attractive option because economic benefits can be felt in tangible ways, such as higher land values and higher wages. At present, the intensification of land use typically focuses on the manufacturing, services, and knowledge industries, leaving out the potential intensification of agricultural land use, which will result in low productivity.

Zoning, which concerns both land use and density, is a viable instrument that governments can use to concentrate and coordinate economic activity in an environmentally, socially, and economically sustainable way.

Principle #5

Value Capture—The government capturing a portion of the incremental economic value created by public investments, activities, and policies.

Public action should generate public benefits. Shifting the focus toward beneficiary funding acknowledges both the direct and indirect beneficiaries, including the government and private sector.

Value capture is a deliberate approach aimed at increasing the benefits of public action by allowing the government to maximize the broader economic, social, and environmental potential of public infrastructure investments and/or land use policies to generate a positive impact on the quality of life.

A focus on beneficiary funding requires the government to be proactive about creating value and, where possible, layering benefits that tend to reinforce the value being created. For instance, transit-oriented development, in which the main revenue stream comes from fares, can derive additional revenue from station development, which could include retail, office, and residential uses. These complementary layers of benefits could reinforce the main revenue stream by creating a strong demand for transit services, increasing ridership to a point where it could benefit the whole of society, due to the resultant lower energy consumption, congestion, and pollution.

The benefits of public investment in infrastructure can be far-reaching, but governments need to plan actively to create these benefits and to align the understanding of the beneficiaries by creating a conducive environment built on fiduciary relationship. Trust is a fundamental basis for government authority, which derives from the duty to ensure the welfare of the governed, without which infrastructure investment can be disrupted or derailed by changes in political direction or by corrupt practices.

Value capture mechanisms (an example shown in Figure 1.7) should thus be established at the outset, so

Figure 1.7: Value Capture Mechanisms—State of Victoria, Australia

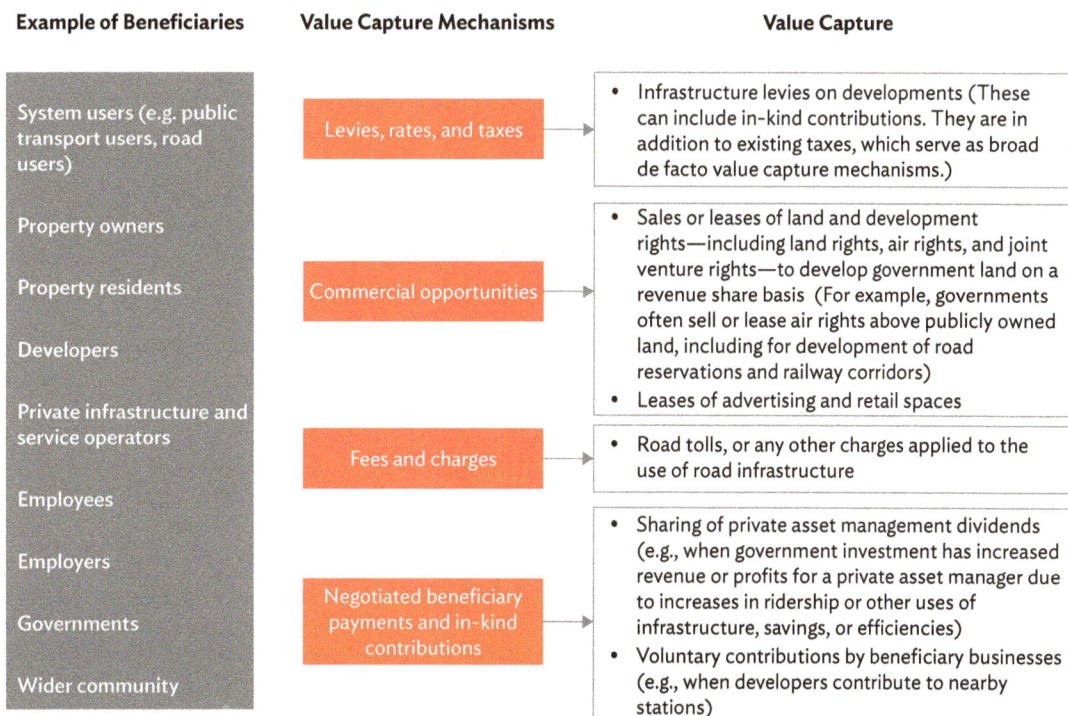

Source: Government of the State of Victoria. 2016. *Victoria's Value Creation and Capture Framework: Maximizing Social, Economic and Environmental Value from Infrastructure Investment* (as modified by the authors). Melbourne. https://www.vic.gov.au/sites/default/files/2019-02/Victorias-Value-Creation-Capture-Framework.pdf.

that governments can be consistent in applying these mechanisms, promoting transparency, and avoiding corruption. To that end, there should be accountability and transparency in the legal framework governing how proceeds are used, considering that value capture can involve substantial sums of money.

Principle #6

Value capture is only possible when value has been created. It should not be preemptive, as this will only increase costs and make economic growth more difficult.

Value can only be captured and shared after it has been created, so the initial focus must be on ensuring a consistent and concerted approach to value creation. Value capture should then proceed after a careful assessment of the benefits and a careful planning of complementary functions that could further increase the benefits created as described in Principle 5. That principle also maintains that the residential and commercial components of transit-oriented development increase ridership, while providing revenues in addition to the fares collected from passengers.

Value creation may require a certain amount of time until the economies of scale are sufficient to be harvested through value capture. The planning of value creation and value capture requires a comprehensive and careful assessment of the benefits that can be generated by public investment in infrastructure, and the means through which these benefits can be captured and reinvested to help fund the infrastructure. Taxation represents an established instrument for value capture that should be implemented as closely as reasonably possible to where the value is created, and targeted at the appropriate beneficiaries. Developers would only accept having to pay a tax if

a direct link can be established and evidenced, and if the tax is consistently applied throughout—within the applicable legal framework.

Value can only be captured and shared after it has been created. Value capture should then proceed after a careful assessment of the benefits.

Our analysis of the Indonesian taxation framework has revealed mechanisms that were already capturing value at various levels, such as the levy in electricity bills that helps defray the costs of public street lighting.[3] It should be noted that value capture can be pursued through incremental steps, starting with low-hanging fruit within existing frameworks, while the government builds more deliberate and proactive mechanisms that require more comprehensive value creation and value capture.

An example of a low-hanging value capture mechanism is the collection of property taxes based on a consistent application of a robust and fair methodology for land valuation. There is a property tax in in almost every jurisdiction, but for most developing countries this tax is not optimized due to outdated tax system and assessment and underreporting of actual sale prices that resulted to a valuation lower than prevailing market value (ADB 2019b).

Principle #7

Value Funding—Confidence in revenues as a means of unlocking financing.

Value capture unlocks financing by boosting the confidence of private investors in infrastructure projects, and enables the recycling and reinvestment of capital into further infrastructure development.

---

3   It should be noted that street lighting is paid for through local taxation under Indonesia's tax regime. Law No. 28 of 2009 on Local Tax and Retribution prohibits the local government from collecting taxes other than those allowed by that law. The law also sets out the upper and lower limits of the tax rates that local governments may collect. A local government may choose its tax rate based on its capacity, so local tax rates may vary from the regional governments to governments on other levels.

The primary beneficiaries of infrastructure investments are users and governments, but also third party beneficiaries that enjoy associated benefits. Users usually benefit directly from the services and may contribute to costs via "user-fees". Governments normally benefit through the improved infrastructure causing an uplift in economic productivity that can boost fiscal revenues. Beneficiaries can be a wide range of third parties, and can accordingly benefit in a wide range of ways.

Value capture principles seek to identify all beneficiaries, then quantify how each party may benefit, then seek to proportionally share the burden of costs through appropriate value capture mechanisms, thus achieving sustainable funding for paying back for the up-front investments in infrastructure.

As governments develop mature regulatory frameworks for land management, taxation, and integrated infrastructure development, opportunities to deploy advanced value capture mechanisms will become available and so also increase investor confidence in the collection of revenues. In their advanced state, value capture mechanisms include financial products that can be recycled into the capital

markets to free up more capital for infrastructure projects, such as governments issuing bonds or the private sector making an initial public offering.

Framework for Assessing Value Capture Readiness

A framework for assessing the current status of value capture, as well as the level of institutional readiness, has been developed based on the seven specific principles of value creation and value capture.

The seven specific principles of value creation and value capture highlighted in this report reflect the shift in paradigm required for the government and the beneficiaries to overcome the challenges identified in Section 1.1. These principles can be used as a framework for assessing the government's readiness to implement value capture, as elaborated in Tables 1.2 and 1.3.

Table 1.2 sets out the tiers of value creation and value capture implementation, with each level of policy-driven interventions (passive, deliberate, and proactive) reflecting a progressively deeper maturity of benefits and associated key development features.

Table 1.2: Tiers of Value Creation and Value Capture Implementation						
Level of Implementation		**Value Capture Mechanism**	**Benefit Zone**	**Key Development Features**	**Advantages**	**Outcomes**
Value Creation	**Passive** Low-hanging	Tax-based and fee-based	Single-plot ("island") developments	Uncoordinated development that strains existing infrastructure	Easy to implement	Low-hanging value capture mechanisms that jump-start a virtuous circle of value creation from public investment
Value Creation	**Deliberate** Entrepreneurial (incremental journey toward a virtuous value cycle)	Tax-based, fee-based, and development-based	Master-planned mixed-use, transit-oriented compact development	Visionary integrated development of growth nodes and corridors, with a focus on population growth, redevelopment, and infrastructure investment	Creates more benefits from complementary functions	Economic, social, and environmental benefits of public investment maximized through value capture
Value Capture	**Proactive** Visionary	Tax-based, fee-based, development-based, and capital markets-based	Highly connected growth nodes and corridors	Strong and sustained economic productivity aided by connectivity	Leverages future value	Recycling and reinjecting of capital into further infrastructure investment

Source: Authors.

For example, at the passive level, the benefit zone will most likely be made up of the single-plot ("island") developments which are characteristic of uncoordinated urban development being poorly plugged into the surrounding urban infrastructure and straining public services.. At this level of implementation, the government can expect to rely only on low-hanging value capture mechanisms to jump-start the journey, while making appropriate reforms that will enable more deliberate policy making, based on an integrated vision of development, to create more value.

In the next section, Table 1.2 will be used to assess the current status of value capture in Indonesia, and then as the basis for selecting the best value creation and value capture approach to be used there.

Table 1.3 describes the lessons learned from a review of case studies (Appendix 4) that can be categorized according to the seven specific principles. The analysis reveals five fundamental enablers of value creation and value capture for a consistent and concerted approach to creating more value from public investments in infrastructure. Taken together, the enablers describe the key challenges, the change in mindset required, and the building blocks for pursuing a value creation and value capture approach. These include:

- a whole-of-government approach, emphasizing the pivotal role of the government;
- visionary economic master plan;
- long-term framework for land use, to serve as the foundation for the plan;
- focus on integrated urban and transport development; and
- a value capture-oriented tax regime, to harvest a share of the economic uplift.

Table 1.3 will serve as the framework for a subsequent analysis of the readiness of institutional enablers within Indonesia. The gap analysis then will be used to develop a further road map for value creation implementation in Indonesia.

Table 1.3: Enablers of Value Creation and Value Capture Implementation					
Enablers of Value Creation and Value Capture	**Whole-of-Government Approach**	**Visionary Economic Master Planning**	**Long-Term Land-Use Planning and Regulatory Framework**	**Integrated Urban and Transport Development**	**Value Capture-Oriented Tax Regime**
Key challenges	Silos within the government resulting from individual ministerial mandates, which may overlap	Project-specific perspectives that do not consider the broader benefits	Long-term view, but short-term approach	• Uncoordinated • Private sector-driven urban development around the catchment areas of transit stations	• Benefits typically not well defined, making value capture difficult to apply
Changes in mindset	• Beyond individual mandates, toward a coordinated effort by government agencies, departments, and/or ministries • Beyond government, toward value sharing with the private sector	• Goal of increasing the benefits from public investment in land development and infrastructure • Beneficiaries of public investment including both the government and the private sector, apart from end users	• Land as a resource that is fixed and limited • Economic productivity derived from land use • Serviced land a source of greater value	• Connectivity involving more than just transportation • Efficient use of urban land through compact development • Creation and leveraging of stable demand for social and economic infrastructure	• Taxes and fees as the most accessible value capture mechanism for government • Option of channeling incremental tax revenues back into the original infrastructure investment
Building block(s)	Institutional changes to facilitate collaboration within the government and with the private sector	• Whole-of-government approach • Long-term land use planning and regulatory framework	Sound land administration and management system	• Visionary economic master planning • Long-term land use planning and regulatory framework • Whole-of-government approach	Robust tax administration and collection framework

Source: Authors.

1.3. Outcomes

Implementing a value capture policy framework will deliver several strategic and tangible outcomes.

Alignment with the United Nations Sustainable Development Goals

The whole-of-government approach required for value capture is closely aligned with the planning and delivery of the United Nations (UN) Sustainable Development Goals (SDGs), especially because it enables the calculation and sharing of the economic and commercial benefits across different parts of the government.

Value creation outcomes also consider the broader economic, social, and environmental benefits arising from public investment in infrastructure and from other government actions. Several definitions of "value creation" can be encountered in practice. For the State of Victoria, Australia, this means creating more value from a public investment than could ordinarily be achieved as a direct consequence of the investment itself. According to the Urban Land Institute (2019), "Value Creation is the unlocking of an increase in the potential value of under-used assets (land and/or structures) as a result of a public sector intervention to stimulate demand from the private sector."

While there are varying definitions it is more useful for practitioners to tailor value creation to be relevant with the real and whole needs of a community. The UN SDGs provide a useful comprehensive framework from which relevant goals and metrics can be drawn to focus areas for value creation as presented in Figure 1.8.

Figure 1.8: Focus Areas of the Sustainable Development Goals in Relation to Value Creation

Industry, innovation, and infrastructure: Build resilient infrastructure, promote inclusive and sustainable industrialization, and foster innovation.

Sustainable cities and communities: Make cities and human settlements inclusive, safe, resilient, and sustainable.

Life below water: Conserve and sustainably use oceans, seas, and marine resources for sustainable development.

Life on land: Protect, restore, and promote the sustainable use of terrestrial ecosystems; sustainably manage forests; combat desertification; halt and reverse land degradation; and halt biodiversity loss.

Climate action: Take urgent action to combat climate change and its impacts.

Partnerships for the goals: Strengthen the means of implementation and revitalize the Global Partnership for Sustainable Development.

Gender equality and **decent work and economic growth**: The combination of these two goals allows for gender-equality policies along with policies on the rights of persons with disabilities. There should be disability-inclusive planning, which, in turn, should be aligned with urban planning and transit-oriented development, as well as gender-transformative policies, to make cities safer, more equal, and more accessible.

Source: PricewaterhouseCoopers. SDG Selector. https://dm.pwc.com/SDGSelector/.

Improved Project Viability and Improved Investor Confidence

The implementation of value capture principles is a more robust approach to the development of economic corridors connected by public transport infrastructure; it will also increase investor confidence in the returns on their investments.

In general, private investors will look for opportunities to optimize the value of their investments, such as a smaller amount of money invested, shorter payback period, and a sufficient return. By ensuring "anchored" sources of revenue from the effective and progressive implementation of suitable value capture instruments, local governments can improve or maintain the attractiveness of their regions to investors.

Robustly implementing value capture principles can assure private investors that they will see returns from their investments.

Especially where tangible economic uplifts are demonstrable through, for example, creation of higher density communities and vibrant economic hubs in and around transit networks. Progressive value capture implementation could also mean that the value captured by the government will increase over time and experience a multiplier effect, thus potentially reducing the payback period of investments. In addition, with dynamic economic centers being created as part of the value capture implementation, an investment could potentially realize significantly higher multifaceted gains, which would ensure an attractive prospect for a return on investment.

Fiscal Discipline and Fiscal Stability

Implementing a value capture policy framework will result in more robust economic planning, with the aim of spurring economic uplift while integrating the value creation implementation mechanisms. The tighter control and monitoring that should arise from this approach will provide enhanced fiscal discipline and fiscal stability.

In general, fiscal discipline, especially regarding a national or local government budget, is understood as a situation in which the government actively works to keep revenue and expenditure in a state of "balance." If a government fails to maintain fiscal discipline, it is likely to see its expenditure exceed its revenue, leading to a deficit.

Consequently, the government will seek to close this gap. While there are multiple ways of doing this, a common approach is to borrow funds, or, in the case of local government, to request support from the national government. But these approaches could have some undesired consequences, for example:

- a depreciation of the currency;
- an increase in overall government interest payments;
- a need to raise taxes to increase revenue, so the government can cover its loan repayments;
- the potential crowding out of the private sector; and
- rising inflation.

The decentralization of public finance in Indonesia has given the provincial and local governments autonomy in their financial management and planning, including their local revenues, expenditures, and overall budgets. These governments are therefore responsible for maintaining the economic stability of their regions or cities. Typically, part of a provincial government's budget may come from the city or regency levels, which are mostly supported by fiscal-sharing funds from the national government.

The concept of fiscal discipline, in common usage, usually only considers one budget cycle, with the ultimate objective of "balancing" the year's revenue and expenditure, thus removing any need for external government borrowing. Fiscal stability, however, is based on a longer-term perspective (i.e., budgets over several cycles).

Conversely, the application of the value creation and value capture principles highlighted here will give a framework for collaboration across line ministries. This collaboration should bring a whole-of-government approach to planning infrastructure investment against real market needs and deliver tangible synergies.

With multiple stakeholders dependent on the outcomes, there will be greater pressure to maintain fiscal discipline over an extended period. Moreover, by addressing real needs in value creation, revenues from all beneficiaries are easier to capture increasing the fiscal revenues that will enhance fiscal stability.

2. The Regulatory and Institutional Frameworks for Value Capture Implementation in Indonesia

The Indonesian regulatory framework provides clear legal references to value capture implementation that govern how the public finance budget is collected, allocated, and spent in Indonesia, applicable to the national and subnational levels of government, including provincial, regional, city, and regency governments. In general, local governments have autonomy regarding the management of their budgets, with potential financial support from the national government.

The existing tax and fee regime prohibits subnational levels of government from introducing new taxes. However, the partial earmarking of revenues from taxes and fees may potentially be assigned to funding for transport and health care within the current regulatory framework, opening the potential for the application of value capture in Indonesia.

2.1. Regulatory Frameworks

The initial assessment of the Indonesian regulatory framework for public finance, and for the planning of urban and transit infrastructure, land administration, and investments, highlighted that while there are restrictions on the government's ability to introduce new types of taxes or fees, the government can implement selected value capture instruments through some existing tax and fee mechanisms.

This section briefly examines some of the regulations in Indonesia that are relevant to the implementation of value capture and land value capture, covering the following regulatory frameworks:

- public (national and local) financing,
- development and spatial planning,
- land management,

- investment, and
- transit infrastructure.

The section also focuses on the regulatory and institutional framework for the financing and funding of transit infrastructure, including:

- the arrangements for financing at the national, provincial, and local government levels, with a focus on revenue sources;
- Indonesia planning's regime, with a focus on the different levels of the spatial planning system, and its features;
- Indonesia's land-management and building-ownership regime, which could be relevant to value capture implementation; and
- The involvement of the private sector in the provision of infrastructure.

A more detailed description of regulations regarding national, provincial, and local public finance is provided in Appendix 1.

Regulatory Framework for Public Finance

National fiscal revenue is predominantly centrally managed through a "melting pot" for subsequent budgetary reallocations. The government budget is allocated annually, with the funds redistributed for all types of spending required to carry out government programs and projects, including infrastructure investments, either through direct spending (capital expenditure [CAPEX] and operational expenditure [OPEX]), indirect spending (through financial assistance and subsidies for infrastructure) or finance spending (through equity injections for infrastructure development). There is no effective process for making multiyear budgetary commitments.

The management of government finance in Indonesia mainly covers the management of revenue and expenditure, with any remaining balance governed by various regulations, depending on the level of government, i.e., national, *kota* (provincial), or *kabupaten* (local).

Law 1/2004, or the *Undang-Undang* on the State Treasury,[4] states that the national government's income and expenditures must be managed through "state accounts," while local revenues must be managed through "local accounts." All payments to the national and regional accounts should be made in a timely manner, and central government revenues derived from the ministries, local work units, or other public agencies may not be used directly by them to finance their expenditures. In short, like many countries worldwide, Indonesia has adopted the general principle of the melting pot, whereby all state revenue goes into one pot and is then allocated for certain purposes. However, this arrangement makes it difficult to obtain government support for the allocation specific tax income, or for increases in tax income, to fund the repayment of financing used for up-front investments in infrastructure projects

National Governance and Public Finance

Law No. 17 of 2003 on State Finance governs how state finances at the national level are managed, and indicates the key roles of the agencies involved. With regard to the implementation of potential value capture instruments, the following terms can be inferred from this regulation:

- The balance of funds from the central government may be allocated to local governments, as determined by Law No. 33 of 2004 on Fiscal Balance between the Central and Regional Governments.
- The central government may provide loans and/or grants to local governments, and vice versa (Art. 22 [2]), with agreement from the local house of representatives under Art. 22 (3).

- Local governments are allowed to offer or receive loans to and from each other under Art. 22 (4).
- The central government may give loans and grants to, or receive the same from, a foreign government or entity with approval from the House of Representatives (Art. 23 [1]), and the same could be forwarded to the local government, or a state-owned enterprise (SOE), or a regional- owned enterprise (ROE).

Law 17/2003 mainly governs state finances at the national level, and provides some descriptions of the roles and positioning of the local governments, for example:

- Local governments (i.e., provincial, city, and regency) are given the authority to manage their finances (Art. 6. [2] c).
- Local governments may collect local revenue in accordance with the local regulations (Art. 10 [2] c.
- Local governments or public agencies may collect nontax revenue under Art. 10 (3) d.
- Local governments manage their own assets under Art. 10 (3) f.

The types of taxes to be collected by each level of government are stipulated by laws and regulations. The introduction of new types of taxes is relatively challenging because it could require the issuance of new laws and regulations, or at least the amendment of existing laws and regulations. The issuance or amendment of laws and regulations will sometimes take a long time, as they involve a long bureaucratic process.

Indonesian regulations on the state budget generally do not recognize the concept of earmarking various revenue sources for specific uses. All state revenue is collected and allocated annually based on the approval of the House of Representatives (or of the local parliament for a local budget). The allocation of the state budget (including the local budgets) is prepared

---

based on the needs and capacity of the state, and is not allocated for specific purposes unless explicitly mandated by the prevailing laws and regulations. For instance, the Constitutional Law mandates that the allocation for education must be at least 20% of the total state budget.

Additionally, Government Regulation No. 12 of 2019 on Regional Financial Management strongly prohibits local governments from collecting fees outside the scope set out under the relevant laws and regulations, as that practice can cause a high-cost economy and impede public mobilization, the interregional traffic of goods and services, and exports and imports that are strategic for the national program.

Law No. 9 of 2018 on Nontax State Revenues specifies that the government can generate nontax revenues from the following areas: the exploitation of natural resources, provision of services, management of separated state assets, the management of state assets, and the management of funds and other state rights. It stipulates that tariffs and some other types of nontax government revenue must be regulated by the relevant ministry for each sector.

Local Public Finances

Law No. 23 of 2014 on Regional Government covers local governance matters, including regional budgets and budget changes, regional mid-term development planning, taxes, fees, and land use. It also updates the descriptions of the local revenue sources as specified in Law 17/2003, as follows:

- locally generated revenue, which includes local government taxes, *retribusi* (fees), asset management revenue, and revenue from other legitimate local sources;
- transfer funds, which include national government transfers and transfers between local governments; and

- other legitimate sources of revenue, including nontax local government revenue and local fees such as those for checking services and the sales of local government assets.

GR 12/2019 governs public finances at the local level and describes the types of revenue that can be collected, in a manner similar to that of Law 23/2014. Art. 32 of Law 23/2014 prohibits provincial and local governments from collecting any types of taxes or fees other than those listed in this law.

Law No. 28 of 2009 on Local Tax and Retribution provides a description of each category of taxes and fees that can be collected at the provincial, regency, and city levels ("retribution" in an Indonesian fiscal context refers to government fees or charges). The law states that the regulation of taxes and fees at these levels of government aims to provide greater certainty for people and businesses. Therefore, Law 28/2009 also states that these governments cannot impose types of taxes other than those specified under this law.[5] However, the law indicates that other types of fees (but not taxes) may be introduced as long as the policy complies with the criteria set out in the law.

In terms of the potential for the earmarking or channeling of revenue, Law 28/2009 states that the utilization of revenue from some of the types of *retribusi* can be allocated to activities that directly relate to the services that generated the revenue (Art. 161 [1]). The terms for the allocation of this fee revenue are to be determined through a local regulation (Art. 161 [2]). Further assessment by a legal specialist may be required to confirm whether this earmarking or channeling could be applied to sectors relevant to value capture implementation in Indonesia. This indicates that there could be ways for subnational governments to optimize their revenue collection, perhaps by adjusting revenue calculations or adjusting their tariff tiers to ensure that the revenue collected is reinvested in the relevant sectors. This, however, must be developed within the terms of the

---

5   While the text of Law 28/2009 states this, the Explanation section of this law mentions that "City/Regency (Local Government)" is authorized to specify other types of taxes, as long as they are in compliance with the criteria set out in the law. A detailed assessment by a legal specialist may be required to determine whether or not there is an opportunity to consider types of taxes other than those mentioned in the text of the law.

regulatory framework, as any application of taxes or fees that conflicts with higher-level legislation will be penalized by delays in, or deductions from, the transferred funds.

At the practical level, the development of the Regional Revenue and Expenditure Budget (APBD) is governed by **Minister of Home Affairs Regulation No. 33 of 2019 on Local Government Budget Development Guidelines**, which is updated for each budget year.

Based on the authors' review of various regulations, Figure 2.1 maps out the government's tax revenue sources, showing the pools of funds at various levels of government, and how these funds are eventually spent on infrastructure.

Based on our review of the relevant regulations, an indicative "flow of money" within the government is presented in Figures 2.1 and 2.2, which show the sources of revenue for all levels of government. Taxes are applicable to business entities, individuals, or both. Some taxes are collected by certain municipalities or regencies and are then remitted directly to the national or provincial tax accounts. These collected taxes are then allocated to national, provincial, and local budgets. The percentages going to the various levels of government vary, depending on the type of tax. For instance, 80% of the collected income tax goes to the national budget, 8% to the province, and 12% to the city and regency where the tax was collected. Meanwhile, some other types of taxes are not shared across all levels of government, but are instead centrally managed. For instance, the value added tax and luxury item tax are managed by the national government, while the underground water exploration tax is managed by officials of the provincial government.

It is also understood that some state tax revenue may be earmarked, for instance, vehicle tax. Article 8 para. (5) of Law No. 29 of 2009 on Regional Taxes and Levies stipulates that 10% of the vehicle tax is allocated to road development and/or maintenance, and to improvements in the mass transit infrastructure.

The earmarking of taxes is legal in Indonesia. However, it requires strong contractual and political commitments from the relevant stakeholders. Unless such earmarking is expressly mandated by law, there are limited sanctions that can typically be imposed on parties refusing to approve budgets consistent with the intended earmarking. Accordingly, while contractual earmarking is possible as a short-term solution, the recognition of such earmarking by the law should be considered so as to secure budgetary commitments despite changes in political power.

Not all types of taxes are earmarked for certain allocations, and those taxes that are not earmarked are centrally managed through the melting pot. Centralized financial management in Indonesia requires all revenue channels to be "mixed" into one government account, except those taxes that have been earmarked for specific uses. The government budget is allocated annually, with the funds redistributed for all types of spending required to carry out government programs and projects, including infrastructure investments, either through direct spending (for CAPEX and OPEX), indirect spending (through financial assistance and subsidies for infrastructure), or though injections of equity financing of infrastructure development.

Figure 2.2 maps out nontax revenue sources, showing pools of funds at various levels of government, and how these are eventually spent on infrastructure, based on the authors' review of various regulations. It also shows other, similar mechanisms for the flow of money under governmental financial management. Aside from taxes, there are three sources of government revenue, collected through different mechanisms. Levies and fees are collected as payment for the provision of commercial services by the government, such as waste collection, parking services, civil registration, and the issuance of building permits. Asset management revenue is obtained from the sharing of profits from national or regional state-owned enterprises (SOEs) and from various financial institutions. Other revenue sources include the local public service agencies (BLUDs) and penalty fees for late tax payments, among others.

Regulatory Framework for the Planning of Urban and Transit Infrastructure

Indonesia carries out regional-level economic planning, and has a well-established regulatory framework for the spatial planning of urban and transit projects. However, economic planning has not been carried out with regard to the economic corridors that are to be linked by transit projects. Further, spatial planning in Indonesia is not efficient at creating value for the government as a whole.

Indonesia's spatial planning system is encapsulated mainly in Law No. 26 of 2007 on Spatial Planning. Figure 2.3 shows the flow of spatial planning and directive strategies from the national to the local governments (either regencies or cities). The first column of Figure 2.3 presents the general spatial planning framework at each level of government, known as the regional spatial plan (RTRW). The national spatial plan informs the provincial plan, and is then translated into the regency and city spatial plans. The second column sets out the detailed spatial plan for each level of planning, including detailed arrangements for zoning, incentives, disincentives, and penalties for spatial plan violations. The national spatial plan is then detailed in island spatial plans and national strategic area spatial plans, which will be referred to as the "area structure." Meanwhile, the area structure also applies to the provincial level, and the provincial spatial plan informs the provincial strategic area, as well as the regency and city levels, which are included in a detailed spatial plan (RDTR), rural spatial plan, and the spatial plans of city and regency strategic areas. The RDTR needs to serve as the foundation for local governments when they develop their urban design guidelines (UDGLs) for urban renewal, urban redevelopment, new urban development, and urban preservation. Along with the local regulations on building design, the UDGLs are the main reference point for local governments when it comes to issuing building permits and monitoring building operations and management processes.

While reinforcing the main sections of Law 26/2007, **Government Regulation No. 15 of 2010 on Spatial Planning Implementation** provides several additional requirements:

- The government wishes to increase public participation in spatial planning: Art. 6. c, Art 7 (4).
- As part of an effort to constrain land use, fiscal disincentives may be applied in the form of higher taxes, while non-fiscal disincentives may include an obligation to provide compensation, the imposition of special requirements for permit applications, obligations to pay *imbalan* (fees), and limits on the provision of infrastructure.

Law No. 32 of 2009 on Environmental Protection and Management states that the analytical process for spatial plan development should be supported by a strategic environmental assessment (KLHS). The KLHS will examine the citywide environmental analysis, which will cover city vulnerability, climate change, groundwater, biodiversity, and other environment-related aspects. As specified by Minister of Environment Regulation No. 69 of 2017 on Environmental Assessment Study Guidelines, the KLHS will determine the basic principles for the utilization of the land, and will examine the constraints on further development.

Figure 2.1: Tax Revenue Sources and Cash Flows through Government Spending Streams

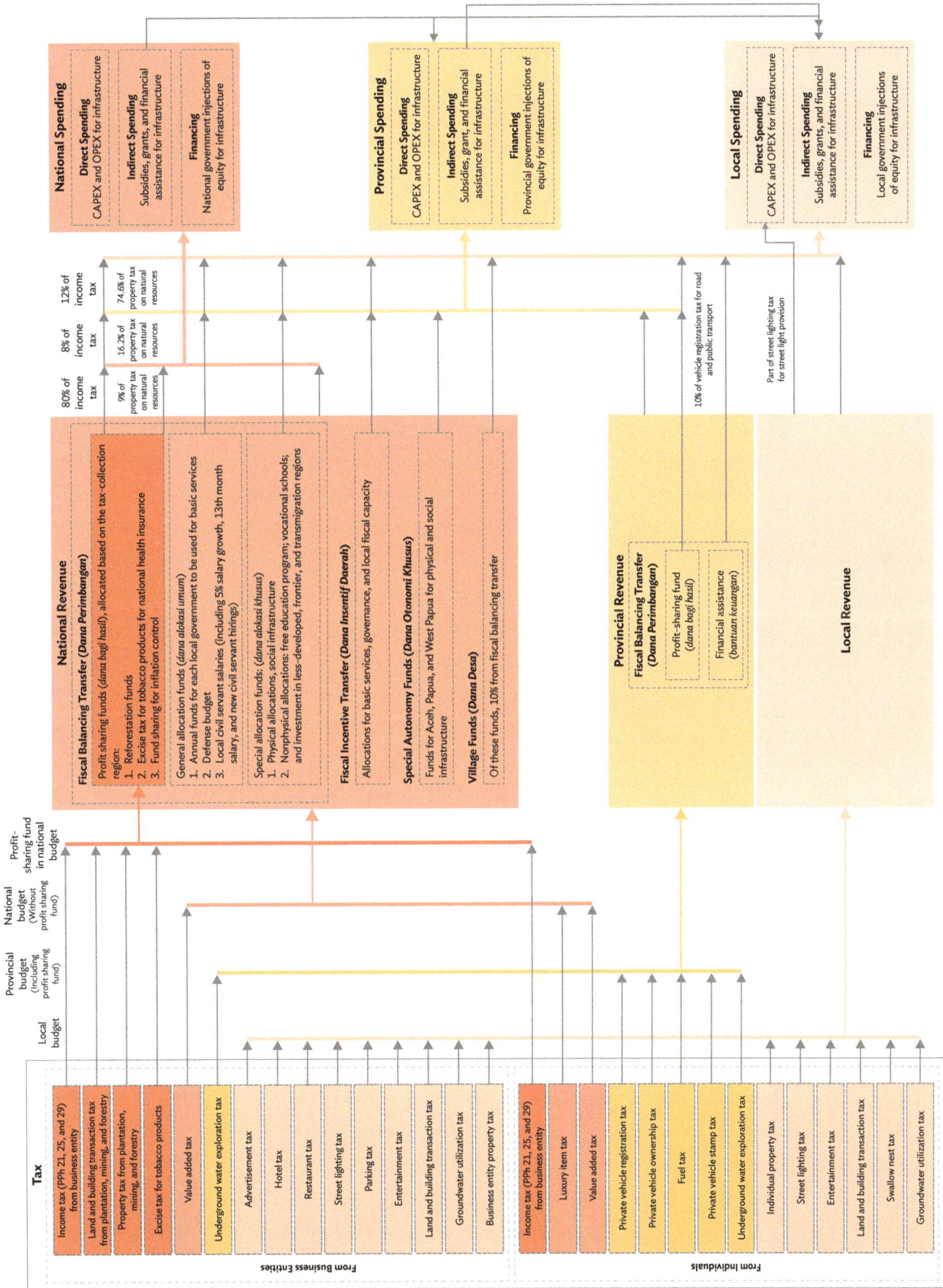

National Spending

Direct Spending
CAPEX and OPEX for infrastructure

Indirect Spending
Subsidies, grants, and financial assistance for infrastructure

Financing
National government injections of equity for infrastructure

Provincial Spending

Direct Spending
CAPEX and OPEX for infrastructure

Indirect Spending
Subsidies, grant, and financial assistance for infrastructure

Financing
Provincial government injections of equity for infrastructure

Local Spending

Direct Spending
CAPEX and OPEX for infrastructure

Indirect Spending
Subsidies, grants, and financial assistance for infrastructure

Financing
Local government injections of equity for infrastructure

80% of income tax | 8% of income tax | 12% of income tax
9% of property tax on natural resources | 16.2% of property tax on natural resources | 74.6% of property tax on natural resources

10% of vehicle registration tax for road and public transport

Part of street lighting tax for street light provision

National Revenue

Fiscal Balancing Transfer (Dana Perimbangan)

Profit sharing funds (dana bagi hasil), allocated based on the tax-collection region:
1. Reforestation funds
2. Excise tax for tobacco products for national health insurance
3. Fund sharing for inflation control

General allocation funds (dana alokasi umum)
1. Annual funds for each local government to be used for basic services
2. Defense budget
3. Local civil servant salaries (including 5% salary growth, 13th month salary, and new civil servant hirings)

Special allocation funds: (dana alokasi khusus)
1. Physical allocations, social infrastructure
2. Nonphysical allocations: free education program; vocational schools; and investment in less-developed, frontier, and transmigration regions

Fiscal Incentive Transfer (Dana Insentif Daerah)

Allocations for basic services, governance, and local fiscal capacity.

Special Autonomy Funds (Dana Otonomi Khusus)

Funds for Aceh, Papua, and West Papua for physical and social infrastructure

Village Funds (Dana Desa)

Of these funds, 10% from fiscal balancing transfer

Provincial Revenue

Fiscal Balancing Transfer (Dana Perimbangan)

Profit-sharing fund (dana bagi hasil)

Financial assistance (bantuan keuangan)

Local Revenue

Provincial budget (Including profit sharing fund)

National budget (Without profit sharing fund)

Profit-sharing fund in national budget

Local budget

Tax

From Business Entities
- Income tax (PPh 21, 25, and 29) from business entity
- Land and building transaction tax from plantation, mining, and forestry
- Property tax from plantation, mining, and forestry
- Excise tax for tobacco products
- Value added tax
- Underground water exploration tax
- Advertisement tax
- Hotel tax
- Restaurant tax
- Street lighting tax
- Parking tax
- Entertainment tax
- Land and building transaction tax
- Groundwater utilization tax
- Business entity property tax

From Individuals
- Income tax (PPh 21, 25, and 29) from business entity
- Luxury item tax
- Value added tax
- Private vehicle registration tax
- Private vehicle ownership tax
- Fuel tax
- Private vehicle stamp tax
- Underground water exploration tax
- Individual property tax
- Street lighting tax
- Entertainment tax
- Land and building transaction tax
- Swallow nest tax
- Groundwater utilization tax

CAPEX = capital expenditure, OPEX = operational expenditure, PPh = Pajak Penghasilan Pasal (Income Tax Article).

Notes:
1. For the purpose of this report, this figure focuses on infrastructure-related spending, rather than providing a complete picture of all government spending.
2. The basic government services (government mandatory affairs) include: education, health, public works and spatial planning, social housing and settlements, social order, and social affairs.

Source: Authors' analysis of various regulations of the Government of Indonesia.

Figure 2.2: Nontax Revenue Sources and Cash Flows through Government Spending Streams

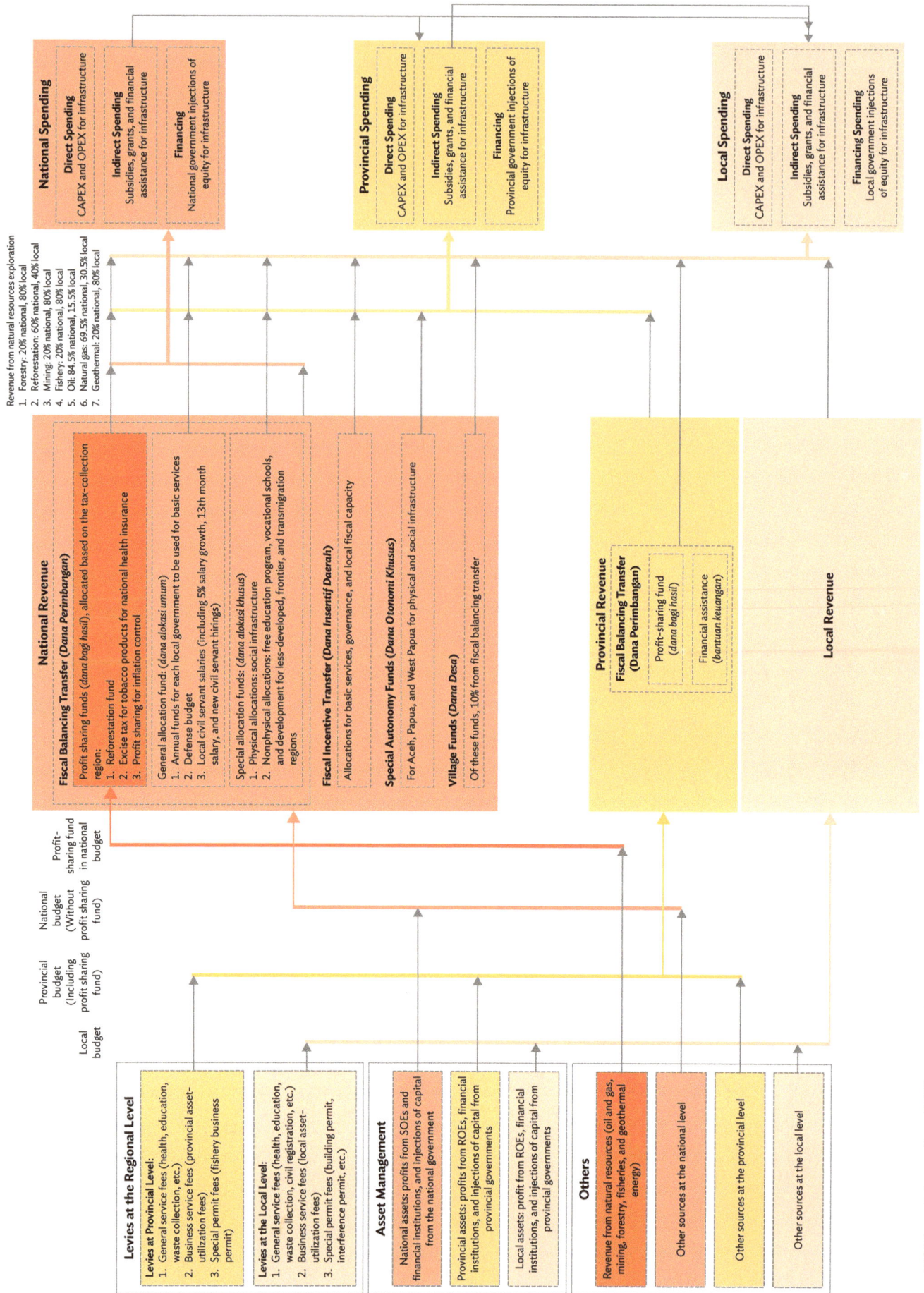

CAPEX = capital expenditure, OPEX = operational expenditure, ROE = regional–owned enterprise (owned by the provincial or regional government), SOE = state–owned enterprise.

Notes:

1. For the purpose of this report, this figure focuses on infrastructure-related spending, rather than providing a complete picture of all government spending.

2. The basic government services (government mandatory affairs) include: education, health, public works and spatial planning, social housing and settlements, social order, and social affairs.

As part of the democratic process, the spatial planning document requires public discussion, as it may affect the development potential of individual land parcels, as well as city livability. Hence, the legislation on spatial planning documents should pass through parliamentary discussions at the relevant levels of government, and then should sign off by the Ministry of Home Affairs and the Ministry of Spatial Planning.

GR 15/2010 specifies that cities should have at least a city or district spatial plan and an RDTR, as described in Appendix 2, Table A2.3.

Minister of Agrarian Affairs and Spatial Planning/ Head of National Land Agency Regulation No. 16 of 2017 on Guidelines for Transit-Oriented Development provides the general requirements for TOD. To support TOD, permissible supporting instruments need to comply with the applicable *peraturan kepala daerah* (head of local government regulation) (Art. 16) in such areas as incentive zoning or bonus zoning, development rights transfers, special fiscal application zoning, and land consolidation.

- **Incentive zoning or bonus zoning** is a limited transfer mechanism in the form of additional allowable floor-area ratio (KLB) to landowners within the TOD area (Art. 17 [1] and [2]),[6] while considering the quality and standards of the facility being developed or improved, environmental bearing capacity, aviation operations safety areas (KKOPs), and skyline requirements of a maximum of 50% of the planned KLB.
- **Development transfer rights** are implemented to encourage the voluntary transfer of development rights according to Art. 18 (1) of MOAASP/NLA 16/2017. These transfers may include (per Art. 18 [2]) the transfer of permitted gross floor area from one land parcel to another within the same zone; the transfer of development rights from protected zones

Figure 2.3: Illustrative Hierarchy of Spatial Planning Regimes in Indonesia

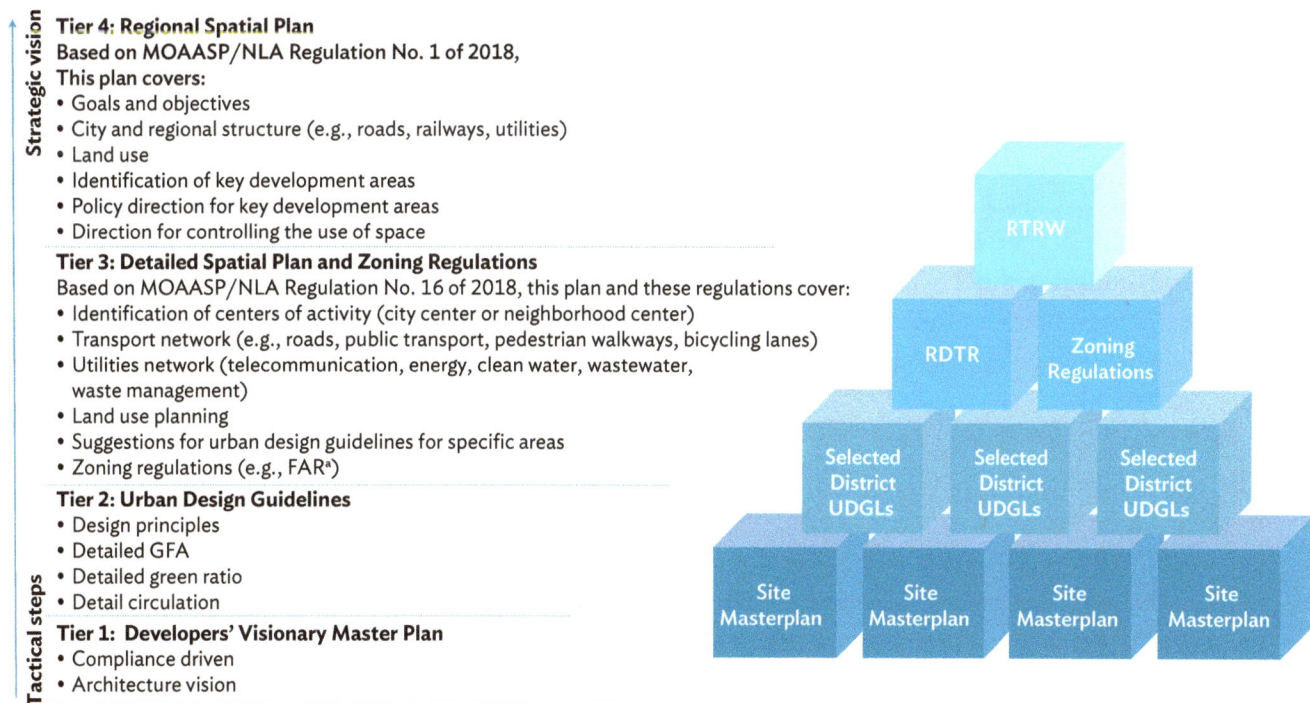

Strategic vision

Tier 4: Regional Spatial Plan
Based on MOAASP/NLA Regulation No. 1 of 2018,
This plan covers:
- Goals and objectives
- City and regional structure (e.g., roads, railways, utilities)
- Land use
- Identification of key development areas
- Policy direction for key development areas
- Direction for controlling the use of space

Tier 3: Detailed Spatial Plan and Zoning Regulations
Based on MOAASP/NLA Regulation No. 16 of 2018, this plan and these regulations cover:
- Identification of centers of activity (city center or neighborhood center)
- Transport network (e.g., roads, public transport, pedestrian walkways, bicycling lanes)
- Utilities network (telecommunication, energy, clean water, wastewater, waste management)
- Land use planning
- Suggestions for urban design guidelines for specific areas
- Zoning regulations (e.g., FAR[a])

Tier 2: Urban Design Guidelines
- Design principles
- Detailed GFA
- Detailed green ratio
- Detail circulation

Tier 1: Developers' Visionary Master Plan
- Compliance driven
- Architecture vision

Tactical steps

FAR = floor area ratio, GFA = gross floor area, MOAASP/NLA = Ministry of Agrarian Affairs and Spatial Planning/National Land Agency, RDTR = detailed spatial plan, RTRW = regional spatial plan, UDGL = urban design guidelines.
[a] The "floor area ratio" is the ratio of a building's total floor area to the size of the plot of land on which it is built.
Sources: Authors' analysis, Government of Indonesia, urban planning regulations.

---

6   *Koefisien lantai bangunan* (KLB) is the ratio of a building's total floor area to the total area of land.

(e.g., conservation areas, green spaces) to more economically valuable or promising land uses; and the transfer of allowable floor areas from one land parcel to another in a different zone, through a floor area conversion based on the economic value of the origin zone or on the "gross floor donors" and on the purpose of the granting of the development rights.

Further requirements related to the transfer of development rights (Art. 18 [3]) include the following:

– The transferable development rights represent a floor area difference between the KLB requirements set out in the zoning regulations and the KLB used in the parcel.
– The maximum allowable transfer of rights received is 50% of the planned KLB.
– A transfer may only be carried out once.
– Once a parcel is subject to a transfer of rights, if a new maximum KLB limit is imposed, it may not transfer the additional KLB.

- **Special fiscal application** zoning may include (per Art. 19) imposing higher taxes and *retribusi* for the use of land that is noncompliant with the character of the TOD area and/or imposing lower taxes and *retribusi* for land use that is compliant with the character of the TOD area.
- **Land consolidation** may be implemented through ownership or use so that it can be used for public infrastructure development projects (per Art. 20 [2]).

The management of the TOD area may be done by the government (or in cooperation with the government) by establishing a new entity to manage the TOD area or by appointing an SOE or ROE as the main operator of a mass transit system (Art. 23 [1 & 2]).

It is widely recognized that, for any value capture mechanisms to succeed, especially those related to the development of infrastructure, there needs to be synergy between the investments coming from the government and those coming from the private sector. This synergy, among other things, could potentially be achieved by ensuring an alignment between the planning documents from both sides. While Indonesia's urban planning regulatory framework provides a planning regime that must statutorily be followed by local governments at the provincial, city, and regency levels, private sector developers conduct the same operations to achieve a different set of goals and objectives. Private sector investment and development planning are often disconnected from the government's urban development vision. Without synergy, the values created by such development could potentially be exclusive, and would not benefit the communities.

Figure 2.4 provides a non-statutory description of the functions of the various types of government planning documents—the RTRW, RDTR, zoning regulations, urban design guidelines (RTBLs)—and discusses how developers' master plans need to comply with the applicable regulations. For example, the RTRW, which generally operates at a strategic level by providing the city structure, such as the road network and utilities, is regulated by the RDTR and zoning regulations, which set out in detail the centers of activity. Select locations covered by the RTRW are detailed in the RTBLs, which describe the requirements, including a detailed green area ratio. These RTBLs usually provide the parameters (and limitations where applicable), with which the master plans proposed by developers must comply.

Table 2.1 provides a non-exhaustive list of relevant articles of Law 26/2007 related to the implementation of value capture.

Figure 2.4: Flow of Spatial and Urban Planning

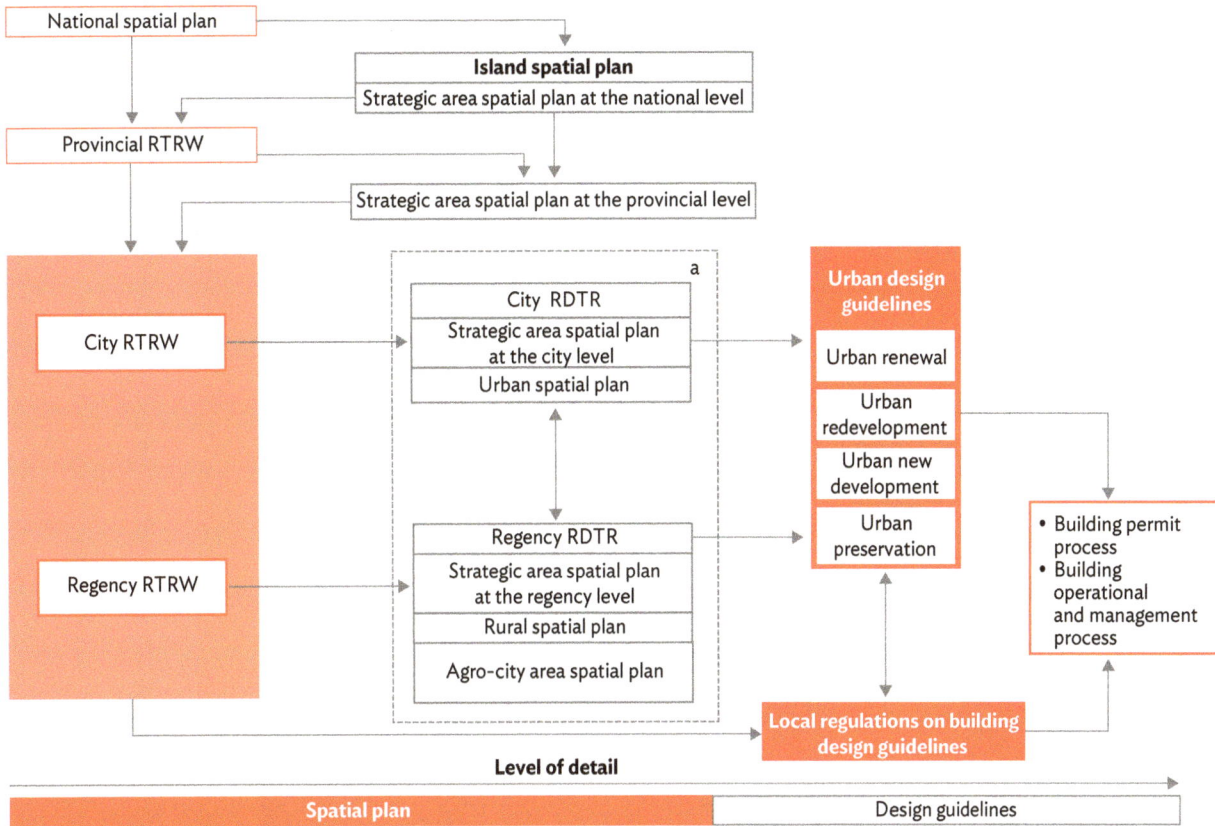

RDTR = detailed spatial plan, RTRW = regional spatial plan (including provincial, regency, and city).

a The seven plans listed in this box and the one below include zoning regulations.

Source: Authors.

Table 2.1: Summary of Law No. 26 of 2007 on Spatial Planning	
Content	**Description**
Classification of spatial planning	Spatial planning can be classified into the following components: • System: regional system and intra-city system; • Main function: conservation and productive areas; • Administrative area: national, provincial, and city or regency; • Activity: urban and rural; and • Area strategic value: national, provincial, and city government strategic spatial planning.
Regulation on sea and air spatial planning	The spatial planning of sea and air is regulated under a separate law.
Scope of spatial planning	• The government is responsible for land use planning, land utilization, and land use control at their respective levels. • The spatial plans of the national, provincial, and city or regency levels also govern the space under the surface of the ground.
Procedure	• The minister coordinates the implementation of spatial planning across sectors, regions, and stakeholders. • Spatial plans can be reviewed and recommended for revision. • The legalization of local governments' spatial planning regulations must be approved or recommended by higher levels of government.
Spatial plan validity and review	Local government spatial plans, which must take the regional mid-term development plan into account, is valid for 20 years, and is reviewed every 5 years.
Mechanisms for land use control	• The mechanisms include: zoning regulations, permit regulations, the provision of incentives and disincentives, and the imposition of penalties. • The zoning regulations include a requirement for the maximum utilization of space (i.e., the green space base coefficient, building coverage coefficient, ratio of the building floor area to the total land area, and the building demarcation lines). • Disincentive mechanisms include: (i) the imposition of a higher tax according to the cost of compensating for the impact of land use; and (ii) limitations on the provision of infrastructure, and the imposition of compensation payments and penalties. • Individuals and entities may enjoy the land value increase resulting from spatial planning. • Noncompliance with spatial planning requirements may result in criminal prosecution.

Source: Authors.

Regulatory Framework for Land Management

There is a well-developed regulatory framework for land management from a spatial planning perspective. However, it is weakly connected with economic planning, value creation, and value capture.

Basic Land Titling and Holding

The ownership of land in Indonesia is principally regulated under Law No. 5 of 1960 on Basic Agrarian Law ("**Basic Agrarian Law**"). Law 5/1960 and its implementing regulations—including Government Regulation No. 24 of 1997 on Land Registration and Government Regulation No. 40 of 1996 on the Right to Cultivate, Right to Build, and the Right of Use over Land—provide various forms of land titles and a registration system to protect legal ownership. The National Land Agency indicated that there have been discussions on the drafting of a new replacement regulation.

The new draft regulation envisages that the National Land Agency will assume the role of land and land use regulator and administrator. The draft is accompanied by several other supporting instruments for land regulation in Indonesia, such as the One Map Policy for the Single Land Registration System, as well as the Complete Systematic Land Register (PTSL). Additional instruments being developed include better support for vertical housing developments, a land banking mechanism, land reform, better management of *tanah adat* (traditional land), as well as the development of the land courts and land law enforcement.

Law 5/1960 sets out some points that are relevant to value capture:

- The existing law remains valid regarding land, air, and space, so long as it does not conflict with national and state interests, per Art. 5.
- Any person or entity that owns rights to farmland must work on it actively, per Art. 10.

- The government shall prevent any organization or individual from holding a private monopoly on the ownership of land, per Art. 13.
- The types of allowable land rights (per Art. 16. [1]) include:
  - *hak milik* (right to own);
  - *hak guna bangunan* (right to build);
  - *hak guna usaha* (right to cultivate);
  - *hak pakai* (right to use);
  - *hak sewa* (right to lease);
  - *hak membuka tanah* (land-clearing rights);
  - *hak memungut hasil hutan* (right to collect forest products); and
  - other rights, excluding the above and will be determined by law, as well as other temporary rights.
- The types of allowable rights for water and airspace (Art. 16 [2]), include:
  - *hak guna air* (right to use water),
  - *hak pemeliharaan dan penangkapan ikan* (right to keep and catch fish), and
  - *hak guna ruang angkasa* (right to use air space).
- In the public interest, including the interests of national government, the rights to land can be withdrawn subject to compensation, according to the regulations, per Art. 18.

The highest form of land title available in Indonesia is *right-to-own* or "**Hak Milik**" which is also the closest to the internationally recognized concept of "freehold" title.

Law 5/1960 also recognizes a form of title based on Indonesian traditional law, commonly referred to as *hak milik adat* (communal rights) or other names, depending on the region. A communal rights title results from the occupation of, or residence on, a piece of land and the payment of taxes and retributions on that land, or through the renunciation of rights by the previous landholder who possessed the communal rights title. The communal rights title is an unregistered form of title, but may be evidenced by certificates registered in the books of the relevant subdistrict office. These certificates include a brief description of the land and the holder of the communal rights title, and provide details of to the payment of taxes and retributions on that land.

In general, the types of land title allowed under Law 5/1960 are as follows:

- *Hak milik*:

  The highest form of land title available in Indonesia is the right to own, or *hak milik*, which is also the closest to the internationally recognized concept of the title of "freeholder." It allows an unlimited period of ownership, and it is transferrable, though it may be encumbered for security reasons.

  The *hak milik* title is available only to (i) Indonesian nationals, (ii) certain religious and social organizations, (iii) government bodies in Indonesia, and (iv) a very limited number of Indonesian legal entities allowed by the government.[7] It is not available to foreign individuals, most Indonesian legal entities, and all foreign legal entities. *Hak pakai* is the only title that may be held by foreign individuals in Indonesia.

- *Hak guna bangunan*:

  A right-to-build (HGB) title is granted for a maximum initial term of 30 years, and may be extended or renewed. It can be used to erect buildings or other structures on a particular parcel of land. It is transferrable, though it may be encumbered for security purposes. An HGB title is available to: (i) Indonesian individuals, and to (ii) legal entities (whether Indonesian or foreign owned) that are incorporated under Indonesian law and domiciled in Indonesia.

Upon the expiry of the initial term, the holder of an HGB title can apply for an extension. An HGB title can be extended for an additional 20 years after the expiration of the initial term. Following the expiration of this additional term, an application for a further extension or renewal must be made. The application for an extension or renewal must be submitted to the land registration office. If the application is approved, the applicant may be granted a renewal of the HGB title over the same plot of land, which in practice can be granted under the same terms. Indonesian land law does not currently limit the number of extensions and renewal cycles allowed for HGB titles.

- *Hak guna usaha*:

  The right-to-cultivate (HGU) title grants the right to cultivate state-owned land or to use it for other agricultural purposes for a certain period of time. GR 40/1996 states that the period of the HGU title is not to exceed 35 years initially, but can be extended for another 25 years. When the extension period expires, the HGU title can be renewed for the same plot of land. The HGU title may only be owned by Indonesian citizens or by companies incorporated under Indonesian law and domiciled in Indonesia.

- *Hak pakai*:

  The right-to-use title represents the right to use and take the fruits of, or simply to take the fruits of, land directly controlled by the government or owned by another party. The right to use can be granted for a definite or indefinite term, as long as the land is used for a specific purpose. When the right to use is granted for a plot of state-owned land, it is valid for a maximum of 25 years, and extendable for another 20 years if the land is still used for a certain purpose.

---

7   In Indonesia, a legal entity is a business in which the assets of the founders are separated from those of the entity itself, which is not the case in the other category of companies: the "business entity." Examples of legal entities are limited liability companies (*Perseroan Terbatas* or PT), cooperatives, and pension funds.

When the right to use is granted for a plot of land that is already subject to a right-to-own title, it is valid for a maximum of 25 years and cannot be extended. However, an extension can be granted based on an agreement between the holder of the right-to-use title and the holder of the right-to-own title.

The right-to-use title may be held by Indonesian citizens, resident foreigners, Indonesian companies domiciled in Indonesia, and foreign companies that have a representative office in Indonesia.

In addition, there are various types of rights over land that do not need to be registered. For instance, no certificate will be issued as evidence of a *hak sewa* (right-to-lease) title. This title grants the holder the right to use a parcel of land, either state-owned or private, in return for compensation. The payment could be one-time or periodical, as determined by a mutual understanding between the parties. Right-to-lease titles may be owned by Indonesian citizens, resident foreigners, Indonesian companies domiciled in Indonesia, and foreign companies that have a representative office in Indonesia.

Under Minister for Agrarian Affairs and Spatial Planning/Head of National Land Agency Regulation No. 17 of 2019 on Location Permits, in order to acquire a parcel of land for business activities, a location permit is necessary, as it grants the holder the right to buy, clear, and develop that parcel of land. Location permits are issued under the One Single Submission system; they are valid for 3 years, and are extendable for a period of 1 year upon the approval of the relevant authorities, on the condition that 50% of the total area applied for has been purchased or obtained by the company holding the permit.

On 16 December 2011, the House of Representatives of the Republic of Indonesia passed the Bill on Land Procurement in the Public Interest, which came into force on 14 January 2012 as Law No. 2 of 2012 on Land Procurement in the Public Interest. Law 2/1012 introduces clear and expedited steps for

the procurement of land in the public interest. It is intended to provide a more effective legal basis for public-interest land procurement. Under Law 2/2012, the term "public interest" is defined as the interest of the Indonesian people, nation, and community, as manifested in the government and used optimally for the welfare of all the people of Indonesia. In order to implement Law 2/2012, Presidential Regulation No. 71 of 2012 on the Implementation of Land Procurement in the Public Interest was enacted and came into force on 7 August 2012, as amended by Presidential Regulation No. 148 of 2015, Presidential Regulation No. 30 of 2015, Presidential Regulation No. 40 of 2014, and Presidential Regulation No. 99 of 2014 ("**Land Procurement Implementation Regulation**"), which revoked the previous implementation law: Presidential Regulation No. 36 of 2005, as amended by Presidential Regulation No. 65 of 2006. PR 99/2014 aims to ensure the smooth execution of development activities in the public interest, for which the purpose is required, and is intended to provide a more effective legal basis for public-interest land procurement.

Under Law 2/2012, the central government and/or the relevant regional government is given the task of ensuring the availability of the land required for public interest uses. The law also clearly stipulates that a party (the "**entitled party**") that owns or otherwise controls the land, space under and/or above the land, buildings, plants, any object related to the land, or other objects that could be expropriated ("**land procurement objects**") is obliged to relinquish its right over this land for the sake of the public interest, following the provision of a fair and reasonable compensation or a legally binding court decision. After such land is expropriated, it becomes the property of the national government, provincial government, city government or a state-owned enterprise (SOE), as the case may be.

Law 2/2012 specifically stipulates the following types of development projects as being in the public interest:

- national defense and security;
- public roads, toll roads, tunnels, railways, train stations, and train-operating facilities;

- water embankments, reservoirs, irrigation systems, drinking water channels, water disposal channels, and sanitation and other water-resource-management construction projects;
- seaports, airports, and terminals;
- oil, gas, and geothermal-energy infrastructure;
- power plants, power transmission stations, switch yards, power networks, and distribution systems;
- government telecommunications and informatics networks;
- waste disposal and processing facilities;
- hospitals owned by the national government or provincial or city government;
- public safety facilities;
- cemeteries owned by the national government or provincial or city government;
- social facilities, public facilities, and open public green spaces;
- wildlife and culture reserves;
- office facilities for the national government, provincial or city government, or subdistricts and villages;
- the structuring of urban slum areas and/or land consolidation, and of rental housing in low-income communities;
- education facilities or schools under the national government or a provincial or city government;
- sports facilities owned by the national government or provincial or city government; and
- public markets and public parking facilities.

Initially, a government entity, an SOE that has been given a special assignment from the government, or a private business authorized by a governmental institution or SOE that plans to procure land for the public interest must have a public consultation with the parties affected with the land procurement objects, including any entitled party under the proposed development plan, until a consensus is reached. If no consensus can be reached, or if there is any objection to the proposed development plan,

the provincial or city governor will establish a team to examine the reasons for the objections. Based on the team's findings, the governor will decide whether the objections are valid. To the extent that such objections are denied, the entitled party may file a legal claim with the State Administrative Court, whose decision can thereafter be subject to a final appeal with the Supreme Court. If, by virtue of a legally binding court decision, the land has been approved for procurement in the public interest, the head of the regional office of the National Land Agency, as the chief executive of land procurement appointed under the land procurement implementation regulations, shall determine the value of the compensation to be paid to the entitled party based on an appraisal by an independent public appraiser licensed by the minister of finance. To challenge the compensation value, if necessary, the entitled party may file a legal claim with a District Court and, if necessary, the decision of the District Court can be filed for a final appeal to the Supreme Court.

Through an inventory and public consultation process, the opinions of the respective title owners and impacted stakeholders need to be considered during the infrastructure development process, and the related opportunity to capture land value needs to be investigated further.

Hak Guna Ruang Angkasa (Space Use Rights) under the Basic Agrarian Law

Based on Law 5/1960 (the Basic Agrarian Law), space is classified as a part of the national patrimony, together with the earth, water, and natural resources contained in it and owned by the public. The government has the right to control this domain—which means that the use of land, water, space, and other natural resources must be aimed at the prosperity of the people of Indonesia.

Related to the right to control, the national government has been authorized by the law to: (i) regulate and carry out utilization, inventory, and maintenance; (ii) determine and regulate the rights that can be owned over (part of) the land, water, and space; and (iii) determine and regulate legal relations between people and legal actions concerning the land, water, and space. Specifically, Article 48 of Law 5/1960 stipulates that *hak guna ruang angkasa* (space use rights) are based on the government's authority to use energy and elements in space to maintain and develop the country's earth, water, and natural wealth.

In order to achieve the use of space that will provide the greatest benefit to the Indonesian people, the government needs to plan the design, use, and supply of land, water, and space while taking various interests into account—both public and private. Article 14 of the Basic Agrarian Law divides planning into (i) the general plan (national planning), which covers Indonesia as a whole; and (ii) the specific plans (provincial and regional planning), which cover each province or region. The provinces must control their use of the land, water, and space within their borders in a manner that complies with the general plan, and in a manner that optimizes community welfare within their borders. The local governments must also ensure that their provisions are in accordance with the general plan.

Regulatory Framework for Building Management

Izin Mendirikan Bangunan (Building Permits)

Based on **Law No. 28 of 2002 on Building ("Building Law")**, every building must comply with the administrative and technical requirements based on its function. Building administrative requirements cover the status of rights over the land, the status of building ownership, and the building permit (IMB).

Article 1 paragraph 1 of the Minister of Public Works and Housing Regulation No. 05/PRT/M/2016 on Building Construction Permits, as amended by the Minister of Public Works and Housing Regulation No. 06/PRT/M/2017, defines the IMB as a license issued by the local government to build, modify, extend, reduce, and/or maintain a building in accordance with the applicable administrative and

technical requirements, except for buildings assigned a particular public function by the government. Any building constructed without a building permit would be subject to the risk of demolition by the relevant authorities.

After a building's construction is complete, the owner has to obtain the function-worthiness certificate (SLF) before the building can be used. An SLF issued by the local regent or mayor is valid for 5 years.

Multistory Building Regulations

The development of multistory, strata-title residential, retail and office buildings are regulated by **Law No. 20 of 2011 on Strata Title Buildings**, which replaced Law No. 16 of 1985 on Strata Title Buildings. On October 30, 2013, the Ministry of Public Works and Housing issued MPWH Regulation No. 10 of 2012, as amended by MPWH Regulation No. 7 of 2013 on the Implementation of Housing and Settlement Areas as the implementing regulation of Law 20/2011.

Law 20/2011 classifies several types of strata title buildings, including: (i) *rumah susun umum* (public strata title buildings), provided for low-income persons; (ii) *rumah susun khusus* (special strata title buildings), provided for special needs; (iii) *rumah susun negara* (state strata title buildings), which are owned and provided by the state for residential purposes, along with other support services for state officials; and (iv) *rumah susun komersial* (commercial strata title buildings), which are for commercial use.

The government is responsible for the development of public strata title buildings, special strata title buildings, and state strata title buildings. Any party developing a public strata title building may receive aid from the government. Public strata title buildings and special strata title buildings may be developed by a nonprofit institution or business entity. A commercial strata title building may be developed by any party. Under Law 20/2011, the developer of a commercial strata title building must provide a public strata title building project with a floor area of at least 20% of the total floor area of the commercial strata title building. The public strata title building project may be located outside the premises of the commercial strata title building, but it is required to be located within the same regency or city. The one exception is the Jakarta province, where under MPWH 7/2013 public strata title buildings may be located in another city different from where the commercial strata title building is located, but it must be within the region. Violation of this requirement may expose the developer to imprisonment of up to 2 years, or a fine of up to Rp20 billion.

A strata title building may be constructed on a parcel of land to which the developer has (i) a *hak milik* title, (ii) an HGB title or *hak pakai atas tanah negara* (right to use state-owned land) title, or (iii) an HGB or *hak pakai di atas hak pengelolaan* (right-to-use over right-to-manage) title. In addition, a public strata title building and/or special strata title building can also be constructed by utilizing land owned by the national, provincial, or regional government (by way of lease or cooperation on utilization) or by utilizing *wakaf* (donated land), by way of a lease or cooperation on utilization pursuant to *ikrar wakaf* (pledged land).

Under this law, the developer may market a strata title building before construction has begun. But prior to marketing the property, the developer must satisfy, at a minimum, the following criteria: (i) the certainty of the space allotment, (ii) the certainty of rights over the land, (iii) certainty of possession of the strata title building, (iv) possession of a construction license, and (v) a guarantee of construction from the relevant surety institution. The developer may enter into a preliminary sale and purchase agreement with a purchaser before a notary prior to the completion of the strata title building. But the preliminary sale and purchase agreement can only occur after the satisfaction of the following requirements: (i) the ownership of the land is clearly established; (ii) the building construction permit has been obtained; (iii) the necessary infrastructure, facilities, and public utilities are accessible; (iv) the construction of the strata title building is at least 20% complete; and

(v) the object of the agreement is clear. In the event that the strata building is constructed on HGB title land, or on land under a *hak pakai di atas hak pengelolaan* title, the developer should settle the ownership title of the land prior to the sale and purchase of units in the strata title building.

Under Law 20/2011, all of the required implementing regulations, including in relation to *surat kepemilikan bangunan gedung* (building ownership certificates), were issued within 1 year of the law's date of enactment. However, the implementing regulation on building ownership certificates was never issued.

Regulatory Framework for Investment

The regulatory framework for investment is broadly aligned with the principles of value capture. However, caution is required to ensure that the incentives given to investors do not undermine the implementation of the planned value capture.

The objectives of investment in Indonesia, based on **Law No. 25 of 2007 on Capital Investment** are to:

- increase national economic growth;
- create job opportunities;
- enhance sustainable economic development;
- increase national competitiveness;
- enhance national technological development capacity;
- drive the democratic economy;
- process the potential economy into economic power, from national and/or international financing sources; and
- improve social welfare.

Law 25/2007 clearly states that investment implementation in Indonesia needs to have a multiplier effect on national economic development (involving the first, third, fourth, and seventh of the above objectives) and social welfare (the second and eighth objectives). In Indonesia, investment has a key role in optimizing its *pendapatan daerah* (regional income) by optimizing the money transferred by private sector players conducting their business in the country. If the level of investment increases, the number of private sector players also increases. In addition to allowing particular private sector players to make profits from their businesses, the infrastructure built by the government (such as roads and public transportation) generates benefits for the private sector as a whole. These benefits need to be captured and transferred to the public treasury, to finance other public infrastructure development in alignment with the objectives of Law 25/2007. For this purpose, the relationship between investments and the value capture mechanism needs to be investigated further.

The law describes how the government aims to create an investment ecosystem that is conducive and attractive to investors. For this purpose, the government has implemented a policy that provides "facilities" and *kemudahan pelayanan dan perijinan* (ease of service and licensing) for investors who comply with some of the criteria provided for under the law. The "facilities" that can be provided to potential investors include:

- net and gross reductions;
- waivers of import duties on goods, raw materials, and machines;
- waivers of the value-added tax (VAT) on imported goods and machines;
- accelerated depreciation; and
- property tax reduction.

At the same time, "ease of services and licensing" includes:

- easier procedures for the private sector to obtain right-to-cultivate, right-to-build, and right-to-use titles;
- easier immigration procedures; and
- easier procedures for the private sector to obtain permits to import goods. (Appendix 1, Table A1.5 provides a detailed description of the relevant facilities and ease of services, as well as the procedures for obtaining permits.)

Based on the above assessment, the government has introduced mechanisms for lessening the administrative burden on potential investors wishing to enter the Indonesian market. The applicability of these mechanisms will need to be carefully explored in relation to the potential implementation of value capture instruments, which, in general, are aimed at increasing the potential revenue from such initiatives.

The government issued Government Regulation No. 24 of 2018 on Electronic Integrated Business Licensing Services, which introduced new business licensing procedures via an operational support system (OSS), launched on 9 July 2018. The OSS is an online business licensing platform intended to accelerate and simplify the process of obtaining business licenses, and it can be accessed online at any time. It is currently operated and managed by the OSS management and organization institution (referred to as the "OSS Body") under the supervision of the *Badan Koordinasi Penanaman Modal* (Capital Investment Coordinating Board) as of 2 January 2019.

The OSS aims to provide businesses with a one-stop shop, with a 24-7 service for receiving all clearances. It can process social security programs, location permits, environmental license, IMBs, and the foreign employee utilization plan.

Any company starting operations in Indonesia must obtain a single business number (NIB) and the relevant business license. The NIB is a mandatory requirement for any businesses seeking to (i) apply for a new business license and/or commercial or operational license; and (ii) to extend or amend an existing business license and/or commercial or operational license through the OSS. A NIB may be obtained by registering in the OSS system via the website (https://oss.go.id/oss/).

2.2. Institutional Framework

The implementation of value capture mechanisms in Indonesia will potentially require the involvement and support of multiple government organizations, while decentralization provides provincial, regional, and local governments with some degree of autonomy. The fact that the relevant sectors are governed by several ministries and state agencies presents a challenge in terms of determining the direction of any collaborative approach.

The existing institutional framework for the planning and procurement of infrastructure and infrastructure services is summarized in Table 2.2.

Table 2.3 describes the responsibilities and structure of local government institutions, which mirror the national level. Local governments have the right to set up their own government structures, though they must be aligned with Government Regulation No. 72 of 2019 on Local Government Structure.

Table 2.2: National Institutional Framework	
Ministry	**General Responsibilities**
Coordinating Ministry for Economic Affairs (CMEA)	• Coordinating and synchronizing the formulation, determination, and implementation of economic policies by ministries and agencies • Controlling and monitoring the implementation of economic policies within the various ministries and agencies • Coordinating the implementation of administrative support among all elements within the CMEA • Managing the state properties and assets under the responsibility of the CMEA • Supervising work performance within the CMEA • Performing certain tasks assigned by the President
Coordinating Ministry for Maritime and Investment Affairs (CMMIA)	• Coordinating and synchronizing the formulation, determination, and implementation of maritime and investment policies by ministries and agencies • Managing and handling national maritime and investment issues • Coordinating the implementation of administrative support for all elements within the CMMIA • Guiding the national priority programs and policies • Managing conflicts of interest among ministries and agencies and ensuring the implementation of each decision • Managing the state properties and assets under the responsibility of the CMMIA • Supervising work performance within the CMMIA
Ministry of Agrarian Affairs and Spatial Planning/National Land Agency (MOAASP/NLA)	• Making and implementing policy decisions in the areas of spatial planning, land infrastructure, legal land relations, land use management, land acquisition, land use control, land tenure control, and landholding • Coordinating the implementation of tasks, providing administrative support for all elements within the MOAASP • Managing the state properties and assets under the responsibility of the MOAASP • Supervising the implementation of tasks within the MOAASP • Providing technical guidance on, and supervision of, the implementation of MOAASP affairs in the provinces and regions
Ministry of Finance (MOF)	• Making and implementing policy decisions with regard to budgeting, taxation, customs and excise, treasury, state assets, fiscal balance, and financing and risk management • Developing fiscal policy and financial sector recommendations • Coordinating the implementation, coaching, and provision of administrative support to all elements within the MOF • Overseeing of the implementation of tasks within the MOF • Providing technical assistance with regard to public finance affairs at the provincial or regional level • Managing and supervising the utilization of state-owned assets
Ministry of National Development Planning/National Development Planning Agency (BAPPENAS)	• Consolidating national development plans • Consolidating the draft state revenue and expenditure budget • Controlling and implementing national development plans • Handling urgent and large-scale problems • Reviewing and designing policies for development, provincial and regional economies, and the planning sector • Strengthening the planning capacity of the central, provincial, and regional governments regarding innovative and creative funding mechanisms • Engaging in participatory planning, including collaboration with universities, professional organizations, and civil society organizations • Coordinating cross-governmental discussions on development planning, national development strategies, policy directions (sectoral, cross-sectoral, and cross-regional), national and regional macroeconomic frameworks, the design of facilities and infrastructure, regulatory frameworks, institutions, and funding, as well as the monitoring, evaluation, and control of the implementation of national development • Coordinating the search for alternative financing options, and allocating funds • Synchronizing the implementation of national development plans and budgeting policies, and preparing facilities and infrastructure designs • Monitoring and evaluating the development process

(continued on next page)

Table 2.2: National Institutional Framework (continued)	
Ministry	**General Responsibilities**
Ministry of Public Works and Housing (MPWH)	• Formulating and implementing policies regarding public works and housing (water resources management, road development, housing and residential area development, infrastructure financing, building arrangement, drinking water supply systems, wastewater management systems, and environmental drainage, as well as solid waste management systems and guidance for construction services) • Coordinating and providing administrative support to all elements within the MPWH • Managing the state properties and assets under the responsibility of the MPWH • Supervising work performance within the MPWH • Implementing technical guidance and supervising the development of public works and housing within local governments • Implementing the technical policies and strategies for integrating the public works and housing infrastructure • Supporting human resources development with regard to public works and housing affairs • Providing substantive support to all elements within the MPWH • Performing certain tasks assigned by the President
Ministry of Transportation (MOT)	• Formulating the substantive, implementation, and technical policies regarding national transportation • Implementing national transportation agendas • Managing the state properties and assets under the responsibility of the MOT • Supervising the work performance within the MOT • Delivering evaluation reports suggestions, and considerations regarding the transportation sector to the President

Source: Authors.

Table 2.3: Local Institutional Framework	
Government Agency	**General Responsibilities**
Regional Planning and Development Board (BAPPEDA)	The BAPPEDA typically has responsibilities similar to those of the Ministry of National Development Planning/National Development Planning Agency (BAPPENAS), but at a more local level.
Treasury Agency (BPD)	The responsibilities of the BPD are generally similar to those of the Ministry of Finance regarding taxation, customs and excise, and treasury collection, but at a more local level.
Regional Financial and Asset Management Agency (BPKAD)	The BPKAD has responsibilities that are similar to those of the Ministry of Finance regarding budgets, state assets, fiscal balance, and financing and risk management, but at a more local level.
Transportation Agency	• Governing transport affairs at the local level, including traffic management, road safety, public transport, and urban mobility • Developing planning documents and budgets related to future transport infrastructure • Developing policies related to transport issues • Issuing permits for heavy vehicle licenses and bus routes • Managing on-street parking and off-street parking in areas that are government assets
Public Works and Spatial Planning Agency	This agency has responsibilities similar to those of the Ministry of Public Works and Housing and the Ministry of Agrarian Affairs and Spatial Planning/National Land Agency, but at a more local level. The agency is also involved in: • Governing public works and spatial planning at the local level • Developing local planning and policies in relation to public works and spatial planning issues.

Source: Authors.

2.3. Identified Barriers, Constraints, and Challenges

Analysis, as well as discussions with relevant stakeholders has shown that the whole-of-government approach to value capture implementation is currently constrained by a regulatory and institutional framework perceived as too rigid and narrow, and difficult to change. Therefore, the challenge is to build the capacity of the relevant parties and to incorporate suitable value capture mechanisms into the development of business cases for large-scale infrastructure projects.

Based on the framework of the enablers of value creation and value capture, as presented in Table 1.3, the key barriers, current constraints, and future challenges are assessed in Table 2.4.

Enablers of Value Creation and Value Capture	Constraints (Current Outlook)	Challenges (Future Outlook)
Table 2.4: Barriers, Constraints, and Challenges Hindering the Whole-of-Government Approach		
Whole-of-government approach	Currently, only the coordinating ministries have the authority to coordinate policies between ministries and government agencies, while the other ministries can only pursue technical policies within their own sectors.	• The future implementation of value capture may become an inter-sectoral affair, which will require strong partnerships and coordination among the relevant ministries and government agencies for both the development and implementation of suitable mechanisms. • The Ministry of Finance and local governments need to be able to capture the benefits of economic uplift.
Visionary master planning of public investments in infrastructure	Investment laws are currently geared toward attracting investors, for example, by providing incentives such as discounted taxes (e.g., income tax and property tax). This could constrain the development of the applicable value capture mechanisms, which aims to optimize the collection of taxes from investors by capturing more value based on the increases in land value in the calculation.	• There might be a need for a detailed assessment of the investment regulations, and it will have to be carefully considered when the government explores the potential implementation of value capture instruments. • Certain value capture instruments may not be applicable to all types of businesses and industries, and will need to be aligned with the relevant investment regulations. • A campaign may be needed to shift public perceptions of value capture mechanisms as an additional "hurdle" to private sector investment.
Long-term land use planning and regulatory framework	Different types of land rights have different characteristics in terms of how those with land rights can access and manage their property. This means that different approaches may be required to evaluate and capture land value.	• The different "levels" of land rights might need to be considered when the government develops the potential future value capture instruments, for instance, the higher potential capture of ownership rights, and potentially the lower capture of rights of use. • The regulations on land provision for infrastructure set out procedures for assessing the impact of infrastructure development. This process could be integrated with the business case for an infrastructure project through the valuing and capture of increases in the land value due to the infrastructure.
Integrated urban and transport development	Regional autonomy means that infrastructure development planning, as well as the implementation of wider value capture mechanisms, may require the involvement and agreement of several local governments.	• Some cities and regencies may face varying degrees of difficulty in developing the detailed spatial plan and zoning regulations suitable for the implementation of value capture mechanisms. • While stakeholders in a more developed region such as Special Capital Region of Jakarta (DKI Jakarta), have already explored various potential value capture instruments, in mid-sized cities (e.g., Palembang) stakeholders will need to look beyond property taxation as a potential instrument for value capture. Significant capacity building and knowledge transfer may be required to raise overall awareness of value capture options in these cities. • Jakarta, Palembang, and other cities could potentially face problems due to urban sprawl, and thus may require a strengthened enforcement of regulations on spatial planning.
Value capture-oriented taxation regime	• There are different channels through which national, provincial, and local revenues are collected. • Each level of government has a different authority concerned with each sector. • The regulations on national and local finance impose restrictions on the collection of taxes and levies outside those stipulated by law. • The current regulations allow allocations to specific infrastructure projects. • The taxes and levies collected by local governments cannot be directly allocated to finance-related infrastructure in areas where the sectoral tax is collected. Taxes are collected through a melting-pot mechanism, and the ability to earmark tax revenue will require a significant reform of the tax system.	• The detailed strategies and arrangements regarding value capture through the collection of taxes and levies might vary for each regency and city, depending on the local financial regulations. • The arrangements regarding spending on infrastructure, sourced from value capture, might need to be fully coordinated among the different levels of government to ensure more effective and efficient spending, considering the limited opportunities for earmarking. • The methodology for calculating taxes and levies might need to be revised to optimize and capture more land value. • Infrastructure investment creates extra economic activity at the local level, but the tax benefits mainly flow to the national government.

Source: Authors.

3.   The Value Creation Framework

For an effective implementation of value creation, a clear value creation framework must be developed, based on the creation of economic infrastructure that will provide industry, commerce, and society with key services to increase their economic productivity. International cases studies on value creation point to four overarching enablers of value creation: land use planning and regulatory frameworks, a whole-of-government approach, economic planning, and an integrated development approach. Several fundamental issues have been identified with regard to the Indonesian long-term land use planning and regulatory framework that will require attention going forward.

3.1.   Economic Theory of Value Creation

Value creation should always be considered during the assessment and improvement of the benefits generated by public investments. Public sector investments create economic infrastructure that provide industry, commerce, and society with key infrastructure services that contribute to economic uplift.

Yoshino and Pontines (2015) studied the economic-productivity effects of infrastructure investment from pre-completion to post-completion of projects, over the years. Their key premise is that, without a given project or policy being implemented, the changes in outcome between the beneficiary and non-beneficiary groups would remain the same over time. They observed that infrastructure projects delivered increased economic productivity relative to a no-project scenario. There were incremental benefits after project implementation, as shown in Figure 3.1 by the orange deviation line. The higher productivity benefited not only direct users, but also third parties and society as a whole.

Value creation should also be planned in parallel with the planning for economic uplift capture.[8] Therefore, value creation requires that all essential infrastructure services work hand-in-hand in order to maximize

Figure 3.1: Economic Productivity Effects on Infrastructure Investment

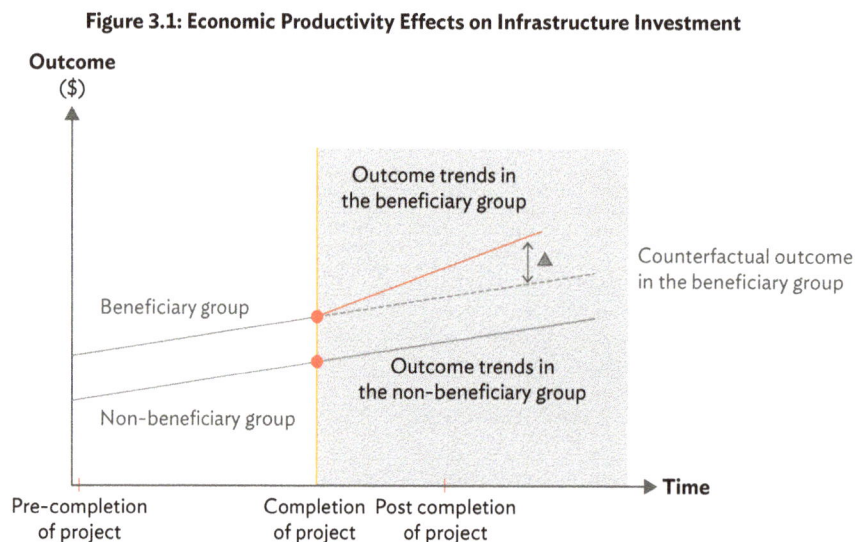

Source: N. Yoshino and V. Pontines. 2015. The "Highway Effect" on Public Finance: Case of the STAR Highway in the Philippines. *ADBI Working Paper Series* No. 549. Tokyo: Asian Development Bank Institute.

---

8   Economic uplift is defined as the tangible positive socioeconomic benefits that accumulate beyond the specific target area of infrastructure development and its direct service delivery through the creation of an asset, function and stakeholder network (UNESCAP 2019). In the literature, "economic uplift" can also be referred to as "externality effects," "spillover effects," "network effects" and/or" indirect effects."

the value created by the economic infrastructure investments, and to make room for business growth.

3.2. Case Studies of Value Creation

While value creation activities are commonplace, their implementation within a policy framework is still relatively new. Reviews of international case studies of policy-based value creation have revealed four value creation enablers: **(i) a whole-of-government approach; (ii) economic planning; (iii) land use planning and a regulatory framework; and (iv) an integrated development approach.**

International Best Practice in Value Creation

Table 3.1 describes the enablers that were derived from reviews of various references, which are listed at the end of the section.

Table 3.1: Enablers Drawn from International Best Practices		
1. Whole-of-Government Approach		
Areas	**Best Practices**	
Enabling framework and legislation	• A value creation and value capture (VCC) framework sets out the expected outcomes, and provides guidance on the application of the appropriate mechanisms for creating and capturing value from public investments in infrastructure. An example is the VCC framework in the State of Victoria, Australia. • Enabling legislation should be enacted to support the value creation and value capture framework.	A strategic VCC plan will outline the VCC opportunities to be pursued, together with their indicative values. A detailed VCC plan will be prepared based on the full business case.
Interministerial and interdepartmental collaboration	• Value capture is often championed by a special entity, but value creation is typically a collaborative effort among competent line ministries to achieve the intended outcomes. • It is necessary to extend the focus beyond the individual project objectives, and to take a broader approach that considers the objectives of other portfolios. • Wider economic, social, and environmental objectives should be considered—including the objectives of other agencies related to the precinct or project under consideration. • An alignment should be ensured among the relevant government policies, strategies, and legislation.	The VCC framework of Australia's State of Victoria defines the parameters for the application of value creation and value capture, such as the types of projects and programs that require a VCC plan.
Innovative procurement and funding	• There should be a shift in mindset from government-pays and user-pays models to the beneficiary-pays model, anchored in a concerted and consistent effort by the government to increase the value generated by public action. • All potential forms of value creation must be considered, as well as a wider group of potential beneficiaries than the immediate user group for the project. • Private sector innovation and expertise must be harnessed through the use of output-based specifications and performance-based payment mechanisms in procurement, to deliver better value assets and services (e.g., higher quality, lower cost, more timely, and safer).	Government ministries and agencies, as the project sponsors, will be responsible for preparing a project-specific statement of intent, setting out the project objectives, as well as a VCC plan for approval by the relevant minister.[a]
2. Economic Planning		
Areas	**Best Practices**	
Creation of nodes of economic activity	• Economic planning creates space for both the public and private sectors to optimize the provision of goods and services for which a tangible demand exists. • The provision of new infrastructure creates new opportunities to expand the goods market for firms and the job market for labor, bringing the market closer to economic agents through better accessibility and improved mobility.[b] • Densification of economic activity results in cost efficiency, thus improving affordability.	The UK's Crossrail financing scheme was based on an in-depth business case study that estimated the benefits and identified the beneficiaries of the Elizabeth Line, in London,[c] allowing the Government of the United Kingdom to negotiate contributions from major businesses identified as gaining from the project through access to a larger labor market and a rise in property values, among other benefits.[d]
Increased benefits of public investment	• A deliberate approach is needed to generate and increase the benefits of public investment in infrastructure, such as resilient job creation, improved accessibility, and improved quality of life. • A comprehensive business case and an economic cost-benefit analysis will provide rigor in the identification of the beneficiaries; they will also help determine the extent to which demonstrations of how planned infrastructure will create economic value within a catchment area will attract beneficiary contributions.	SASEC is a cooperation program that brings together Bangladesh, Bhutan, India, Maldives, Myanmar, Nepal, and Sri Lanka in a project-based partnership that aims to promote regional prosperity, improve economic opportunities, and build a better quality of life for the people of South Asia. Aware of its immense economic potential, South Asia has also recognized that it is home to more than 800 million of the world's poor, and is thus in dire need of effective industrialization and job creation.[e]
Collaboration between the public and private sectors	• Economic planning should aim to create mutually beneficial partnerships for both the public and private sectors. • There should be a clear and transparent framework for private participation that will make use of performance incentive models such as output-based specifications and performance-linked payment mechanisms.	
Economic data on flows of materials	• Government data banks and statistics gathered consistently from the national to the city level will enable a robust economic analysis of public investments at various levels of government. • There should be integrated, complete, up-to-date, and fully representative data, based on consistent scoping and methodologies, that are made available to the public.	
3. Land Use Planning and a Regulatory Framework		
Areas	**Best Practices**	
Integrated master planning and development geared toward a high quality of life, competitive economy, and a sustainable environment	• There should be a visionary master plan anchored in a long-term view (from 2021 to 2060 or 2070) of land use and transportation, to ensure that development is sustainable, and that present and future needs are met. • Spatial plans are often out of date or nonexistent, and sometimes there are gaps (e.g., a provincial plan exists but not a lower-level one). • There should be a long-term land- and water-use plan setting out broad strategies to support the projected population growth and economic growth, ensuring that there is adequate land and water for posterity, while also ensuring a high quality of life in the present. • Government strategies are translated into a master plan to guide development over 10–15 years, promoting the better integration of economic activity, land use, and transport infrastructure.[f]	The Government of the State of Victoria has recently introduced new planning controls that allow for an increase in floor area in return for providing public amenities.[a]

(continued on next page)

Table 3.1: Enablers Drawn from International Best Practice *(continued)*

3. Land Use Planning and a Regulatory Framework

Areas	Best Practice	
Flexible zoning geared toward mixed-use, compact developments near transit stations	• Zoning concerns both land use and density, and can be a viable government instrument that enables public and private developers to concentrate economic activity and increase property values within a planned area. • A robust regulatory framework to enforce the long-term land and water use plan should specify where development can occur, and at what density level, to prevent the unsustainable conversion of land, especially land initially intended for conservation, preservation, and protection. • Land speculation makes land acquisition expensive for the government. To prevent this, rules should clearly set out the process for exercising eminent domain, including the rules for determining reasonable compensation. • Flexible zoning in terms of the FAR can help achieve optimal land use intensity at the city level, and around transit stations. In this case, it does not relate solely to "flexible land use conversion." For example, FARs can be finely tailored to be proportional to the proximity to transit stations.[g] • A margin of flexibility should be included both for the transfer of development rights between different uses as the market changes and allowing private developers to adjust the intensity of development based on market needs.[g]	Hudson Yards, in New York City, was re-zoned into a very dense mixed-use urban development that has now become a central business district for the creative and knowledge industries. Hudson Yards adopted a flexible zoning scheme in which the FAR that determines the density of land use was set as a range between the base and maximum FAR. That range is intended to provide flexibility, while capturing maximum value.[g]
Robust system of land administration and management to allow clarity and certainty regarding ownership, and a forward-looking view of the acquisition and disposition of land	• The land administration and management system should be transparent, accurate, responsive, and efficient. • A system of land registration and surveys, and subsequent improvements thereto, increases clarity and certainty regarding ownership, allowing the land market to function effectively and efficiently. • For example, through INLIS, a service of the Singapore Land Authority, the general public can obtain access to property information and land survey information, among other types of information, in the form of plans and cadastral maps.[h] • Forward-looking and effective land acquisition policies and legislation are needed, as well as a strategic view regarding the disposition of core and noncore public assets.	The BCDA, in the Philippines, is charged with transforming former military bases and properties into centers of economic growth, in partnership with the private sector, based on the principles of integrity, excellence, and efficiency in the stewardship of government resources. Its goal is to create sustainable urban communities to improve the lives of Filipinos.[i]

4. Integrated Development Approach

Areas	Best Practice	
Placemaking	• Place value for residents arises from vibrant, sustainable communities where they can access jobs, shopping, and services on foot or by bicycle, and enjoy a range of benefits, such as reduced transportation costs; easier access to amenities, including high-quality schools; and improved public health.[g] • Urban regeneration is intended to increase the place value of promising areas that have stagnated.[j]	Hong Kong, China's spatial planning is based on TOD (rail-based) and a commitment to doing more with less. TOD in Hong Kong, China embraces the idea that locating amenities, jobs, shops, and housing around transit hubs promotes the use of public transit and nonmotorized transport. Land in Hong Kong, China is zoned according to the maximum FARs, with extremely dense building permitted directly above and adjacent to rail stations. The integration of land use and transit planning has placed 75% of people and 84% of jobs less than 1 kilometer from a mass transit station. The government-controlled MTRC operates a rail-plus-property business model that captures any rises in property value resulting from new railway infrastructure, using revenue from property development to fund the railway's construction and operations.[g]
Integrated transport planning	• Enabling transfers between different modes of transport, such that a deeper and broader network of mobility can be provided, will increase the potential service coverage from origin to destination. It will also promote higher ridership.	
Public commons	• Public commons can be leveraged when optimizing land use benefits and improving the efficiency of public works installation.[j] • For example, public commons such as parks and greenways connect the elements of sustainability, housing, and livelihood, while the underground space can accommodate utilities and transport, creating commercial value capture opportunities.	Singapore's success as a trading port city in colonial times left it overpopulated, resulting in urban slums. Singapore has focused not only on economic growth and jobs, but also on social development. Measures such as relocating street hawkers to specially designated areas and the adoption of mixed-use buildings have minimized the hardship of displacement for residents and businesses. Increasing green spaces and reducing pollution have further improved the quality of life.[j]

BCDA = Bases Conversion and Development Authority, FAR = floor area ratio, INLIS = Integrated Land Information Service, MTRC = Mass Transit Railway Corporation, SASEC = South Asia Subregional Economic Cooperation, TOD = transit-oriented development, UK = United Kingdom, VCC = value creation and value capture.

Note: The floor area ratio (FAR) is the ratio of a building's total floor area to the size of the plot of land on which it is built.

[a] Government of the State of Victoria, Australia. 2017. *Victoria's Value Creation and Value Capture Framework: Maximising Social, Economic and Environmental Value from Infrastructure Investment*. Melbourne. https://www.vic.gov.au/sites/default/files/2019-02/Victorias-Value-Creation-Capture-Framework.pdf.

[b] N. Yoshino, M. Helble, and U. Abidhadjaev, eds. 2018. *Financing Infrastructure in Asia and the Pacific: Capturing Impacts and New Sources*. Tokyo: Asian Development Bank Institute. https://www.adb.org/sites/default/files/publication/394191/adbi-financing-infrastructure-asia-capturing-impacts-and-new-sources.pdf.

[c] In 2001, Crossrail Limited was established to build the new Elizabeth Line through Central London. It is a wholly owned subsidiary of Transport for London, as part of London's integrated transport network. Over 60% of Crossrail's funding requirement of £17.8 billion in 2019 (£14.8 billion in 2010) has been provided by identified beneficiaries, including other parts of the public sector, London residents, and London businesses. One of the biggest sources of revenue was the Business Rate Supplement, which was paid by all businesses in London. The Business Rate Supplement provided a secure revenue, on which Transport for London raised £3.5 billion of debt with an initial repayment tenure of 15 years.

[d] M. Buck. 2017. Crossrail Project: Finance, Funding and Value Capture for London's Elizabeth Line. *Proceedings of the Institution of Civil Engineers* 170(CE6): 15-22. https://www.icevirtuallibrary.com/doi/pdf/10.1680/jcien.17.00005.

[e] In this subregion, urban population growth has outpaced urban infrastructure development, with 200 million living in slums. Responding to these problems requires further development and SASEC aimed to invest $2.4 trillion by 2020 to address the subregion's infrastructure gap. Building transport corridors, while developing the areas alongside and between those corridors, is part of the goal of sustainable development. This approach extends the benefits of economic transformation and growth to more of the population in the development corridors. Planning and/or development is currently underway for three economic corridors in Bangladesh, India, and Sri Lanka. The developments in the corridors include: (i) a high-speed transportation network (rail and road), (ii) ports with state-of-the-art cargo-handling equipment, (iii) modern airports, (iv) special economic regions and industrial areas, (v) logistics parks and transshipment hubs, (vi) knowledge parks focused on industrial needs, and (vii) complementary infrastructure such as townships and real estate. SASEC: South Asia Subregional Economic Cooperation. Economic Corridor Development. https://www.sasec.asia/index.php?page=economic-corridors in.

[f] Urban Redevelopment Authority (Singapore). Concept Plan 2011 and MND Land Use Plan. https://www.ura.gov.sg/Corporate/Planning/Concept-Plan/Land-Use-Plan.

[g] S. Salat and G. Ollivier. 2017. *Transforming the Urban Space through Transit-Oriented Development: The 3V Approach*. Washington, DC: World Bank. https://openknowledge.worldbank.org/handle/10986/26405.

[h] Government of Singapore, Singapore Land Authority, Integrated Land Information Service (INLIS). https://www.sla.gov.sg/inlis/.

[i] Government of the Philippines, Bases Conversion and Development Authority (BCDA). https://www.bcda.gov.ph/.

[j] Centre for Liveable Cities (CLC). 2016. *Urban Redevelopment: From Urban Squalor to Global City*. Singapore: CLC. https://www.clc.gov.sg/docs/default-source/urban-systems-studies/uss-urbanredevelopment.pdf.

Source: Authors.

Value Creation in the Financing of Infrastructure

Value creation is enabled by financing productive infrastructure investments that enable growth in economic productivity.

The main sources of financing for infrastructure are summarized in Table 3.2 and Table 3.3, together with their relative appetites for development risk. One main difference between public finance and private capital is who bears the risk of default on public infrastructure projects. Private investors seek recourse to the government through payment mechanisms such as availability payments and guarantees on revenue shortfalls. With regard to public financing, the Ministry of Finance determines its capacity to meet government obligations, including availability payments and government guarantees on infrastructure projects.

The case studies show that whether within the government or the private sector, decision-makers need to be confident that there is a strategic case for any investment decision and that the investment can provide the required returns. Value creation and value capture provide the basis for this confidence, through a comprehensive economic cost-benefit analysis.

Any attempt to shift away from a reliance on government funding for infrastructure projects will face various challenges. For example, in the case of conventional real-estate developments and conventional townships, the limitations are described in the subsequent sub-sections.

Financing Conventional Real-Estate Developments

Private developers are limited by their having to rely on off-the-books sales or on their corporate balance sheets to finance development projects, so they tend to invest in real estate for which the demand is immediate and tangible. This tendency promotes single-plot/"island" developments characteristic of uncoordinated urban development being poorly plugged into the surrounding urban infrastructure and straining public services.

Table 3.2: Sources of Infrastructure Financing

Main Sources	Sub-Sources	Mechanisms
Public	National	Bond financing (backed by taxes, user fees, and beneficiary contributions)
	Subnational	
	Development institutions	Loans and grants
Private	Corporate finance	Public companies
		Private companies
		Bond financing
	Project finance	PPP
		Non-PPP

PPP = public–private partnership.
Source: Authors.; N. Yoshino, M. Helble, and U. Abidhadjaev, eds. 2018. *Financing Infrastructure in Asia and the Pacific: Capturing Impacts and New Sources*. Tokyo: Asian Development Bank Institute. https://www.adb.org/sites/default/files/publication/394191/adbi-financing-infrastructure-asia-capturing-impacts-and-new-sources.pdf

Table 3.3: Public Finance vs. Private Capital

Public finance	Public capital comes from central, provincial, regional, and local governments, as well as from other government institutions, plus national development banks and multilateral development banks such as the World Bank, Asian Development Bank, and the Islamic Development Bank.
Private capital	Private capital is provided in two main forms: corporate finance (on the balance sheet, from infrastructure companies' own resources) and project finance, a contractual financing arrangement used for infrastructure.

Public finance generally dominates in emerging Asia, especially in the People's Republic of China. Among the ASEAN countries, Goldman Sachs estimated in 2013 that the government's share of infrastructure financing was 90% in the Philippines, 80% in Thailand, 65% in Indonesia, and 50% in Malaysia. Efforts are being made to shift this balance toward a greater participation by the private sector.

ASEAN = Association of Southeast Asian Nations.
Sources: Goldman Sachs. 2013. ASEAN's Half a Trillion Dollar Infrastructure Opportunity. *Asia Economic Analyst* No: 13/18. New York; N. Yoshino, M. Helble, and U. Abidhadjaev, eds. 2018. *Financing Infrastructure in Asia and the Pacific: Capturing Impacts and New Sources*. Tokyo: Asian Development Bank Institute. https://www.adb.org/sites/default/files/publication/394191/adbi-financing-infrastructure-asia-capturing-impacts-and-new-sources.pdf.

Financing Conventional Townships

The conventional focus is on granting concessions for land plots to certain companies, but this intrinsically limits integration, and thus diminishes the scope for value realization.[9] There is also a significant reliance on attracting anchor investors to create a core of employment or reliance on transport networks for "dormitory towns".

However, this narrow and limited focus has led to something of a chicken-and-egg conundrum. Because of limited integration, there is often no supporting economic and social infrastructure within conventional townships, making it difficult to obtain commitments from anchor investors, which aggravates the problem of having no commitment to the creation of supporting economic and social infrastructure.

Without the supporting social infrastructure, demand for economic infrastructure that could spur economic activity is dampened. Demand risk limits investments, so developers have to rely on their own corporate balance sheets for financing.

These challenges limit the value creation potential of infrastructure development and, because the benefits cannot be maximized, it will be difficult for the government to introduce value capture mechanisms apart from those that already exist, such as taxes and fees.

A few of the financial products that could be leveraged through value creation and value capture policies are:

- **Bonds and green bonds**. Stable revenues from social and economic infrastructure can be securitized and offered as bonds. The bonds typically offer the bond issuer flexibility for long-term project financing.
- **Lending products**. Social and economic infrastructure with strong user demand that can give robust revenues will increase lenders appetite to loan to the infrastructure projects. Some examples of lending products include: sovereign lending, blended financing, structured financing, and project financing.
- **Equity divestments and initial public offerings**. Stable property rentals and confidence in the maximum capital productivity, as a result of value creation, would provide opportunities for equity divestment or real estate investment trusts.

Among these financial products, bond financing by the government has been successfully implemented for Hudson Yards, in New York. See the case study on Hudson Yards in International Case Studies (Appendix 4).

3.3. Assessment of the Indonesian Value Creation Framework

While the Indonesian regulatory framework presents some obstacles to value creation, a potentially suitable entry point would be to incorporate value creation principles into planning documents and into business cases for infrastructure projects.

Indonesia's regulatory and institutional framework as described in Section 2 is evaluated within the value creation framework drawn from this review of international best practice as set out in Table 3.4, in order to identify areas where value creation can be supported and areas where changes may be required.

9 Winarso (2016) observed that new township development in suburban Jakarta has created significant urban segregation and profit-oriented development. Social infrastructure built with the permit requirements has only served middle upper-class citizens, and is not affordable to most local residents. The emergence of townships is driven by profit, but local communities end up paying for the negative externalities, through such means as green space reduction, congestion, and gentrification.

Table 3.4: Assessment of Indonesian Value Creation Framework	
Whole-of-Government Approach	
Enabling framework and legislation Legal references: • Law No. 28 of 2009 on Local Tax and Retribution • Government Regulation No. 12 of 2019 on Regional Financial Management • Law No. 26 of 2007 on Spatial Planning • MPWH Regulation No. 6 of 2007 on Building Blocks and Neighborhood Plan Guidelines • MOAASP/NLA Regulation No. 16 of 2017 on Guidelines for Transit-Oriented Development	• Creating new tax instruments will require significant amendments to the legislation on the Indonesian taxation system. City governments are restricted from innovating new taxation mechanisms. Taxes or fees other than those specified under the law are prohibited. For certain types of taxes (e.g., property taxes), the local government may increase the statutory base value to raise property taxes. • There is an inconsistency between the law regarding the regional tax and fee system and the regulations governing the spatial planning system, in terms of the local government's right to charge fees on development rights transfers. • Law 28/2009 does not recognize the trading of development rights as a permissible source of revenue for local governments. On the other hand, the spatial planning regulations allow local governments to engage in the transfer of development rights.
Interministerial and interdepartmental collaboration	• Complex stakeholder discussions are typically required for various types of urban project preparation or permits for businesses. • In practice, discussions between different levels of government do occur (e.g., between provincial and city-level governments), especially at the preparation stage of some infrastructure projects.
Innovative procurement and funding Legal reference: Presidential Regulation No. 38 of 2015 on Cooperation between Government and Business Entities in Procurement of Infrastructure	• Indonesia has recognized PPPs as a possible financing scheme for the provision of infrastructure. However, the regulations do not yet specify how beneficiary-pays models will able to support PPP repayment schemes directly (by improving the GCA's financial ability to repay under government-pays or availability-payments models) or provide viability gap funding to create more viable user-pays business models.
Economic Planning	
Creation of nodes of economic activity	• There are several cases of overlapping and conflicting economic visions in the current spatial plan regulations. Some ad hoc economic planning may lead to an unsustainable investment environment.
Increased benefits from public investment Legal reference: Minister of National Development Planning/Head of National Development Planning Agency Regulation No. 4 of 2015 on the Procedure of Cooperation between the Government and Business Entities in Infrastructure Procurement	• Current infrastructure project preparation has not yet required the project teams to identify the project beneficiaries. Economic impact analysis is merely used to understand the rationale for the project.
Public and private sector collaboration	• No gap identified
Economic data on materials flows	• Data and statistics have been consistently collected from the national to city levels to allow for a robust economic analysis of public investment. The Central Bureau of Statistics, or *Badan Pusat Statistik*, is the leading agency for the collection of data and information on various sectors. A budget pipeline has been allocated to update the data annually, and to carry out a national census at least every five years. However, there are particular types of data that may require enhancement to support value capture and value creation analysis.
Long-Term Land-Use Planning and Regulatory Framework	
Integrated master planning and development Legal references: • Law No. 26 of 2007 on Spatial Planning • MOAASP/NLA Regulation No. 1 of 2018 on Guidelines for the Organization of Spatial Planning for Province, Regency, and City • MOAASP/NLA Regulation No. 16 of 2018 on the Instruction Guide, Detailed Spatial Plan and Regency/City Zoning Regulation	• Indonesia's planning system takes into account a visionary master plan anchored in a long-term view (over 20 years) and updated every 5 years. The document has been developed based on development studies, environmental impact analyses, and infrastructure planning. The RTRW strategies have been translated into a detailed spatial plan, which is intended to guide development over 10–15 years. However, transport infrastructure planning usually occurs through ad hoc decisions at the political level, which may not align with the agreed-upon spatial plan. • There is a mismatch between the regional spatial plan and the government's regional long-term economic strategy. And short-term economic factors accounted for in the Regional Medium-Term Development Plan might not continue in the event of a change in political leadership. • Spatial plans are often out of date or nonexistent, and sometimes there are gaps, for instance, when there is a provincial plan, but no regency or city plans. • Each regional government has based its planning regime on the administrative boundaries of the respective provinces and regions, in line with the government's policy of decentralization, whereby each province or region has the autonomy to plan development in their respective areas. While this enables local governments to focus their planning on optimizing local assets, often the potential economic uplift from activities along certain economic corridors crosses one or more administrative boundaries. • This gap is particularly observable during the planning of large-scale transit projects such as railways or roads, when the resulting economic impact around the transit economic corridors is not properly assessed or effectively captured due to planning coordination issues.
Flexible zoning Legal references: • MOAASP/NLA 16/2018 • MPWH 6/2007 • DKI Jakarta Governor Regulation No. 67 of 2019	• Law 26/2007 and the related regulatory guidance strictly prevent the unsustainable conversion of land, especially land slated for conservation, preservation, and protection. However, there are still problems with enforcement. Flexible zoning in terms of the FAR aimed at achieving optimal land use intensity, as well as transfers of development rights, has been recognized in the Indonesian planning system. However, there is no guidance on implementing FAR trading mechanisms at the city level.
Sound system of land administration and management Legal reference: Presidential Regulation No. 9 of 2016 on the Acceleration of the Implementation of the One Map Policy	• Indonesia is currently transforming its land management system through its "One Map Policy," and digitizing all land data into a single integrated system, updated annually. • However, the modernization process requires more trained personnel on the ground and a greater budget commitment. • Indonesia's land management system recognizes several types of land rights, for instance the, "right to use" and "right to lease." • A different land value capture strategy may apply, based on the type of landholding.
Integrated Urban and Transport Development	
Placemaking	• Placemaking has been adapted as one of the strategies for developing a detailed spatial plan. • However, tactical urbanism may occur due to a lack, or slow implementation, of formal urban development plans.
Public commons	• The national guidelines have suggested that infrastructure planning be aligned with land use planning. But due to the low enforcement of planning regulations, unexpected urban development projects sometimes occur, which represent a trade-off between the city's investment targets and current infrastructure capacity.

DKI = Special Capital Region (Jakarta), FAR = floor area ratio, GCA = government contracting agency, MOAASP/NLA = Minister of Agrarian Affairs and Spatial Planning/Head of National Land Agency, MPWH = Ministry of Public Works and Housing, PPP = public–private partnership.
Note: The floor area ratio (FAR) is the ratio of a building's total floor area to the size of the plot of land on which it is built.
Source: Authors.

4. The Value Capture Framework

For the effective implementation of value capture, there must be a clear identification and quantification of the positive effects on economic productivity—e.g., on tax revenues, gross domestic product (GDP), GDP per capita, rates of return, and employment—arising from the economic uplift caused by a policy change or infrastructure investment. Additionally, the key beneficiaries of these economic and commercial gains need to be identified. The value capture framework provides a range of tools that can be used to harvest a share of the economic uplift. This chapter lists value capture mechanisms, such as various categories of taxes and fees, and identifies low-hanging fruits that can be implemented by national and local government.

4.1. Economic Theory of Value Capture

Value capture is a mechanism whereby the public captures a portion of the incremental economic value created by the government's investment activities and policies as an additional funding source beyond the typical government-pays and user-pays models.

The focus is not on increasing the rate of taxation, but on increasing economic productivity so that the volume of fiscal revenue can be increased.

In a contrast to the current passive approach, value capture is an actively planned, sophisticated, and layered approach to improving fiscal revenue, one that identifies the beneficiaries and quantifies the benefits, then uses not only government-pays and user-pays mechanisms, but also beneficiary-pays.

In economic terms, value capture can mean capturing the positive effects on economic productivity—e.g., on tax revenues, gross domestic product (GDP), GDP per capita, rates of return, and employment—arising from the economic uplift caused by a policy change or an infrastructure investment.

According to a study conducted by Yoshino and Pontines (2015) of a major highway development in the city of Batangas, Philippines, tax revenues in Batangas increased from ₱490 million to ₱622 million and then to ₱652 million during the construction period. While the construction was going on, workers came to the area, increasing its GDP. After the highway was finished, tax revenues diminished, but then increased drastically after the fourth year, when they reached ₱1.2 billion, more than twice as much as before the construction had begun. Neighboring cities such as Ibaan and Lipa also benefited from the highway. For instance, Lipa saw a tax revenue gain of ₱371 million in the fourth year.

The case study of the highway in Batangas demonstrates important aspects of value capture. For instance, value capture takes into account the ramping-up period before user demand kicks in, and therefore requires long-term planning. Eventually, the infrastructure investment was shown to benefit not just the city where the highway was built, but also neighboring cities, which benefited from the improved connectivity.

Tax collection in developing countries has been ineffective due to a lack of technology, insufficient governance, and the costs of auditing and administration. Governments are facing complex problems not only in implementing and enforcing their tax policies, but also in quantifying the real impacts of incremental tax revenue in the case of many infrastructure projects.

Aside from utilizing incremental tax revenues, governments could capture additional revenues through direct collection via three models: user pays, government pays, and beneficiary pays. They are described in Table 4.1.

Table 4.1: Sources of Value Capture from Different Stakeholders	
Model	**Source of Value**
User pays	Usage-based charges for the use of infrastructure (e.g., public transportation fees, toll charges, public utility service charges)
Government pays	Local, provincial, and national taxes; fiscal balancing transfers of income and property taxes; subsidies; up-front public funding; and grants (e.g., viability gap funding)
Beneficiary pays	Private sector investment or various types of property or business taxation

Source: Authors.

Developing countries have struggled to create an appropriate and efficient governance framework for capturing value through additional tax revenue. To begin with, the taxes and fees should be based on an assessment of the public's willingness to pay and on voluntary efforts (by users, the government, private infrastructure investors, and operators). There must also be a proper tax-collection mechanism and a highly efficient collection process.

A framework for value capture has to therefore encompass a more sophisticated and layered approach to the deployment of mechanisms aimed at capturing value from each source.

4.2. International Best Practices for Value Capture

Both the government and the private sector can deploy value capture mechanisms to recover wider economic, social, and environmental benefits from investments in infrastructure. International best practice indicates that governments typically employ tax- and fee-based mechanisms, while the private sector could benefit from employing mechanisms that are development-based.

Both the government and the private sector can deploy value capture mechanisms to recover wider economic, social, and environmental benefits from investments in infrastructure.

It is an accepted practice for the government to recover a portion of the economic uplift resulting from public infrastructure investments and other government actions. In most developing countries, private landholdings are usually significant, and private companies try to strategically acquire land banks that allow them to capture the benefits of connectivity enabled by government infrastructure investments. For example, private developments located within the catchment area of a transit station can charge higher commercial rents because of the improved access to customers and to a larger talent pool.

This section provides examples of value capture mechanisms for the government and for landowners and master developers. It should be noted that the grouping of value capture mechanisms here distinguishes between those mechanisms that only the government can deploy and those that are available both to the government and the private sector. A number of examples exist in which the government acts as a landowner and master developer through state-owned enterprises (SOEs).

The value capture mechanisms listed in Table 4.2 are mostly development-based tools that require a level of maturity in land-use planning and regulation that would allow the government to use zoning as an instrument for value capture without eroding its long-term sustainable targets for the sake of medium-term gains.

Table 4.2: Examples of Value Capture Mechanisms for the Private Sector Landowners and Master Developers and for the Government

For Landowners and Master Developers	For the Government
1. Land sales	1. Betterment levies
2. Land leases	2. Development impact fees
3. Sales of concession rights	3. Developer contributions
4. Revenue from the provision of services	4. Leveraging of government land
6. Equity dividends	5. Leveraging of government fiscal expenditure
7. Equity divestments and IPOs	6. Taxes on property transactions
8. Sales of development rights and air rights	7. Taxes on land value
9. Land readjustments	8. Business tax
	9. Tourism tax
	10. Income tax

For the Government

Low-hanging fruit for value capture by the government typically involves tax- and fee-based mechanisms that already exist within the existing legal and regulatory framework. The taxes and fees mentioned here are present in most countries. However, differences in application can provide ideas for leveraging tax- and fee-based mechanisms for value capture.

For Landowners and Master Developers

Landowners and master developers can be from the public sector, the private sector, or in some cases a collaboration between the two. The value capture mechanisms can best be deployed by the government when it embarks on land-development projects as a landowner and/or master developer.

IPO = initial public offering.
Source: Authors.

Tables 4.3 and 4.4 provide descriptions of the value capture mechanisms, including the key requirements for their implementation, and case studies of applications of these mechanisms.

4.3. Assessment of the Indonesian Tax System in Line with the Value Capture Framework

The Indonesian regulatory framework for public finance presents a multilayered set of tax- and fee-based instruments that are being used to capture value from individuals as well as businesses, through a national finance system that generally uses a melting-pot approach, with limited potential for earmarking. A readiness analysis of the potential for the introduction of value capture instruments through existing mechanisms is also discussed in this section.

Public Flow of Money

The flow and quantities of public funds have been mapped out from their sources through to their budgeting for expenditure. This analysis shows the effectiveness of taxation and the opportunities for adjusting the burden of taxation to encourage behavioral changes, including a shift away from private vehicles and toward public transport. However, tax revenues rely considerably on the use of private vehicles, and this reliance could become a dependency for local governments that will conflict with their policies to encourage public transport use (policies that could reduce their fiscal revenues).

Jakarta receives a significantly greater relative contribution from property taxes than does Makassar. This in part reflects the greater building density in the core city, which results in a higher economic productivity.

The authors of this study analyzed flow-of-funds diagrams for Jakarta and the city of Makassar to identify the optimal value capture approach in each case. The diagrams show the pools of funds at the various levels of government, and how these funds are eventually spent on infrastructure, based on the authors' review of various regulations and the relevant data on Makassar and Jakarta. The analysis would have covered the city of Palembang, as well. Unfortunately, at the time of the drafting of this report, the full detailed data on government revenue and spending for Palembang was not available.

In the case of Makassar, Figure 4.1 shows that the private-vehicle-ownership tax has become the highest revenue contributor among the various taxes, at Rp3.24 trillion per year, while the second-highest contributor is the income tax. However, these taxes do not directly flow into the local budget, as they need to be accounted for in the national and provincial budgets, as well. According to the regulations on taxes and fees, these taxes are shared across all levels of government. Moreover, the property-related taxes (property tax and property transactions tax) also make

Table 4.3: Value Capture Mechanisms for the Government			
Value Capture Mechanisms	Description	Key Requirements	Examples
Betterment levies (currently not recognized in Indonesia)	Betterment levies are a form of tax or fee levied on land that has gained in value because of improvements in certain areas or neighborhoods due to public infrastructure investment. It is designed to capture a part of the increase in the market value of the land attributable to infrastructure investment.	• Systemwide fiscal regulations should allow special tax assessments and collections at the municipal level. • There should be robust property appraisals and land cadastre systems.[a] • Typically, betterment levies are charged at around 30%–60% of the gain in land value, so a betterment levy requires great certainty regarding the underlying land value gains.[b]	Bogotá has garnered about $1 billion worth of investments in public works from this type of levy, and eight smaller Colombian cities have obtained a combined $1 billion. More importantly, the recent imposition of levies on 1.5 million properties in Bogotá has been generally accepted by taxpayers, with relatively low default rates. Regarding levy collection, the Washington-based Urban Land Institute defines the area of influence and measures the benefits resulting from a project or set of projects. This is done for each city zone, taking into account the identified benefits from each project.[c]
Development impact fees (applied in Jakarta, based on Governor Jakarta Regulation No. 210 of 2016)	Development impact fees are designed to charge developers the market costs of the infrastructure expansion necessitated by their development projects. Growth generates demand for systemwide expansion in infrastructure for roads, water supply, wastewater removal, parks, and other facilities.[b] Typically, governments levy these fees as one-time, up-front charges, and the receipt of payment is a precondition for public approval for the development of a particular parcel of land.[d]	• Strong planning and analytical capacity at the local level are needed for the preparation and costing of infrastructure upgrades, along with a solid approach to allocating benefits across different locations and projects. • There should be a strong execution of public investment plans. • The formulas for calculating impact fees should be transparent and stringent, so that developers can project the fees credibly.[a]	Impact fees will have to be simplified to capture the broad differences in infrastructure costs. In Mumbai, it has been estimated that a 10% development fee added to the cost of new construction could finance 40%–50% of all regional infrastructure investments required by 2040.[b]
Developer contributions (a scheme that has been applied in Jakarta,[e] and is partly recognized in DKI Jakarta Governor Regulation No. 67 of 2019 on the Implementation of Transit-Oriented Areas and by MOT Regulation No. 75 of 2015 on Traffic Impact Assessments)	Developer "exactions" can be defined as developer contributions. It is usually an obligation of the developer to build "physical" infrastructure for the public.[d] This typically works as a compensation for exemptions from building regulations for a project (e.g., allowing more intensive land use, higher densities, or a relaxation of the building code). In contrast to impact fees, which are applied systemwide on a formula basis, exactions are typically applied on a case-by-case basis, and determined through negotiations.[a]	• Clear land-use and town-planning regulations are required, as well as strong construction norms (for the setting of baseline conditions). • Local government should build its capacity for planning and implementation, to be able to fulfill its infrastructure obligations. • A comprehensive public outreach approach should be used to explain the process of developer exactions, noting what can be gained.[a]	In Cairo, Arab Republic of Egypt, developer exactions in the form of the installation of "public" infrastructure in return for free transfers of developable desert land is expected to provide a range of urban infrastructure services for more than 3,300 hectares of newly developed land, without any financial cost to the government. The expected proceeds amount to $1.45 billion of private investment in internal and external infrastructure. In addition, 7% of serviced land will have to be turned over to the government for middle-income housing.[b]
Leveraging government land (examples in Indonesia including spaces within railway stations rented to commercial tenants for shops)	The transfer of publicly owned assets (land, buildings) to a private developer, whereby value is realized either directly (e.g., sales proceeds) or through the creation of future development value or socioeconomic benefits.[a]	• Excess or underutilized public assets should be made available, either individually or through asset consolidation for optimization. • The market value of the public assets can be clearly established, and has the potential to generate additional value. • The government must communicate effectively to citizens its rationale for disposing of public assets. • A publicly owned entity must have a negotiating capacity on a par with that of private sector developers, so it can achieve fair pricing.[a]	Cairo's municipal government auctioned 2,100 hectares of desert land for new towns in May 2007. The $3.12 billion proceeds, equal to approximately 10% of the total national government revenue, were intended to be used to reimburse the costs of internal infrastructure and to build connecting highways to the Cairo Ring Road.[b]
Taxes (applicable in Indonesia, for example in the form of land and building taxes, property sales tax, land registration tax, hotel room tax, and amusement tax)	Taxes represent a recurring, stable source of revenue for the government. Apart from taxes on land values and property transactions, governments may also consider accessing other tax revenue streams such as corporate taxes, income taxes, and sales taxes, all of which could generate increased revenues as a result of the externality effects of newly developed infrastructure.[f] Additional taxes have also been negotiated and levied by governments on property owners identified as benefiting from specific public improvement(s).	• There should be a robust land cadastre, land assessments, and a regular reassessment process. • Local governments should have the capacity for effective tax administration. • The local real estate market should be able to accurately gauge the value of land in unimproved condition, based purely on the location, quality of the property, and its development potential.[a] • The majority of owners must agree to self-assessments. • For taxes to serve as a source of value capture, the economy must be strong and the real estate market robust. • There will be the need for primary legislation and tax hypothecation.[g]	An incremental supplement to the national nondomestic business tax rate, the BRS, was used in London to finance Crossrail. In April 2010, the mayor of London levied a £0.02 supplement on the business tax rates for properties with a ratable value of over £55,000 per year. This threshold ensured that smaller premises would be exempt, with the burden falling on the larger businesses, which were more able to absorb the costs, and most of which were located along the lines of the proposed route, in any case. The BRS generates around £225 million per year, which could support GLA borrowing of around £3.5 billion. The levy is expected to fall away once the bonds are fully repaid, which is forecast to be in the 2030s.[g]

BRS = business rate supplement, CMMIA = Coordinating Ministry for Maritime Investment and Affairs, DKI = Special Capital City Region, GLA = Greater London Authority, MOT = Ministry of Transportation, SEZ = Special Economic Zone.

[a] World Bank, City Resilience Program. n.d. Land Value Capture: Investment in Infrastructure. Washington, DC. https://www.gfdrr.org/sites/default/files/publication/Land%20Value%20Capture.pdf.

[b] G.E. Peterson. 2009. Unlocking Land Values to Finance Urban Infrastructure. Trends and Policy Options No. 7. Washington, DC: World Bank. http://documents1.worldbank.org/curated/en/723411468139800644/pdf/461290PUB0Box3101OFFICIAL0USE0ONLY1.pdf.

[c] O.B. Ochoa. 2011. Betterment Levy in Colombia: Relevance, Procedures, and Social Acceptability. Land Lines. April. https://www.lincolninst.edu/sites/default/files/pubfiles/1899_1213_LLA110404.pdf.

[d] R. Amirtahmasebi, M. Orloff, S. Wahba, and A. Altman. 2016. Regenerating Urban Land: A Practitioner's Guide to Leveraging Private Investment. Washington, DC: World Bank.

[e] The development of the new elevated roundabout in the Semanggi district of Jakarta provides a precedent for compensation from a private sector developer in the case of a public infrastructure project. The private developer, Mori Building Co., Ltd. wanted to build an office tower in Semanggi, a prime area of the city, but the total proposed gross floor area of the building exceeded the zoning regulation's maximum limit. After evidence was provided that the increase could be done within the environmental parameters, the Jakarta municipal government allowed the building construction to proceed. However, the developer had to provide compensation based on the government's standard of calculation. Recognizing the lack of transparency in the determination of compensation in previous cases, the Jakarta government enacted the Gubernatorial Regulation No. 175 of 2015 (later updated by Gubernatorial Regulation No. 251 of 2015), which allowed compensation to be provided in the form of public infrastructure and was considered to be more accountable, as well as a direct benefit for the citizens of Jakarta.

[f] N. Yoshino. 2019. Sustainable Development in Asia. Presentation prepared for a meeting at the Asian Development Bank Institute. Tokyo. May. http://pubdocs.worldbank.org/en/509981557878951936/051419-sustainable-development-in-asia-Naoyuki-Yoshino.pdf; United Nations ESCAP. 2019. Infrastructure Financing for Sustainable Development in Asia and the Pacific. ESCAP Financing for Development Series No. 3. Bangkok: United Nations. https://www.unescap.org/sites/default/files/publications/Infrastructure%20financing-high.pdf.

[g] M. Buck. 2017. Crossrail Project: Finance, Funding and Value Capture for London's Elizabeth Line. Proceedings of the Institution of Civil Engineers 170(CE6): 15–22. https://www.icevirtuallibrary.com/doi/pdf/10.1680/jcien.17.00005; World Bank, City Resilience Program, Land Value Capture.

Source: Authors.

Table 4.4: Value Capture Mechanisms for Landowners and Master Developers			
Value Capture Mechanisms	**Description**	**Key Requirements**	**Examples**
Development rights and air rights	Development rights have an economic value, and can be sold by public authorities or transferred between private landowners under a transferable development rights scheme.[a] Saleable development rights fall into two categories: the right to convert less productive (lower) use land to a higher use, and the right to build at higher densities than would normally be allowed by existing zoning regulations.[b]	• This mechanism applies to larger urban areas with strong real estate markets that maintain enough demand and growth potential for high density development. • Rigid land use controls, property records (cadastre), and property appraisal systems must be in place.[b]	The municipal government of Sao Paolo in Brazil, sold additional construction rights to help finance public investments in designated growth areas within the city. The municipal government's attempt to use this approach to finance its metro system failed because of institutional fragmentation, with the municipal government unwilling to use the funds for a project that was the responsibility of the state government.[c]
Density bonuses	Density bonuses provide incentives for developers to build public amenities in return for the right to build higher-density properties than are permitted under the existing zoning.[d]	• This mechanism applies to larger urban areas with strong real estate markets that maintain enough demand and growth potential for high density development. • Rigid land use controls, property records (cadastre), and property appraisal systems must be in place.[b]	A density bonus program was introduced in New York City in 1961. It granted developers the right to build 3 additional square feet of construction in return for every square foot of public space improvements that they carried out at the street level within their property (usually a setback to create a plaza or arcade). This density bonus was later revised to 10 square feet for every square foot of public space improvement, up to a certain upper threshold. This program was responsible for the development of over 500 privately built public spaces in Manhattan over three decades.[a]
Land asset management	This refers to the management of land development, sales, leasing, acquisitions, and allocations. Land asset management strategies include doing an inventory of publicly owned land; establishing the market value of all significant parcels; and making strategic decisions on whether to retain, sell, jointly develop, or convert land to public use.[c]	• The municipal government and infrastructure agencies must offer a policy rationale for adopting these strategic methods for land asset management • There should be well-established rules for the equitable exercise of eminent domain.[c]	In 1995, the BCDA formed a joint venture with private sector partners to develop part of Fort Bonifacio, the last large remaining tract of undeveloped land in Metro Manila. BCDA sold 150 hectares of land to the newly formed joint venture, the Fort Bonifacio Development Corporation, for ₱30.4 billion (roughly $800 million at the time). The BCDA also retained a 45% economic interest in the joint venture, which was managed by the private partners. The sales proceeds were invested in the development of the Subic and Clark SEZs (50%), the modernization of military housing (32.5%), and in the construction of housing for the homeless (4%); of the remainder, 2.5% was allocated to the city government and 10% to the national government.[c]
Land readjustment	This is a participatory process in which landowners or occupants voluntarily contribute a certain percentage of their land for infrastructure development and for sale to cover part of the project costs. In return, each landowner or occupant receives a serviced plot in the same neighborhood that is smaller in size, but higher in value.[b]	• Generally, land readjustment requires the consent of a supermajority of landowners to approve the project. • There should be an appropriate legal framework that empowers the local authority to take land from dissenting landowners when a supermajority agrees. • Land readjustment is more feasible in areas with high land values, where the land readjustment has the potential to increase the land value after completion, guided by the city's master plan. • The quality of property records and cadastral maps are important for expediting implementation.[b]	Land readjustment has been extensively used in Japan as a means of reorganizing and consolidating landholdings to achieve rational patterns of urban development. Land readjustment was carried out in almost 30% of Japan's urban areas as of 30 March 2003. That was accomplished through 11,400 projects covering a total of 368,313.5 hectares, including land-readjustment projects completed before 1954 (under an old law), all projects completed since 1954 (under the subsequent law), and all projects still in progress.[e]
Granting of Concession Rights	Additional revenue can be derived from the granting of concession rights for power and water services as part of land development. Concession agreements may follow output-based specifications and performance-linked payment mechanisms, and other procurement conditions that can be negotiated with the concessionaire.	• Concession agreements, especially under PPPs, typically follow output-based specifications, performance-linked payment mechanisms, and other procurement conditions that can be negotiated with the concessionaire.	The BCDA entered into a joint venture with a private consortium to develop the power distribution system in New Clark City. The BCDA awarded the contract to the Meralco-Marubeni consortium (90% stake) based on its lowest tariff bid of ₱0.6188/kWh, besting the ₱0.9888/kWh bid by the Aboitiz-KEPCO Consortium, which comprised the Olongapo Energy Corporation and KEPCO Philippines Holdings, Inc.[f]

BCDA = Bases Conversion and Development Authority, kWh = kilowatt-hour, PPP = public–private partnership, SEZ = special economic zone.

[a] R. Amirtahmasebi, M. Orloff, S. Wahba, and A. Altman. 2016. *Regenerating Urban Land: A Practitioner's Guide to Leveraging Private Investment*. Washington, DC: World Bank.

[b] World Bank, City Resilience Program. n.d. *Land Value Capture: Investment in Infrastructure*. Washington, DC. https://www.gfdrr.org/sites/default/files/publication/Land%20Value%20Capture.pdf.

[c] G.E. Peterson. 2009. Unlocking Land Values to Finance Urban Infrastructure. *Trends and Policy Options* No. 7. Washington, DC: World Bank.

[d] H. Buensuceso and C. Purisima. 2018. *Funding Transport Infrastructure Development in the Philippines: A Roadmap Toward Land Value Capture*. Singapore: Milken Institute. https://milkeninstitute.org/sites/default/files/reports-pdf/LVC-Whitepaper.pdf.

[e] Y. Hong and B. Needham, eds. 2007. *Analyzing Land Adjustment: Economics, Law, and Collective Action*. Cambridge, MA: Lincoln Institute of Land Policy. https://www.lincolninst.edu/sites/default/files/pubfiles/analyzing-land-readjustment-full.pdf.

[f] BCDA. 2018. Meralco Consortium Submits Lowest Tariff Bid for New Clark City Power Distribution. News release. 21 December. https://bcda.gov.ph/news/meralco-consortium-submits-lowest-tariff-bid-new-clark-city-power-distribution.

Source: Authors.

a significant contribution to local revenues, at more than Rp300 billion per year. Figure 4.1 thus shows the potential for capturing more value from these revenue channels in the future.

In the case of Jakarta, Figure 4.2 shows that the income tax has become the highest contributor among the various taxes there, having reached Rp74.81 trillion per year, while the joint second-highest contributors are transport-related and property-related taxes, each of which contributes more than Rp13 trillion. However, the income tax revenue does not directly flow into the local budget, as it needs to be accounted for within the national budget. Of the surplus tax revenues for the Special Capital Region, 20% is shared with Jakarta (as Jakarta is the Special Capital Region). Nevertheless, Figure 4.2 shows that transport-related, property-related, and business-related taxes have the potential for higher collection totals in Jakarta due to the greater density of buildings and population in the core city.

Brief Quantitative Analysis of Tax Collection in Jakarta, Makassar, and Palembang

Tax-to-Gross Domestic Product Ratio in Indonesia

The ratio of the national tax revenues to the gross domestic product (GDP) is referred to as the "tax-to-GDP ratio," and it is often used to measure the government's capacity to control its economic resources. In 2017, Indonesia's tax-to-GDP ratio was 11.5%, lower than those of the other Southeast Asian countries, as shown in Figure 4.3.

The tax-to-GDP ratio also indicates delays in tax revenues in Indonesia, compared with those of other middle-income countries in Southeast Asia.

Between 2010 and 2017, the compound annual growth rates (CAGRs) of the country's GDP and tax revenues were comparable, at 10.25% per year for GDP and 10.49% for the tax revenues, as shown in Figure 4.4. At this rate, the current Indonesian tax collection framework can maintain, but not improve, the government's slice of economic growth. The International Monetary Fund (IMF) concurs with the Organisation for Economic Co-operation and Development (OECD) that Indonesia should stimulate growth in order to harness its economic potential through comprehensive tax reform and rigorous tax implementation and collection.

The Performance of Cities

Table 4.5 shows a comparison of the total local tax revenues in Jakarta, Palembang, and Makassar relative to their respective gross regional domestic product (GRDP) in terms of nominal value. By definition, the higher the GRDP, the more tax the city or region should be able to collect and use in part to fund infrastructure development.

Aside from the historical trend of GRDP relative to tax revenue in each city, this analysis also presents the CAGR of each variable to show the estimated average increase over the period under observation. It was noted that all three cities experienced an economic slowdown in 2015, and that the rate of GRDP growth has not returned to the level prior to 2015.

Figure 4.1: Flow of Public Money in Makassar, Budget Year 2018

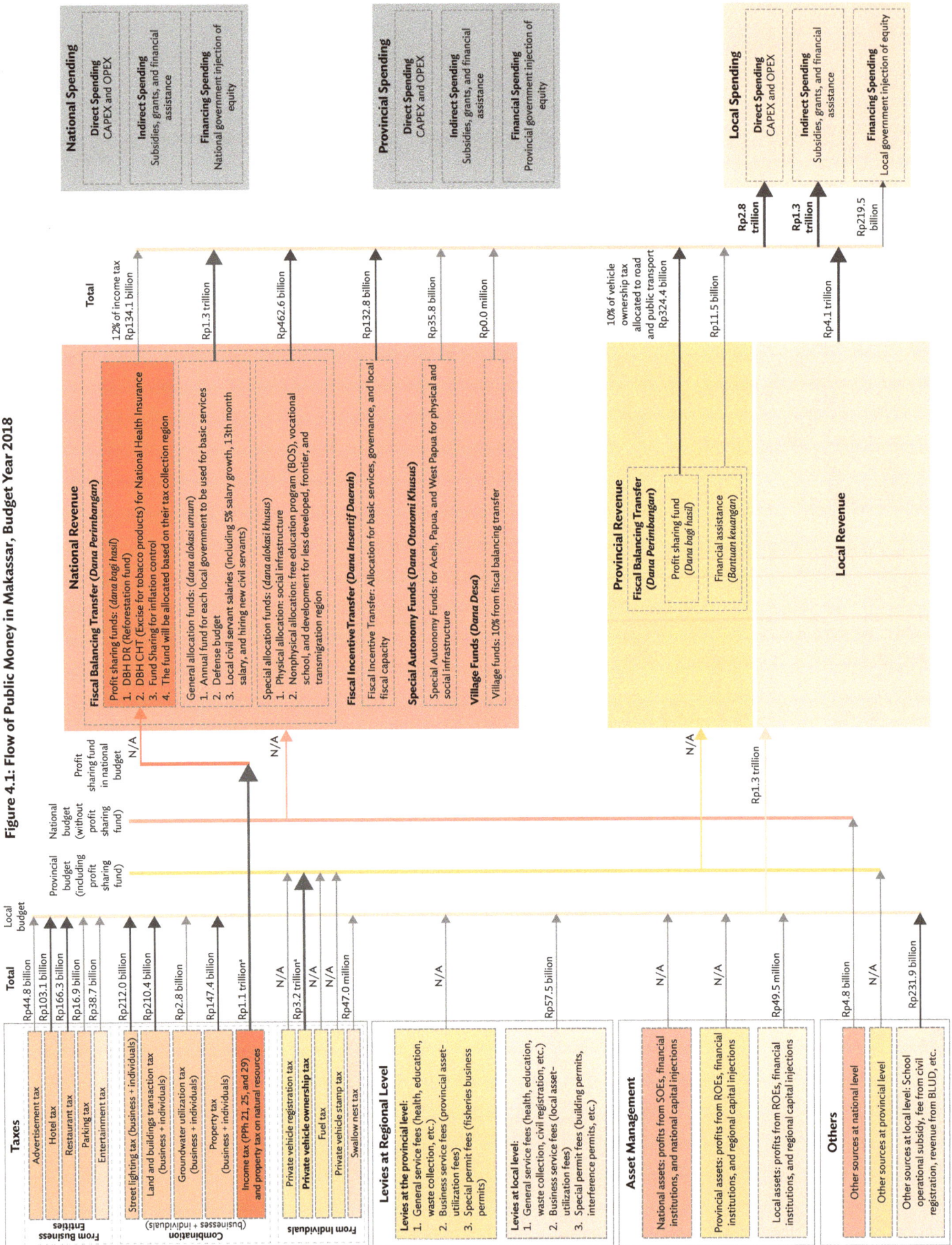

National Spending
- Direct Spending: CAPEX and OPEX
- Indirect Spending: Subsidies, grants, and financial assistance
- Financing Spending: National government injection of equity

Provincial Spending
- Direct Spending: CAPEX and OPEX
- Indirect Spending: Subsidies, grants, and financial assistance
- Financing Spending: Provincial government injection of equity

Local Spending
- Direct Spending: CAPEX and OPEX
- Indirect Spending: Subsidies, grants, and financial assistance
- Financing Spending: Local government injection of equity

Arrows to Local Spending: Rp2.8 trillion; Rp1.3 trillion; Rp219.5 billion

Total (flows):
- 12% of income tax Rp134.1 billion
- Rp1.3 trillion
- Rp462.6 billion
- Rp132.8 billion
- Rp35.8 billion
- Rp0.0 million
- 10% of vehicle ownership tax allocated to road and public transport Rp324.4 billion
- Rp11.5 billion
- Rp4.1 trillion

National Revenue

Fiscal Balancing Transfer (Dana Perimbangan)

Profit sharing funds: (dana bagi hasil)
1. DBH DR (Reforestation fund)
2. DBH CHT (Excise for tobacco products) for National Health Insurance
3. Fund Sharing for inflation control
4. The fund will be allocated based on their tax collection region

General allocation funds: (dana alokasi umum)
1. Annual fund for each local government to be used for basic services
2. Defense budget
3. Local civil servant salaries (including 5% salary growth, 13th month salary, and hiring new civil servants)

Special allocation funds: (dana alokasi khusus)
1. Physical allocation: social infrastructure
2. Nonphysical allocation: free education program (BOS), vocational school, and development for less developed, frontier, and transmigration region

Fiscal Incentive Transfer (Dana Insentif Daerah)
Fiscal Incentive Transfer: Allocation for basic services, governance, and local fiscal capacity

Special Autonomy Funds (Dana Otonomi Khusus)
Special Autonomy Funds: for Aceh, Papua, and West Papua for physical and social infrastructure

Village Funds (Dana Desa)
Village funds: 10% from fiscal balancing transfer

Provincial Revenue

Fiscal Balancing Transfer (Dana Perimbangan)
- Profit sharing fund (Dana bagi hasil)
- Financial assistance (Bantuan keuangan)

Local Revenue

Middle labels / flows:
- Profit sharing fund in national budget — N/A
- National budget (without profit sharing fund)
- Provincial budget (including profit sharing fund)
- Local budget
- N/A; N/A; Rp1.3 trillion

Taxes

From Business Entities
Item	Total
Advertisement tax	Rp44.8 billion
Hotel tax	Rp103.1 billion
Restaurant tax	Rp166.3 billion
Parking tax	Rp16.9 billion
Entertainment tax	Rp38.7 billion

Combination (businesses + individuals)
Item	Total
Street lighting tax (business + individuals)	Rp212.0 billion
Land and buildings transaction tax (business + individuals)	Rp210.4 billion
Groundwater utilization tax (business + individuals)	Rp2.8 billion
Property tax (business + individuals)	Rp147.4 billion
Income tax (PPh, 21, 25, and 29) and property tax on natural resources	Rp1.1 trillion*

From Individuals
Item	Total
Private vehicle registration tax	N/A
Private vehicle ownership tax	Rp3.2 trillion*
Fuel tax	N/A
Private vehicle stamp tax	N/A
Swallow nest tax	Rp47.0 million

Levies at Regional Level

Levies at the provincial level: N/A
1. General service fees (health, education, waste collection, etc.)
2. Business service fees (provincial asset-utilization fees)
3. Special permit fees (fisheries business permits)

Levies at local level: Rp57.5 billion
1. General service fees (health, education, waste collection, civil registration, etc.)
2. Business service fees (local asset-utilization fees)
3. Special permit fees (building permits, interference permits, etc.)

Asset Management
Item	
National assets: profits from SOEs, financial institutions, and national capital injections	N/A
Provincial assets: profits from ROEs, financial institutions, and regional capital injections	N/A
Local assets: profits from ROEs, financial institutions, and regional capital injections	Rp49.5 million

Others
Item	
Other sources at national level	Rp4.8 billion
Other sources at provincial level	N/A
Other sources at local level: School operational subsidy, fee from civil registration, revenue from BLUD, etc.	Rp231.9 billion

BLUD = local public service agency, CAPEX = capital expenditure, N/A = not applicable, OPEX = operational expenditure, PPh = income tax, ROE = regional-owned enterprise, Rp = Indonesian rupiah (national currency), SOE = state-owned enterprise.

Note: The basic government services (government mandatory affairs) include: education, health care, public works and spatial planning, social housing and settlements, social order, and social affairs.

a These are estimated values.

Figure 4.2: Flow of Public Money in Jakarta, Budget Year 2018

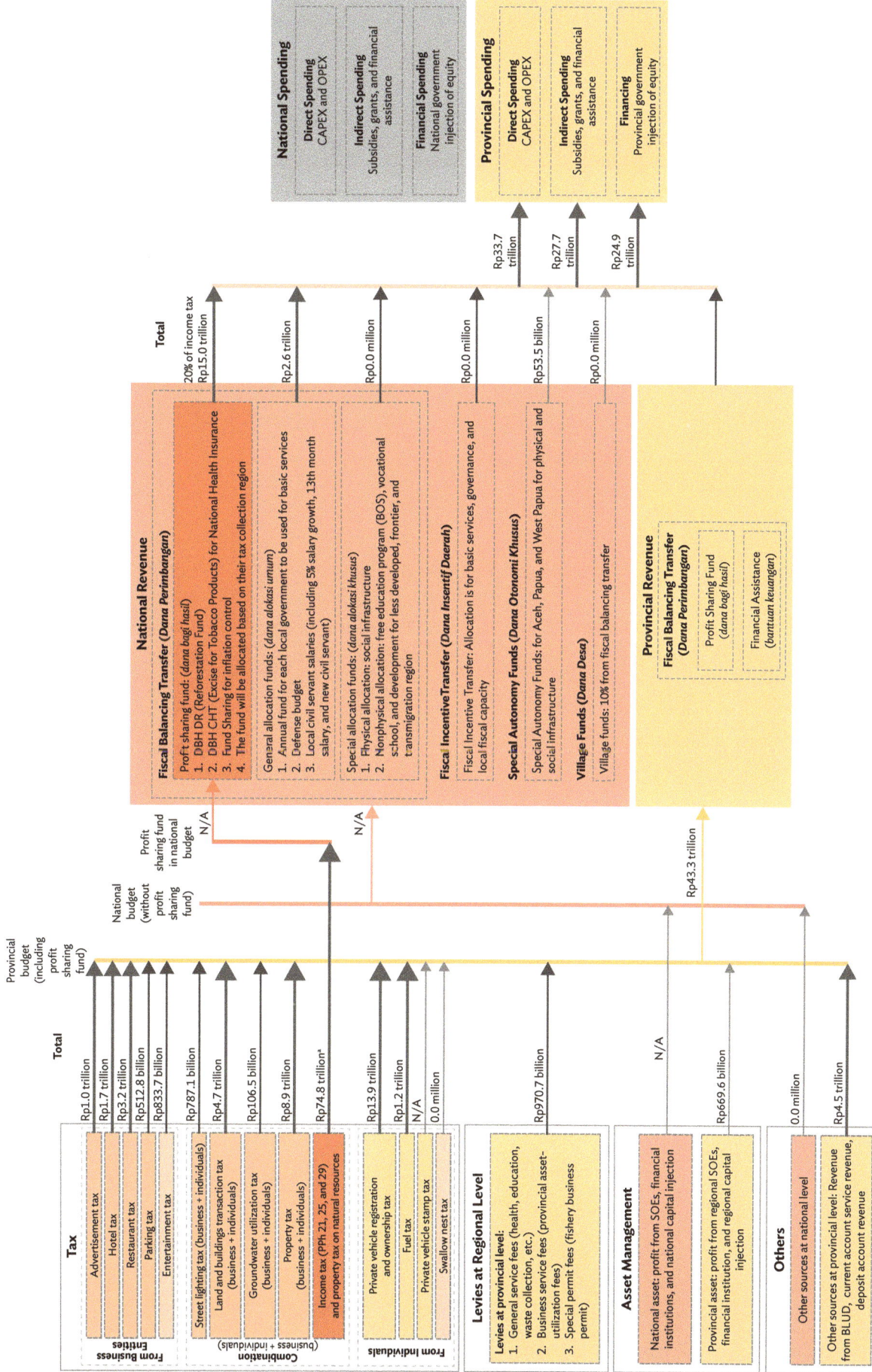

BLUD = local public service agency, CAPEX = capital expenditure, N/A = not applicable, OPEX = operational expenditure, PPh = income tax, ROE = regional-owned enterprise, Rp = Indonesian rupiah (national currency), SOE = state-owned enterprise.

Note: The basic government services (government mandatory affairs) include: education, health care, public works and spatial planning, social housing and settlements, social order, and social affairs.

a This is an estimated value.

Source: Government of the Special Capital Region of Jakarta, Indonesia. 2018. *Midterm Development Plan 2017–2022.* Jakarta.

Figure 4.3: Indonesia's Tax-to-GDP Ratio Compared with the Ratios for Other Southeast Asian Countries, 2017

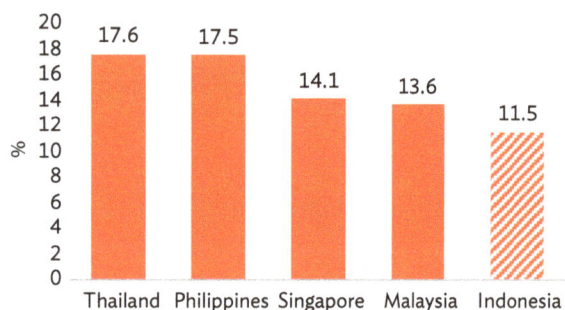

Source: Organisation for Economic Co-operation and Development (OECD). Revenue Statistics in Asian and Pacific Economies 2019—Indonesia. https://www.oecd.org/tax/tax-policy/revenue-statistics-asia-and-pacific-indonesia.pdf.

Figure 4.4: Indonesia's Nominal Gross Domestic Product Relative to Tax Revenues, 2010-2017

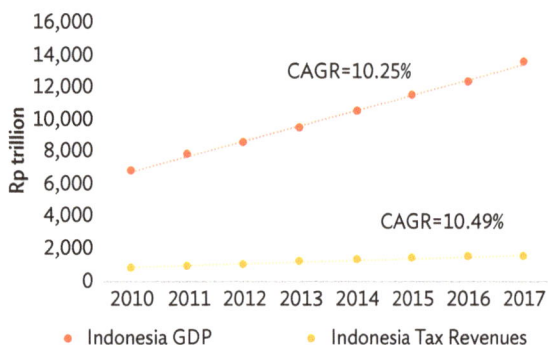

CAGR = compound annual growth rate, GDP = gross domestic product, Rp = Indonesian rupiah (national currency).
Sources: Government of Indonesia, Statistics Indonesia; Organisation of Economic Co-operation and Development (OECD).

Table 4.5: Gross Regional Domestic Product Relative to Tax Revenues in Jakarta, Makassar, and Palembang, 2013–2017 (%)

Indicator	DKI Jakarta	Makassar	Palembang
Total local taxes relative to GRDP (2017)	3.25	0.75	0.59
CAGR of GRDP (2013–2017)	11.20	12.68	11.03
CAGR of total local taxes (2013–2017)	13.30	15.37	14.00

CAGR = compound annual growth rate, DKI = Special Capital Region, GRDP = gross regional domestic product.
Note: The period of 2013–2017 has been selected based on data availability for the three cities.
Source: Authors.

Tax revenue variables that are considered in the analysis consist of the total original local/regional tax (*pajak daerah*) and tax sharing revenue (*bagi hasil pajak*).

Jakarta

The municipality of Jakarta saw a consistent upward trend in both GRDP and tax revenues during 2012–2018. The CAGR for GRDP was 11.27%, and for tax revenues it was 10.61%. Therefore, despite the directly proportional trends of both variables, the growth in tax revenues can be boosted by improving the tax calculation and collection process.

As Jakarta is an autonomous provincial-level jurisdiction—formally the Special Capital Region of Jakarta, or Daerah Khusus Ibukota Jakarta (DKI Jakarta)—the available tax data show a clear separation between transport-based taxes (which are indicated as part of the regional tax) and property-based taxes (included in tax-sharing revenue).

Figure 4.5: Nominal Gross Regional Domestic Product Relative to Tax Revenues in Jakarta, 2012–2018

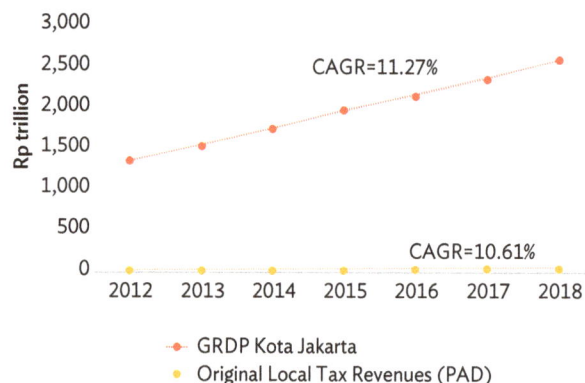

CAGR = compound annual growth rate, DKI = Special Capital Region, GRDP = gross regional domestic product, Rp = Indonesian rupiah (national currency).
Sources: Statistics Indonesia; Medium-Term Development Plan DKI Jakarta Province; DKI Jakarta Regional Tax and Retribution Agency.

The transport-based taxes consist of the:

- vehicle tax (*pajak kendaraan bermotor*),
- vehicle ownership transfer tax (*bea balik nama kendaraan bermotor*),
- vehicle fuel tax (*pajak bahan bakar kendaraan bermotor*), and the
- parking tax.

The taxes on land and buildings consist of the:

- land and buildings tax (*pajak bumi dan bangunan*),
- duty on the acquisition of land and building rights (*bea perolehan hak atas tanah dan bangunan* [BPHTB]).

The data are presented in Table 4.6.

Transport- and property-related tax revenues as shares of the total local tax revenue are presented in Figure 4.6. The figure shows that transport-related tax revenue decreased as a share of total local tax revenue, while the share of property-related tax revenue increased at the same rate during the period under observation.

Revenue generated from property-based taxes could be further accelerated if vertical and high-density development took place. The reason is that, although the size of a parcel of land would remain constant, the gross floor area (GFA) of the building on top would be a multiple of the land area.

Table 4.6: Transport-Related and Property-Related Tax Revenues in Jakarta, 2012–2018							
Expenditure and Revenue	2012	2013	2014	2015	2016	2017	2018
Transport-Related Spending (Rp billion)			21.18		48.51	61.73	78.25
Transport-Related Tax Revenue							
Vehicle tax/*pajak kendaraan bermotor* (Rp billion)	4.11	4.61	4.98	6.09	7.14	8.01	8.55
Vehicle ownership transfer tax/*bea balik nama kendaraan bermotor* (Rp billion)	5.51	6.14	5.53	4.69	5.00	5.03	5.35
Vehicle fuel tax/*pajak bahan bakar kendaraan bermotor* (Rp billion)	0.88	1.03	1.17	1.23	1.10	1.15	1.25
Parking tax (Rp million)	221	319	407	451	466	486	513
Transport-related taxes as a share of total local tax revenue (%)	37.3	37.5	33.3	35.8	31.2	27.6	29.8
Total (Rp billion)	**10.72**	**12.10**	**12.08**	**12.46**	**13.71**	**14.67**	**15.66**
Property-Related Tax Revenue							
Duty on the acquisition of land and building rights (Rp million)	3.23	3.42	3.70	3.70[a]	3.90	6.76	4.72
Land and Buildings Tax P2/*Perdesaan dan Perkotaan*) (Rp million)	...	3.38	5.66	5.66[a]	7.02	7.72	8.89
Tax sharing revenue, minus income taxes (Rp million)	2,787	271	117	136	107	156	65
Property-related taxes as a share of total local tax revenue (%)	20.9	21.9	26.1	27.3	25.1	27.5	26.0
Total (Rp billion)	**6.01**	**7.07**	**9.48**	**9.49**	**11.03**	**14.63**	**13.68**

Rp = Indonesian rupiah (national currency).
Notes:
1. A blank cell indicates that the column head does not apply
2. ... = no data available.
[a] Data for 2015 were not completely available.
Source: Jakarta Open Data. https://data.jakarta.go.id/ (accessed 15 December 2020); Authors.

Figure 4.6: Transport-Related and Property-Related Tax Revenues as Shares of Total Local Tax Revenue in Jakarta, 2012–2018

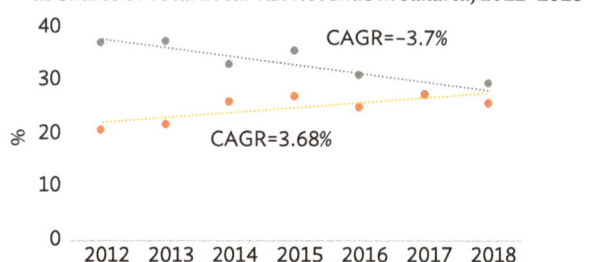

- Share of transport-related tax revenue to total local tax revenue
- Share of property-related tax revenue to total local tax revenue

CAGR = compound annual growth rate.
Source: Jakarta Open Data. https://data.jakarta.go.id/ (accessed 15 December 2020); Authors.

Table 4.7: Transport-Related Tax Revenue and the Number of Registered Vehicles, 2012–2016					
Variable	2012	2013	2014	2015	2016
Transport-related tax revenue (Rp billion)	10.72	12.10	12.08	12.46	13.71
Registered cars (million)	2.74	3.01	3.27	3.47	3.53
Registered motorbikes (million)	10.83	11.95	13.08	13.99	13.31
Total registered vehicles (million)	13.57	14.96	16.35	17.46	16.84
Transport-related tax revenue per registered vehicle (Rp'000)	0.79	0.81	0.74	0.71	0.81

Rp = Indonesian rupiah (national currency).
Source: Authors.

Figure 4.7 shows the trends in the numbers of registered vehicles, which include cars and motorbikes, and in the transport-related tax revenues during 2012–2016. Even though both variables showed an upward trend, the higher growth rate in the number of vehicles compared with the growth rate of transport-related tax revenues meant a decreasing value in taxes collected per vehicle.

While vehicle-based taxes make a significant contribution to the overall tax revenue, the authors' analysis found that there is significant potential for optimization, given that the nominal value of the vehicle-based tax revenue is very low, at less than Rp1,000 per vehicle. In discussions held for this study, relevant local government stakeholders noted that this could partly be the result of poor law enforcement related to vehicle tax compliance. As a benchmark, in England the surplus revenue from on-street and off-street parking alone contributes up to 22% of the government's annual net transport expenditure (RAC Foundation 2018).

Palembang

Palembang showed an upward trend in both GRDP and local tax revenue during 2013–2017, but the local tax revenue accounted for only a very small percentage of GRDP. The CAGR for GRDP was 11.03%, while for tax revenue it was 14.00%. This indicates that the local tax revenue was growing at a higher rate than the city's economy as a whole. However, at 0.5%–0.6% of GRDP, local tax revenue had a significant potential for growth that was yet to be captured by the city's tax collection and enforcement mechanisms.

The collection of property-related taxes is under the authority of Palembang municipality, whereas the transport-related taxes for Palembang is collected by the South Sumatra provincial government. Due to the unavailability of any detailed breakdown of total local tax revenue, further analysis of transport-related and property-related tax revenues was not possible.

Makassar

Makassar showed an upward trend in both GRDP and local tax revenue during 2012–2018, but the local

Figure 4.7: Transport-Related Tax Revenue and Number of Registered Vehicles, 2012–2016

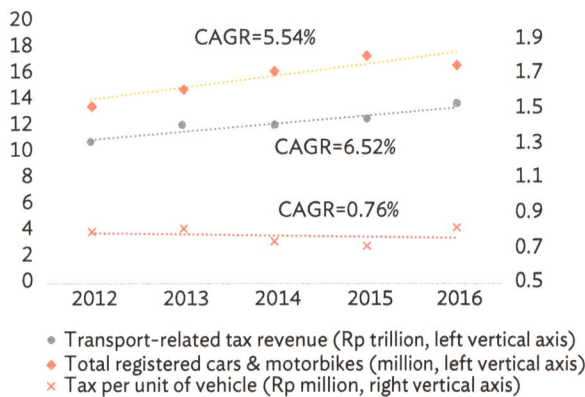

Transport-related tax revenue (Rp trillion, left vertical axis)
Total registered cars & motorbikes (million, left vertical axis)
Tax per unit of vehicle (Rp million, right vertical axis)

CAGR = compound annual growth rate, Rp = Indonesian rupiah (national currency).
Source: Jakarta Open Data. https://data.jakarta.go.id/ (accessed 15 December 2020); Authors.

Figure 4.8: Nominal Gross Regional Domestic Product and Tax Revenues in Palembang, 2013–2017

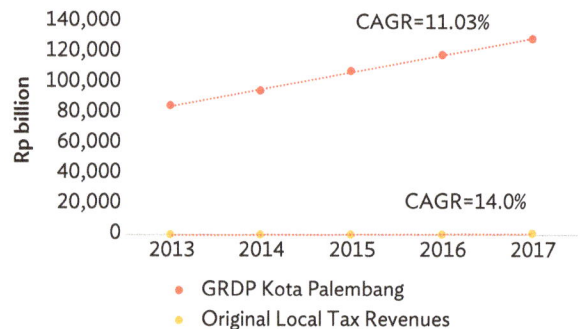

GRDP Kota Palembang
Original Local Tax Revenues

CAGR = compound annual growth rate, GRDP = gross regional domestic product, Rp = Indonesian rupiah (national currency).
Source: Central Bureau of Statistics for the City of Palembang, *Medium-Term Development Plan of the City of Palembang*.

tax revenue accounted for only a small percentage of GRDP. The CAGR for GRDP was 24.22%, while for tax revenue it was 29.06%,[10] more than double those of other cities. This indicates that the local economy was growing rapidly compared with those of other cities. However, at 0.6%–0.7% of GRDP, local tax revenue had a significant potential for growth that was yet to be captured by the city's tax collection and enforcement mechanisms.

Due to the limited availability of detailed data and the inconsistency of tax statements between regional and provincial tax mechanisms, the authors focused on key private transport-related and property-related tax components:

- local taxes: parking;
- separately managed local assets: regional parking company (*perusahaan daerah parkir*);
- BPHTB; and the
- land and buildings tax P2 (*perdesaan dan perkotaan*).

The relevant data are presented in Table 4.8.

Figure 4.10 shows that, as shares of total local tax revenue, transport-related and property-related tax revenues both decreased at a similar rate during 2014–2018. The data in Table 4.8 show that parking revenue and landownership revenue are nearing zero growth.

Figure 4.9: Nominal Gross Regional Domestic Product and Local Tax Revenue in Makassar, 2012–2018

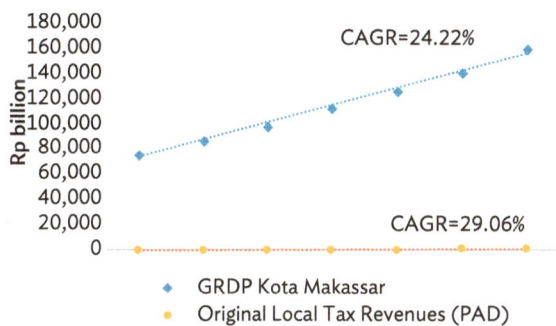

CAGR = compound annual growth rate, GRDP = gross regional domestic product, Rp = Indonesian rupiah (national currency).
Sources: Makassar City Government Office; Authors.

Figure 4.10: Transport-Related and Property-Related Tax Revenues and Total Local Tax Revenue in Makassar, 2014–2018

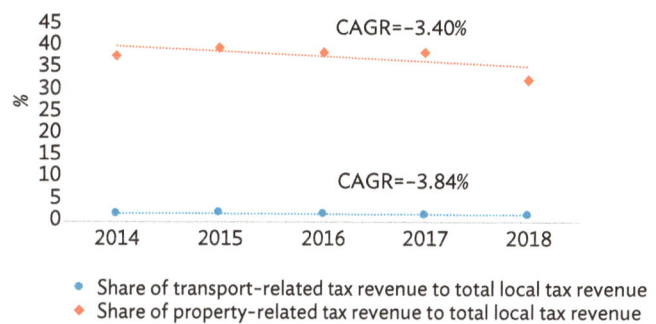

CAGR = compound annual growth rate.
Source: Authors.

Table 4.8: Parking-Related and Property-Related Tax Revenues in Makassar, 2014–2018					
Tax Revenue	**2014**	**2015**	**2016**	**2017**	**2018**
Parking-Related Tax Revenue					
Parking (Rp billion)	12.17	14.14	15.26	16.50	16.91
City parking company (Rp million)	175	160	247	1,300	1,094
Parking-related taxes as a share of total local tax revenue (%)	1.90	2.03	1.80	1.66	1.65
Total (Rp billion)	**12.34**	**14.30**	**15.51**	**17.80**	**18.00**
Property-Related Tax Revenue					
BPHTB (Rp billion)	153.18	150.46	188.86	272.83	210.36
PBB P2 (Rp billion)	96.64	132.51	148.52	146.51	147.43
Property-related taxes as a share of total local tax revenue (%)	38.43	40.27	39.15	39.09	32.85
Total (Rp billion)	**249.82**	**282.97**	**337.37**	**419.34**	**357.79**

PBB P2 = Land and Buildings Tax P2, BPHTB = duty on the acquisition of land and building rights, Rp = Indonesian rupiah (national currency).
Sources: Makassar City Government Office; Authors.

---

10   The significant growth of Makassar's tax revenue was caused by increases in property tax and the significant additional tax revenue sharing from the provincial government in 2016.

The collection of property-related revenue is under the authority of the Makassar municipality, whereas transport-related revenue for Makassar is collected by the South Sulawesi provincial government. Due to the unavailability of any detailed breakdown of total local tax revenue, further analysis, particularly of transport-related and property-related tax revenues, was not possible.

The sources of local tax revenue listed in Table 4.8 include hotels, restaurants, advertising, entertainment, and street lighting. Of particular note is the high amount of tax revenue from street lighting, which was jointly invoiced by the provincial government and the state-owned power company, Perusahaan Listrik Negara (PLN), which also took care of the collection. This process exemplifies the importance of collection methods in capturing value.

Tax- and Fee-Based Value Capture Readiness

A detailed analysis of Indonesia's tax-based and fee-based readiness for value capture is presented in this section, together with commentary on how they can be applied or improved from a regulatory, technical, and institutional perspective. The potential for each revenue category to be used as a value capture channel is also described.

Analysis of Tax- and Fee-Based Value Capture Readiness in Indonesia

Table 4.9 assesses Indonesia's tax-based readiness for value capture, and Table 4.10 assesses Indonesia's fee-based readiness for value capture—both from a regulatory, technical, and institutional perspective. The potential value capture channels are also described. There is more discussion on this topic in Appendix 6.

It is generally recognized that the implementation of any new or innovative forms of taxes or levies aimed at improving the quality of services could potentially have a negative impact on the actual rate of use if the new tariff is set above the users' average willingness to pay, let alone their ability to pay. For example, increasing the tourist tax may discourage tourists, and therefore reduce the revenue. Similarly, if the tariff for solid waste collection is increased, people may object to using the service. This report recommends further assessments of the applicability of the various potential tax-based and fee-based value capture instruments, including in terms of public acceptance, which could vary among services and among regions.

Table 4.9: Tax-Based Value Capture Readiness Analysis	
Type of Tax	**Anticipated Potential Value Capture Channel**
Property tax	Property taxes could potentially be channeled into tax increment financing by updating the NJOP to reflect improvements, and by using the proceeds to fund up-front investments. An up-front tax increment is not possible, however, as the NJOP should be based on the current value. Hence, a robust NJOP value projection should be estimated when the government intends to refinance a project through this scheme.
Property transaction (rights transfer) tax	The capital gains tax could be channeled into fiscal revenues by updating the formula to account for the property transaction.
Income tax	Significant regulatory changes would be required to enable funds to be earmarked for specific projects.
Transport tax	Vehicle title registration fees in value capture-target areas could be increased, with the increment allocated to value capture-related expenditures.

NJOP = sales value of a taxable object.
Source: Authors.

Table 4.10: Fee-Based Value Capture Readiness Analysis	
Type of Fee	**Anticipated Potential Value Capture Channel**
Solid-waste service fees	• Solid-waste service fees in value capture-target areas could be increased, with the increment allocated to value capture-related expenditures.
On-street parking fees	• On-street parking fees in value capture-target areas could be increased to improve the accessibility of the nearby public transport system, with the increment allocated to value capture-related expenditures. • Meanwhile, parking rates at designated off-street facilities may be reduced to incentivize their use as park-and-ride entry points to the nearby public transport system.
Market service fees	• Market service fees may not be suitable as value capture channels, as they could be seen as too capitalistic. • However, public perceptions may change if the local government can provide evidence that it has reinvested the money collected in public infrastructure improvements.
Wastewater treatment fees	• The incentive-and-disincentive mechanism could be considered as a way to motivate building managers to develop their own treatment plants or to develop them jointly with the managers of adjacent buildings, compensated through an increased FAR, though taking environmental requirements into account. • With careful and equitable calculations, funding collected through these *retribusi* (fees) could be allocated to improvements in the wastewater-treatment infrastructure and support services.
Telecom tower control fees	• The following could be considered: – imposing higher tower-control fees in value capture-targeted areas, and – modifying the calculation of the fee, to take into account not only the space needed to construct the tower, but also the number of operators that will be using the tower.
Local asset-utilization fees (*retribusi pemakaian kekayaan daerah*)	• Local asset-utilization fees have a significant potential as value capture channels, and there is a growing precedent for them. But the regulatory framework has not kept pace. For instance, there are still no clear regulations concerning the development rights for parcels of land under or above a certain size.
Wholesale market or trading complex fees	• Different tariff bands could be applied based on the proximity of the wholesale market facility to the value capture-target areas.
Bus terminal fees (*retribusi terminal*)	• Bus terminal fees could be developed as value capture channels where premium bus service operators have higher terminal fee tariffs imposed when serving high-density demand areas. • The local government must clearly demonstrate that it is reinvesting the money collected through the fees in such improvements as better access to the terminal, therefore maintaining the overall sustainability of the bus services. • Depot- and workshop-type services could be provided at the bus terminals where there is extra land available, to provide a new channel for government revenue.
Dedicated parking fees (*retribusi tempat khusus parkir*)	• The fact that many citizens keep their cars on the street in front of their houses, often impacting the traffic capacity of the surrounding road network, provides an ample opportunity to impose parking fees on car owners, as a supplement to the annual vehicle taxation mechanism.
Hotel, resort, and villa fees (*retribusi hotel, resor, dan vila*)	• With careful and equitable calculations, the funds collected through these retribusi could be allocated to improvements in the infrastructure surrounding tourism areas.
Port and harbor service fees (*retribusi layanan pelabuhan dan pelabuhan*)	• There are no significant channeling opportunities for port and harbor service fees.
Recreation and sports facility fees (*retribusi tempat rekreasi dan olahraga*)	• There are no significant channeling opportunities for fees charged at recreation and sports facilities. An affordable price may be charged to ensure operation cost recovery.
Building permit fees (*izin mendirikan bangunan*)	• The function of building permit fees could be expanded to facilitate the implementation of a development impact fee. • Depending on the results of a legal assessment, there could also be a tariff based on incremental increases in property value, rather than on just the proposed construction. For instance, the permit fee for constructing an additional 100 m^2 room in a building that originally had 200 m^2 would differ from the fee for a building that originally had 500 m^2.
Route permit fees (*retribusi izin trayek*)	• An increase in fees imposed on road-construction permits could be considered for the operation of high-demand areas or value capture-target areas. • Support for value capture-related infrastructure financing could also be linked to the ease of route expansion or fleet development, as a way of incentivizing operators.

FAR = floor area ratio (the ratio of a building's total floor area to the size of the plot of land on which it is built), m^2 = square meter.
Source: Authors.

Summary of Value Capture in Indonesia's Current Regulatory Framework

Apart from the assessment of taxes and fees in the preceding Tables 4.9 and 4.10, the illustrative taxation framework shown in Table 4.11 presents a set of potential types of taxes that could be adopted. The gaps that are indicated by "x" in the table are potential tax revenue sources that can be captured to make funding sources more robust.

Immovable taxes consist of taxes that are related to land and/or buildings, and are inflexible in terms of asset mobility, or where the assets remain inside a tax catchment area; whereas **movable taxes** are considered highly footloose, or the asset has flexible mobility and is dependent on the current domicile of individual taxpayers.

Table 4.11 indicates how the Indonesian taxation framework recognizes some of the key tax objects, and the levels at which they are recognized or collected. It also provides the type of tax and the beneficiaries for each instrument.

Table 4.11: Comparison of Tax and Fee Collection in Indonesia with Best Practices					
Best Practices			Indonesian Practices		
Immovable[a]	Movable[b]	Sharing Characteristics of Both[c]	Immovable[a]	Movable[b]	Sharing Characteristics of Both[c]
Property tax, land rates, fixed assets tax (residential and commercial division)	Vehicle license fee and tax increment	Special taxes and assessments (additional taxes on special regions surrounding infrastructure)	√ Local	√ Provincial	x
Hotel room tax or surcharge	Vehicle registration fee	Developers' contribution	√ Local	√ Provincial	√ National x Provincial
Parcel tax and flat rate assessment on property, regardless of value or size	Truck tonnage tax	Amusement taxes (on cinemas and theatres)	x	x	√ Local
Betterment levies and assessments	Other taxes on vehicles, including motorcycles	Business/corporate tax (as businesses can move out or removed, but at a slower pace than people)	x	√ Provincial	√ Fiscal balancing transfer
Naming rights to fixed infrastructure (one-time fee)	Gasoline, diesel, and lighting oil taxes	Value-added tax (local) on consumption	x	√ Provincial	√ National
Heating oil for premises tax	Personal income tax (collected by the central, provincial, and/or city governments)	Payroll tax and fee	x	√ Fiscal balancing transfer	√ Fiscal balancing transfer
Tax on registration and licensing of landownership		Local commercial garage fee	√ Local		x
Real estate acquisition tax		Estate or wealth transfer tax	x		x
Urban planning tax		Commercial advertisement space fees (including billboards)	x		√ Local
PILOT (i.e., payments by landowners in lieu of property taxes)		Other regulatory fees and user charges	x		x
On- and off-street parking fees			√ Local		
Local and urban road taxes			x		
Congestion fees and peak use surcharges			x		
Sports stadium seating fees (seat licenses)			x		
Environment or nature reserve or national park tax			x		
Tourism tax			x		
Departure tax (at airports and seaports)			x		

PILOT = payment in lieu of taxes.
Notes:
√ = Taxes and fees that are recognized and collected in Indonesia at local, provincial, or through fiscal balancing transfer.
x = Taxes and fees that are not recognized and not collected in Indonesia.
A blank cell indicates that the column head does not apply.
[a] "Immovable" refers to taxes and fees that are fixed or that are related to land and/or buildings inside a tax catchment area.
[b] "Movable" refers to taxes and fees that are highly flexible. They depend on the current domicile of each taxpayer.
[c] To a certain extent, the shared characteristics would include instances when taxes and fees are movable outside a tax catchment area over the medium to long term.
Sources: Authors; N. Yoshino, M. Helble, and U. Abidhadjaev, eds. 2018. *Financing Infrastructure in Asia and the Pacific: Capturing Impacts and New Sources.* Tokyo: Asian Development Bank Institute. https://www.adb.org/sites/default/files/publication/394191/adbi-financing-infrastructure-asia-capturing-impacts-and-new-sources.pdf.

Further Analysis on Property Tax

When implementing a strategy to increase the overall collection of property taxes (i.e., on land and buildings), the relationship between the applicable tax rates and the building density of the area must be considered. A density-based analysis should be performed to assess the property tax productivity of the selected city. For instance, the current property tax calculation methodology, based on the sales value of a taxable object (NJOP), considers the value of the land and the building(s) on it. The building quality would be difficult to determine at this stage, as it would probably be too complicated to perform a citywide analysis. Instead, the total gross floor area (GFA) could be the more appropriate basis on which to determine tax rates.

The total GFA for each land plot would be required as the main input for the density-based analysis. While information regarding the total GFA, especially in DKI Jakarta, is made publicly available on the Jakarta Satu website, the data are not publicly available for other Indonesian cities. The authors intend to request assistance from the Coordinating Ministry for Economic Affairs (CMEA) in obtaining further data. They will then conduct a density-based analysis, including an assessment of the ratio of the current property tax rates to total GFAs. If the analysis shows that properties with significantly higher GFAs generate the same level of tax income as those with lower GFAs, the conclusion will be that property tax collection could be increased by including the GFA in the tax rate calculations. Including the GFA in the calculations is a potential low-hanging fruit for value capture, an instrument for optimizing property tax collection. This ensures land plots with higher GFAs, which would presumably yield higher overall values (either from the land itself or from other drivers, such as economic activity), would generate higher value capture for the government that could then be reinvested in infrastructure, goods, or services for communities.

Figure 4.11 shows a partial analysis of the property tax in Jakarta. A geographical information system (GIS) analysis was carried out to discover the increments of increases in market-based value from the initial construction of Jakarta MRT (in 2014) to the pre-operation of the system (in 2017). The time frame was selected to illustrate how the perception of MRT construction influenced the actual future land value. The figure indicates that there was a significant increase of more than Rp10 million ($800) per square meter of land in the areas around the selected MRT stations, which in Figure 4.11 are indicated by the maroon spaces.

Increasing the property tax per unit might not be politically preferable, as most of the land use within a 700-meter radius of Jakarta MRT's stations is residential (Appendix 2). Moreover, increasing the unit costs will encourage gentrification by raising living costs. Thus, increasing revenue from property taxes should be carried out by:

- increasing property taxes through updated property value assessments; and/or
- increasing transit connectivity, thus enabling denser urbanization to increase the total gross floor area.

Figure 4.11: Incremental Increases in Market-Based Land Values in the Jakarta Mass Rapid Transit Corridor, 2014–2017

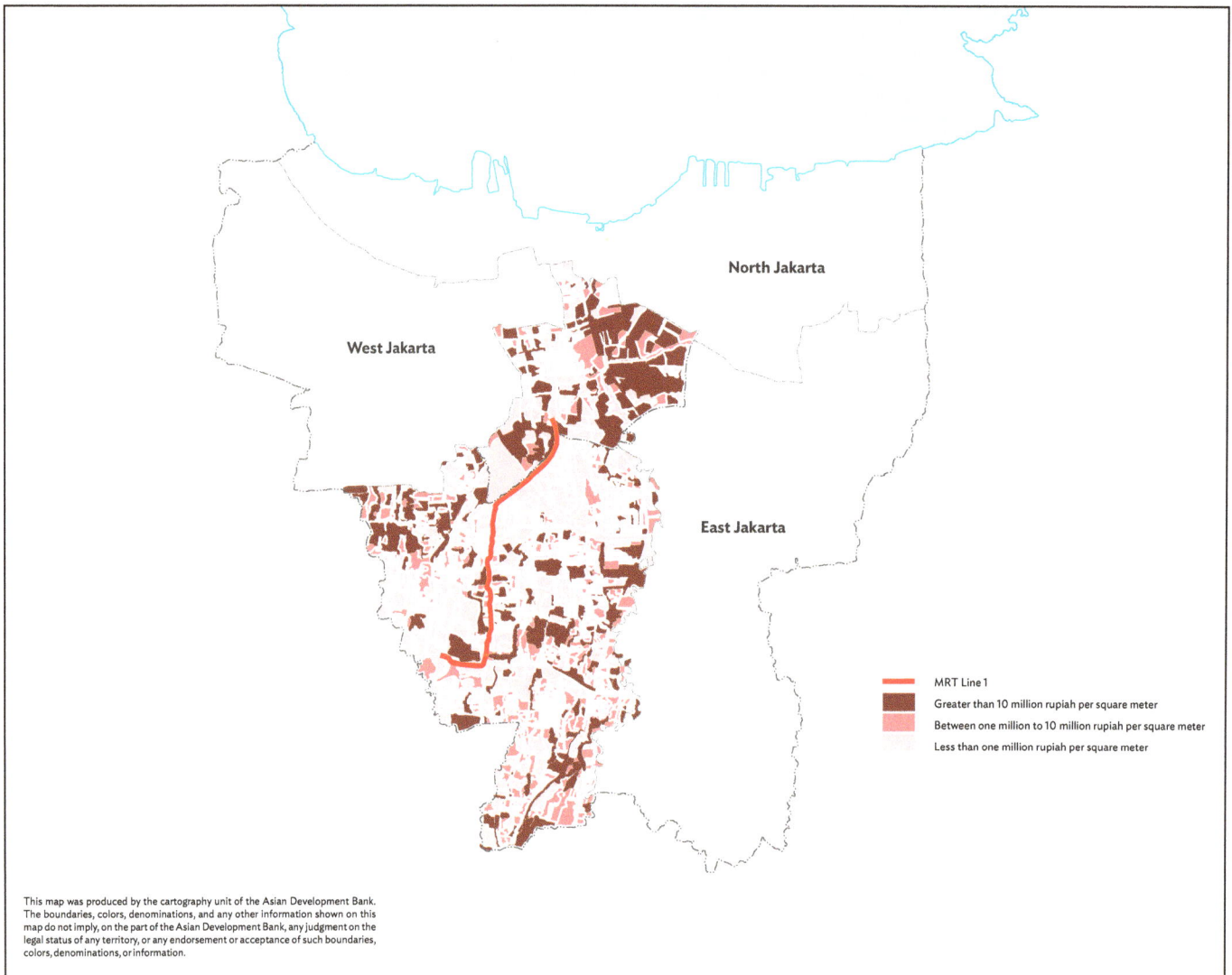

North Jakarta

West Jakarta

East Jakarta

MRT Line 1
Greater than 10 million rupiah per square meter
Between one million to 10 million rupiah per square meter
Less than one million rupiah per square meter

This map was produced by the cartography unit of the Asian Development Bank. The boundaries, colors, denominations, and any other information shown on this map do not imply, on the part of the Asian Development Bank, any judgment on the legal status of any territory, or any endorsement or acceptance of such boundaries, colors, denominations, or information.

MRT = Mass Rapid Transit.
Source: Authors.

5. Value Funding Framework

"Value funding" means using value capture to bolster confidence in the returns to public and private investments.

The virtuous cycle of value creation, value capture, and value funding can enhance private-sector financing appetite and participation in infrastructure development by increasing the investors' confidence in the returns from value capture, and from the leveraging of the positive externality effects of the newly developed infrastructure. An assessment of the data from the case study locations—DKI Jakarta, Palembang, and Makassar—suggests that the current Indonesian tax collection activities could maintain, but not improve, the government's share of the proceeds of economic growth, which has been deemed as lower than in some of the neighboring countries. Value capture presents an opportunity to alleviate the fiscal burden caused by the under-collection of taxes, and to secure the potential value resulting from infrastructure development that is not yet captured by the existing tax-collection activities.

According to ADB (2017b), to keep the momentum of economic growth and poverty reduction, and respond to climate change, developing economies in Asia will need to invest $26 trillion from 2016 to 2030, or $1.7 trillion per year.[11] The main challenge in doing so is the infrastructure investment gap—i.e., the difference between investment needs and current investment levels.

In the case of Indonesia, estimated infrastructure spending amounted to $23 billion in 2015 (or 2.6% of GDP), while its annual needs over the 5-year period from 2016 to 2020 were estimated at $74 billion. Assumed unchanged spending levels, the resulting annual investment gap of $51 billion represents around 5.1% of the average annual projected GDP over 2016 to 2020 (ADB 2017b). The challenge of filling an infrastructure funding gap of such magnitude—a

gap that has probably widened due to the COVID-19 pandemic and its resultant stress on public finances from both the revenue and expenditure sides—is formidable. The value creation and capture framework presented in this report identifies the key principles that could enable the government to recover its fiscal capacity by reinvesting in infrastructure a portion of the economic growth arising from public investments.

5.1. Public Sector-to-Public Sector Commitments within the Traditional Tax Framework

Public sector-to-public sector commitments within a traditional tax framework are relevant where one part of the government is responsible for making infrastructure investments and other part(s) of the government would, under normal circumstances, enjoy the benefits arising from an economic uplift.

The virtuous value cycle involves a policy-based and planned process in which the proposer (a government agency or state-owned entity) borrows from the public sector to finance an infrastructure project, and the infrastructure later creates benefits for others. There would be a contractual agreement between the benefiting public-sector entities and the proposer, normally brokered by the Ministry of Finance, under which the proposer implements the appropriate value capture mechanisms to recover revenue (user pays, government pays, and beneficiary pays), thus creating funding channels for repaying the financing used for the initial investments (Figure 5.1).

As an illustration, consider an area that has been prone to flooding for many years. The planning agency and Ministry of Public Works then regenerates the area with sustainable measures to reduce the flood risk. It is envisaged that the land value in the area will improve after the regeneration, and thus the treasury agency

---

11 This includes climate change mitigation and adaptation investments of $241 billion per year.

Figure 5.1: Public Sector Commitment

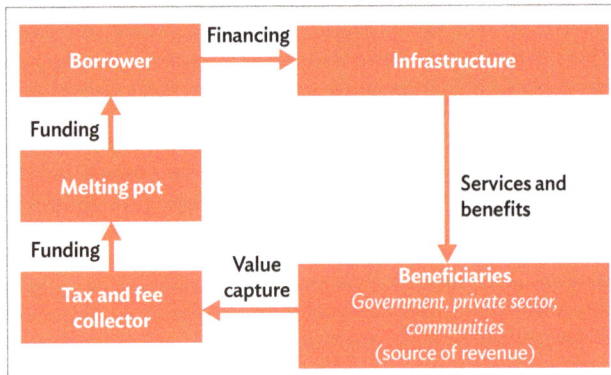

Source: Authors.

Table 5.1: Public Sector Commitment Readiness Analysis

Enabler	Readiness[a]	Requirements
Whole-of-government approach		• Clear contract with the treasury agency under which funds from certain tax revenues will be allocated to debt repayment • Strong inter-government consensus and political will • If local taxes are involved, a possible issuance of a new local law to secure the political commitment of the local parliament
Visionary economic master plan		• A clear economic zone or corridor strategy attached to the project's implementation, which also identifies the project beneficiaries
Long-term land-use planning and regulatory framework		• Clear and legitimate land use planning ("RTRW") for specific purposes.
Integrated urban and transport development		• A clear and legitimate transport master plan integrated with land use planning for specific purposes • Authorization for the local government to set the property tax and land transaction tax rates, as long as the rates are not greater than the maximum rate set out under the law
Value capture-oriented tax regime		• Clear incremental tax revenue, with the project beneficiaries identified • Multiyear budget commitments to fund the project that will be drawn from the anticipated incremental tax revenue

a The readiness assessment is based on a review of the cities of Jakarta, Makassar, and Palembang, as well as on a national regulatory review. A more detailed explanation of city readiness is available in Appendix 2.
Source: Authors.

will receive an incremental increase in property tax revenue. Under the contract, the expected revenue increase must be used to repay the finance or funding of the infrastructure that had been installed to reduce the flood risk. Due to the melting pot arrangement, the contract may have to include a guarantee of approval from the local parliament.

To implement this scheme, several general requirements would have to be fulfilled. They are presented in Table 5.1.

The following are value capture mechanisms that could create funding channels to support this scheme:

- **Property tax**. Generally, property value—and thus property tax revenue—is expected to increase with the development of new infrastructure. Higher building density can also increase property tax revenue.
- **Developer fees**. Master developers that will benefit from an infrastructure project could be charged an up-front fee as part of their construction permit or through fees on property sales or leases. The revenue gained from these fees could then be used toward the repayment of the finance or funding of the new infrastructure.

The legal aspects of this scheme would include the following points:

- The existing legislation recognizes the concept of earmarking, although its application varies depending on the types of government revenue.
- Proceeds from regional retributions must be used to fund the operation of the relevant services (Law 28/2009, Art 161.1). The proceeds from regional taxes are not typically earmarked for this purpose, except for the proceeds from the vehicle ownership tax, cigarette tax, and street lighting tax, which shall be earmarked for certain government activities (Law 28/2009, Arts 8.5, 31 and 56.3).
- Proceeds from national taxes are not typically earmarked. Revenues from the income tax, property tax on plantations, taxes on mining

and forestry operations, and excise taxes on tobacco products are shared with provincial or regional governments at the rate stipulated in the legislation. Each provincial or regional government has the authority to determine the use of the shared revenue, subject to budgetary approval from the parliament.

- The existing legislation does not expressly stipulate that the proceeds from nontax state revenue (PNBP) can be earmarked. However, the legislation adopts a mechanism whereby relevant ministries that generate the PNBP may propose the use of such proceeds, subject to approval from the Ministry of Finance (and by the parliament, during the approval of the annual state budget). This relationship between the Ministry of Finance and the relevant ministries allows for contractual arrangements for the earmarking of PNBP proceeds.
- Without any amendments to existing laws, the earmarking of certain types of revenue might still be possible. For certain types of revenue, earmarking is mandated by the legislation; and, accordingly, the relevant stakeholders are bound to allocate some funds as earmarked in the annual budget.
- For other revenue, earmarking is still possible through contractual or coordination arrangements among stakeholders. To implement this, strong political will be required. As such arrangements are not mandated in the legislation, the parliament should agree to the budget earmarking scheme. Changes to the legislation to provide express statements allowing earmarking should be considered.
- Local governments are generally authorized to manage their own financial affairs, so they may allocate incremental tax revenues to specific projects. The allocation of the funding must be included in the provincial or regional budget, which requires approval from the parliament on an annual basis. Securing a long-term political commitment from the parliament is key, and can be done through the issuance of a local law.

5.2. Hypothecated Taxes

Tax hypothecation is the ring-fencing of tax revenue into a special account for a specific purpose. Tax hypothecation is generally relevant and acceptable when incremental tax increases have only arisen due to an infrastructure investment, the beneficiaries can be clearly identified, the benefits can be clearly quantified, and there are appropriate taxes that can be used as targeted value capture mechanisms.

As mentioned above, the virtuous value cycle includes a process in which the proposing state-owned entity borrows from the public sector to finance an infrastructure project. The proposer may implement an appropriate value capture mechanism to recover

The town of Milton Keynes, in the United Kingdom, was able to borrow money from the Homes and Communities Agency to forward-fund infrastructure against expected tariff receipts, as HM Treasury was confident of the long-term certainty of the receipts. In 2004, Milton Keynes established a building tariff, called a "Strategic Land and Infrastructure Contract," to fund social and physical infrastructure in its strategic expansion areas. Developers agreed to pay standardized contributions of £18,500 per residential dwelling and £260,000 per hectare of commercial land, under the legal framework.

Developers pay 75% of the charges upon completion, rather than up front, reducing their need to borrow and allowing greater certainty for both partners. Some payments can be delivered "in kind," whereby developers provide specified infrastructure or public spaces.

revenue (user pays, government pays, and beneficiary pays). But with tax hypothecation, a portion of tax revenue is ring-fenced in a separate account to provide a discrete additional funding source to complement the direct payments, thus creating funding channels for repaying the financing used for the initial investments (Figure 5.2).

Figure 5.2: Hypothecated Taxes

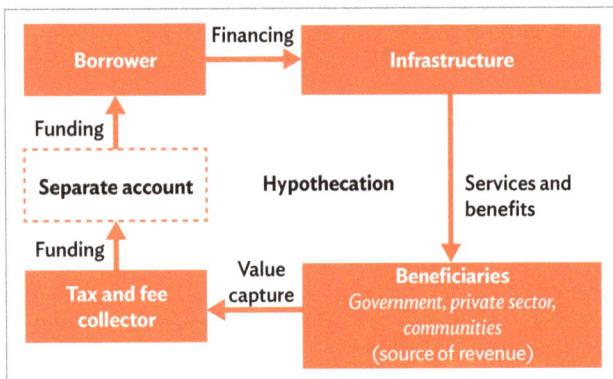

Source: Authors.

Hypothecated taxes can also provide taxpayers with in-built accountability for public spending.

To implement this scheme, several general requirements would have to be fulfilled. They are presented in Table 5.2.

The following value capture mechanisms have the potential to create funding channels to support this scheme:

- **Fuel tax, parking tax, and parking fee**. Incremental revenue from these taxes and fees can be hypothecated for the financing of transport infrastructure.
- **Property tax**. For example, land values in areas surrounding transport infrastructure built by public–private partnerships (PPPs) are expected to increase after project completion. The project sponsor or borrower can provide greater viability gap funding (VGF), and thus more attractive PPP yields, if the expected incremental property-tax revenue is committed specifically to refunding the VGF expenses.

Table 5.2: Hypothecated Tax Readiness Analysis		
Enabler	Readiness[a]	Requirements
Whole-of-government approach		• Transparency and accountability of the sponsors or the borrower, as they will be using taxpayer funds • Clear contract with the treasury agency under which funds from certain tax revenues will be allocated for debt repayment to separate accounts • Creation of a separate account for hypothecated tax funds, will require a change in the Law No. 17 of 2003 on State Budgets
Visionary economic master plan		• A clear zone or corridor economic strategy attached to the project's implementation, which also identifies the project beneficiaries • A business case that analyzes the strategic case, economic benefits, commercial case (deals), financial case, and management case
Long-term land-use planning and regulatory framework		• Clear and legitimate land use planning
Integrated urban and transport development		• Clear and legitimate transport master plan integrated with land use planning
Value capture-oriented taxation regime		• A clear type of hypothecated tax revenue that will be secured to finance the project • Changes in the No. 17 of 2003 on the Public Finance and Budgeting System to enable public money earmarking and ring-fencing • Multiyear budget commitments to fund the project to be allocated from the anticipated incremental tax revenue

[a] The readiness assessment is based on a review of the cities of Jakarta, Makassar, and Palembang, as well as on a national regulatory review. A more detailed explanation of city readiness is available in Appendix 2.
Source: Authors.

- **Hotel tax and entertainment tax**. Infrastructure development can potentially improve the businesses surrounding the project area, resulting in a greater tax base for hotel and entertainment taxes.
- **Congestion fees**. Electronic road pricing can be applied in relevant or appropriate corridors.

Legal mitigation:

- Under the current prevailing laws and regulations, all regional tax revenue must be deposited in a regional general cash account, and such revenue is not allowed to be used directly. The creation of a separate account for hypothecated taxes will require changes in Law No. 17 of 2003 on the Public Finance and Budgeting System.

• Note that local public service agencies (BLUDs) are allowed to receive revenue that has been deposited into a separate account, and to use the proceeds from that revenue to directly fund BLUD operations.

5.3. Payment in Lieu of Taxes

Payment in lieu of taxes (PILOT) is relevant when the role of proposer of an infrastructure project can be assigned to the state-owned entity or private developer responsible for planning, financing, and implementing of the project. The government can concede its tax collection privileges, and instead grant concession rights to the proposer to collect fees from the project's direct beneficiaries that would otherwise have been paid in taxes to the government. Under this arrangement, the proposer has concession rights under which it may implement appropriate value capture mechanisms to recover revenue (user pays, government pays, and beneficiary pays), but in this case part of the revenue comes from the fees that were paid in lieu of taxes. The fees are deposited into a separate account, thereby providing a discrete funding source in addition to the direct tax payments, thus creating funding channels for repaying the financing of the initial investments (Figure 5.3).

Figure 5.3: Payment in Lieu of Taxes

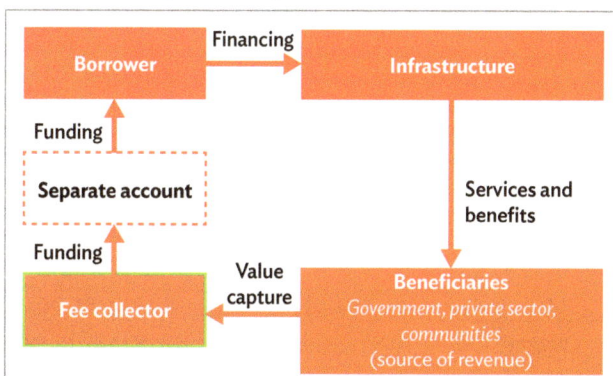

Source: Authors.

PILOT provides users and beneficiaries with in-built accountability for public spending.

This scheme works by giving a state-owned enterprise (SOE) the role of a master developer of an infrastructure project. This SOE is given the authority to manage specific areas within the infrastructure corridor, such as transit-oriented development areas, for aspects such as:

• land zoning and land use;
• provision of ancillary infrastructure;
• facilitation of taxes, permits, and licensing for business tenants; and
• the raising or reduction of charges or rental fees, possibly reducing these fees in exchange for future tax revenue.

Given the above authority, the assigned SOE may provide incentives to the private sector who will contribute to the infrastructure development. The formula for incentives should at least consider the characteristics of the population, area density, and the revenue-sharing mechanism.

As an illustration, a toll road project may be bundled with an industrial estate located in the toll road corridor. An SOE is given not only a mandate to build the infrastructure, but also the right to relax property taxes and to collect fees from businesses within the industrial estate. The expectation is that lower property taxes and discounted fees will attract manufacturers to invest in the industrial estate, and propel traffic growth along the toll road. Once there is a healthy level of economic activity, the SOE can start charging normal fees in any parts of the infrastructure corridor under its management. Revenue from these fees is deposited into the special account used to repay the project financing or to cover the operational expenditure (OPEX) of the infrastructure.

To implement this scheme, several general requirements would have to be fulfilled. They are presented in Table 5.3.

Table 5.3: Payment-in-Lieu-of-Taxes Readiness Analysis		
Enabler	**Readiness[a]**	**Requirements**
Whole-of-government approach		• Clear contract between the government and the assigned SOE or ROE, which is legitimate and acknowledged by the parliament • Clear contract between the government and the assigned SOE, which is legitimate and acknowledged by parliament • Parcel of land (greenfield or brownfield) acquired by the government or by an assigned SOE, so the SOE has the legitimacy to collect the fees and regulate the area[b] • SOE or ROE established or assigned to manage the public investment, as well as implementing the project (with the two functions split between two SOEs or ROEs in some cases)[c] • The relevant SOE required to include this scheme in its long-term strategic plan (*rencana jangka panjang perusahaan*), with income collected from specific sources allocated to specific infrastructure expenditure.
Visionary economic master plan		• Clear zone or corridor economic strategy attached to the project implementation, which also identifies the project beneficiaries • A business case that analyzes the strategic case, economic benefit, commercial case (deals), financial case, and management case
Long-term land-use planning and regulatory framework		• Clear and legitimate RTRW • Clear urban design guidelines, comprising building density land use and technical design guidelines that comply with the RTRW and RDTR • Flexible density regulated in the urban design guidelines • Improvements in the regulatory framework relating to the optimization of state assets and the ownership titles to apartments built on state land, to allow the mixed use of land (combining infrastructure assets in residential and commercial areas)[d] • Higher possibility of assigning contractual rights for the utilization of national or regional government assets for security purposes, for the benefit of financiers
Integrated urban and transport development		• Clear and legitimate transport master plan integrated with the RTRW • Clear transport and urban renewal project business case and master plan • The imposition of a new mandatory levy (in lieu of a tax) required to be set through the enactment of a new law or government regulation
Value capture-oriented taxation regime		• Commitment under the local law (*perda*) to relax the taxation regime or use discretion in its application in corridors or zones managed under the PILOT scheme • Multiyear budget commitment to fund projects, to be allocated from the anticipated incremental tax revenue • Areas exempt from local taxation to be determined by the RTRW and RDTR (ideally, those for which the national and regional (provincial and city) government is responsible for overall management), with the exemption stipulated in the local law, which requires approval from the local parliament

PILOT = payment in lieu of taxes, RDTR = detailed spatial plan, ROE = regional-owned enterprise, RTRW = regional spatial plan, SKBG = building ownership certificate, SOE = state-owned enterprise.

[a] The readiness assessment is based on a review of the cities of Jakarta, Makassar, and Palembang, as well as on a national regulatory review. A more detailed explanation of city readiness is available in Appendix 2.

[b] The land required for the building of is typically owned by the national or regional government. The law is silent on whether the developer is allowed to retain the infrastructure built on land owned by the government, and the practice differs across sectors. For more information, see Appendix 7, under "Infrastructure assets."

[c] Generally, an SOE or developer is allowed to issue debt instruments (e.g., bonds) through capital markets, subject to compliance with certain requirements. For more information, see Appendix 7, under "Debt securities issued by state-owned enterprises."

[d] Under Law No. 20 of 2011 on Strata Title Buildings, a developer is allowed to sell an apartment to a buyer, who then holds an SKBG (building ownership certificate), which is different from the *SHM Sarusun* (apartment ownership title). Detailed operating procedures for the administration of SKBGs have not been issued, and no SKBG titles is known to have been issued. SKBG ownership should be considered in the PILOT initiative.

Source: Authors.

The following value capture mechanisms which have the potential to create funding channels to support this scheme:

- **Rental fee**. Project beneficiaries may be charged an annual rental fee, which will be used to fund the infrastructure project.
- **Transfer development rights fee**. The master developer SOE can sell development rights to landowners or developers who aspire to obtain higher allowable density construction on their land. This scheme is highly regulated and should comply with the regional spatial plan (RTRW) and urban design guidelines (UDGLs).

Legal mitigation (a full legal mitigation analysis of PILOT is available in Appendix 7):

- The applicable legislation provides guidance on the development of housing complexes or apartment complexes by an SOE or ROE, as well as transit-oriented development (TOD) zones.

However, the imposition of new mandatory fees on the project beneficiaries (e.g., property owners, registered businesses) will need to be regulated by additional laws or government regulations.[12]

- The local government is authorized to set the property-tax and land-transaction-tax rates, as long as the rates are not greater than the maximum rate set by national law. In addition, as part of the TOD policy, the government may establish fiscal zones, in which the tax rate could be differentiated. Uses of space that do not comply with the TOD policy may be charged a higher tax or retribution, under MOAASP/NLA 16/2017.

- This requirement could be revised to allow the substitution of the property tax for other PILOTs as part of the fiscal zoning policy.

- The issuance of bonds by an SOE or ROE will typically require that the underlying land be used as collateral.[13] The existing state finance regime does not allow for national or regional government assets to be encumbered to secure bonds issued by an SOE or ROE. Accordingly, the procurement of assets must be on the SOE's or ROE's account, or if the assets are procured by the state, they must be injected as an in-kind equity contribution to the SOE or ROE. Taxes must also be considered.

- Alternatively, the SOE or ROE could potentially procure the contractual right to utilize land through the national and regional government asset-utilization regime, for instance, through a Build–Operate–Transfer (BOT) or a Build–Transfer–Operate (BTO) contract, or an optimization cooperation contract (*kerjasama pemanfaatan*). If this route is to be pursued, some improvements in the existing legislation may need to be considered, in order to: (i) combine infrastructure assets and vertical residential areas, (ii) improve the regulatory regime for air rights, (iii) allow the sale of the strata title over national or regional government-owned land, and (iv) allow the assignment of the contractual rights for security purposes.

> The redevelopment of Hudson Yards is one of New York's most important responses to the demand for new office space, to keep New York competitive with other global markets and to maintain agglomeration economies within the highly concentrated employment areas in Manhattan. In 2005, the City Council approved the Hudson Yards' rezoning, transforming the low-density manufacturing area into a high-density, mixed-use district. By the end of 2006, $3 billion in Hudson Yards bonds had been sold, making the project fully financed, primarily through a scheme called "payment in lieu of taxes" (PILOT).

5.4. Concessions

A concession is a straightforward scheme whereby an ROE or private sector entity is given the right to build and operate infrastructure. Essentially, the concessionaire invests in a project and collects the revenue subsequently generated by the infrastructure. This can be done, for instance, by assigning the ROE or private company as the master developer for an urban development or renewal project.

---

12 Law No. 1 of 2011 on Housing and Settlement Areas does not specifically authorize the imposition of additional fees (under the beneficiary-pays principle) by the developer on property owners within a complex. Accordingly, the introduction of PILOT, which serves as a mandatory fee payable to an SOE or ROE, may require certain amendments to Law 1/2011. For more details on housing or apartment complex funding and development, see Appendix 7, under "Development Rights."

13 Assets owned by regional governments can be used as collateral only for projects or assets financed or purchased through the issuance of municipal bonds. For more details, see Appendix 7, under "Asset collateral."

As an illustration, an ROE could be given a concession to build toll roads and industrial estates, after which it will have the right to collect all the revenue within the infrastructure corridor, including capital gains on property sales. If the concession scheme leads to profits for the ROE, the government could choose to divest its shares in the ROE and recycle the money into other infrastructure projects.

To implement this scheme, several general requirements would have to be fulfilled. They are presented in Table 5.4.

The following value capture mechanisms have the potential to create funding channels to support this scheme:

- **Service fee**. Businesses that own property in the area of an infrastructure project could be charged an annual or monthly service fee, which would be used to fund the infrastructure OPEX or even capital expenditure (CAPEX).
- **Parking fee**. The ROE may control the collection of on-street parking fees within its concession area or corridor.
- **Capital gains**. The ROE may profit from sales of land and buildings that it has developed.

Legal mitigation:

- Most infrastructure sectors are open to infrastructure delivery by an SOE, ROE, or private sector entity under a public–private partnership (PPP) scheme. In most cases, tariffs are regulated by the government, and the criteria will include the consumers' ability to pay and the need for political interventions. Accordingly, the project must have a very strong business case for relying fully on tariffs for funding.

Table 5.4: Concession Readiness Analysis		
Enabler	**Readiness[a]**	**Requirements**
Whole-of-government approach		• The establishment or assigning of an SOE that is capable of implementing a project, and is legally authorized to carry out business activities such as industrial area management or building management • Clear contract between the government and the assigned SOE • Acquisition by the government or assigned SOE of a parcel of land (greenfield or brownfield), so the SOE can then resell the land or property to a private sector entity • The completion by the relevant SOE of the required land-acquisition procedures, with the expenditure for these procedures included in the SOE's long-term corporate plan and/or budget, which must be approved by its shareholder (i.e., the minister of SOEs) • Concession agreements, especially under PPPs, following output-based specifications and performance-linked payment mechanisms, as well as other procurement conditions that can be negotiated with the concessionaire • Clear contract with the treasury agency to securely allocate the proceeds from divestment, the signing bonus, and other concession fees for infrastructure development • Clear inter-government consensus and political will (if the contracting agency for the concession agreement and the licensing issuer are different government agencies, then with consensus and stakeholder support documented in a memorandum of understanding)
Visionary economic master plan		• Clear zone or corridor economic strategy attached to the project implementation, which also identified the project beneficiaries • A business case that analyzes the strategic case, economic benefit, commercial case (deals), financial case, and management case • Area divestment strategy for the future, when the company's value reaches a reasonable level for sale to the public
Long-term land-use planning and regulatory framework		• Clear master plan or urban design guidelines that comply with the RTRW
Integrated urban and transport development		• Clear and legitimate transport master plan that is integrated with the RTRW
Value capture-oriented taxation regime		• No requirement to change the current tax regime • Some adaptations to the local laws (*perda*), depending on the project case • Land acquisition by the SOE to develop infrastructure, such as industrial zones

PPP = public–private partnership, RTRW = regional spatial plan, SOE = state-owned enterprise.

[a] The readiness assessment is based on a review of the cities of Jakarta, Makassar, and Palembang, as well as on a national regulatory review. A more detailed explanation of city readiness is available in Appendix 2.

Source: Authors.

- A combination of an infrastructure project and a revenue-generating project is theoretically possible, although such project proposals must be analyzed on a case-by-case basis. The two projects would typically be under different authorities, and thus political support from these authorities would have to be secured in the form of a memorandum of understanding, joint decree, or agreement.

- The proceeds from the divestment of an SOE or ROE, signing bonuses, or concession fees shall constitute national or regional government revenue, which must be deposited in the national or regional government accounts. These proceeds cannot be directly used for infrastructure spending. Instead, they must become part of the annual budget, which must be approved by the treasury agency and parliament.

The Mactan Cebu International Airport (MCIA) Authority, in the Philippines, signed a public–private partnership (PPP) contract with a private concessionaire for the expansion of the airport in 2014. The bidding parameter for the PPP project was the highest up-front payment to the government for the grant of a concession. The winning bidder paid 80% of the project cost, or ₱14.4 billion, which is being used by the MCIA Authority to finance other developments required for the airport. The premium to the government was paid in anticipation of the revenue to be earned from the commercial development rights granted to the private sector partner under the PPP contract.

6. Value Creation and the Capture Policy Road Map

This study's analysis, as well as discussions with the relevant stakeholders on implementing value capture in Indonesia, has concluded that a well-established "lead policy institution" should be appointed to lead cross-government collaborative initiatives. This institution would be tasked with optimizing the current development planning and management system (which is the entry point for an effective value capture mechanism), and ultimately with strengthening tax and fee collection in general. Additionally, a "lead implementing institution" should be appointed to support the line ministries and local governments in operationalizing value capture.

This study found that gaps exist between value capture best practices and the current institutional and regulatory framework in Indonesia. The approach to value capture can best be divided into short-term and long-term action plans.

Five institutions have been identified essential for developing a successful value capture policy framework:

- **Ministry of Finance** (MOF), which has oversight and ultimate discretionary control of fiscal budgeting for investments in infrastructure projects, as well as control of fiscal revenue. The MOF should assign a team to evaluate whether the business cases for proposed infrastructure investments have made sufficient use of value capture mechanisms to provide the public sector with "value for money," and to ensure that a fiduciary mechanism is in place for channeling funds into repayments of up-front investments.
- **Coordinating Ministry for Economic Affairs** (CMEA), which has a strategic coordination function in economic policy making. It is therefore well placed to drive the creation of an overarching policy framework, and to coordinate among ministries and agencies in the formulation of value capture-related regulations, as part of the National Medium-Term Development Plan (RPJMN) and value capture guidelines. The CMEA also provides guidance to the relevant ministries and agencies on developing value capture policies within their own organizations and on monitoring their implementation.
- **Coordinating Ministry for Maritime and Investment Affairs** (CMMIA), which has a strategic coordination function in transport and investment policy making. It is therefore also well placed to drive the creation of an overarching policy framework and to coordinate among ministries and agencies in the formulation of value capture-related regulations, as part of the RPJMN and value capture guidelines. The CMMIA also provides guidance to the relevant ministries and agencies on developing value capture policies within their own organizations and on monitoring their implementation.
- **Ministry of Agrarian Affairs and Spatial Planning/National Land Agency** (ATR/BTN), which has a strategic role in coordinating the management of land use; this could be leveraged to maximize value creation and value capture.
- **Ministry of National Development Planning/National Development Planning Agency** (BAPPENAS), which oversees investments in nationally strategic infrastructure projects that have significant economic value. BAPPENAS has a key role in the preparation of business cases for infrastructure investments and in the evaluation of these cases before their submission to the MOF. BAPPENAS is well placed to drive innovation and explorations of alternative infrastructure funding mechanisms, and to refer to established precedents for new projects, while it is also able to identify synergies between investments proposed by parallel line ministries.

Achieving the broader benefits of value capture in infrastructure financing will require:

- **a lead policy institution**, to be appointed to drive the preparation and adoption of a value capture policy; and
- **a lead implementing institution**, to be appointed to drive the implementation of value capture practices by line ministries and local governments.

This study has identified a short-term action plan that could create the momentum for mainstreaming value capture tools into infrastructure planning, as well as a long-term action plan that that could then roll the best practices, to maximize the benefits to the Indonesian economy.

Hong Kong, China Case Study on Assigning Lead Institutions

In the case study of Hong Kong, China (Appendix 4), the city's Mass Transit Railway (MTR) was designated the value capture lead under the Rail + Property model in the areas around the MTR stations. Jakarta's Mass Rapid Transit (Jakarta MRT) system is heading in a similar direction, as it has recently been appointed to manage that city's urban design guidelines and transfer development rights within the catchment areas of its stations.

However, considering the limited scope and authority of transport operators (such as the Hong Kong, China MTR or Jakarta MRT), it would be more appropriate if the role of lead institution were assigned to a national-level organization that could manage the subnational stakeholders more effectively, and provide capacity building where required. Additionally, the organization could overcome the different implementation challenges in the various regions (e.g., social, political, and economic), from which lessons could be learned for future implementations.

6.1. Short-Term Action Plan

The short-term action plan could begin immediately, and could be fully implemented within a 24-month period, with a focus on:

- establishing the policy framework,
- building capacity, and
- implementing smaller pathfinding projects within the existing regulatory and tax framework.

The proposed short-term action plan is illustrated in Figure 6.1.

The proposed detailed short-term actions are listed here:

(i) **Selecting the lead policy institution**. The lead policy institution should be selected from among the existing coordinating ministries, and the roles and responsibilities described below should determine the criteria for the selection. Value capture implementation is by nature an inter-sector effort, so strong partnerships between ministries will be necessary for the implementation of the relevant policies in each ministry's domain. **The CMEA is considered the best fit for this role**.

(ii) **Preparing the legal framework for land value capture**. The **lead policy institution** should prepare a legal framework (e.g., in the form of a presidential regulation) for national and local governments, and for other relevant stakeholders. The framework should:

Figure 6.1: Short-Term Action Plan

Select lead policy institution	Prepare national LVC legal framework	Select lead implementing institution	Select specific pilot project(s)

LVC = land value capture.
Source: Authors.

(a) conceptualize the value capture framework, with a particular focus on the mechanisms for capturing or monetizing economic benefits, and for channeling the proceeds into the funding or repayment of the initial infrastructure financing;

(b) institutionalize the process of project screening, selection, preparation, and implementation with regard to value capture, through a special mandate given to a lead implementing institution to coordinate and oversee the overall project cycle;[14]

(c) formulate a coordination framework among the key stakeholders for the preparation of the project business case, the preparation of the enabling legislation, and the implementation of the project;

(d) authorize the development of pilot projects, guiding the preparation of project business cases that recognize the potential for value creation in particular cities, such as Palembang or Makassar;

(e) formulate the process for identifying the key entity (government authority, SOE, or ROE) that could potentially be the value capture manager, and provide the local government with some commercial-structuring options for framing the network manager; and

(f) provide guidance on the national level, for instance through the issuance of a presidential regulation, with consideration given to:
- fair and lawful value capture instruments for different situations, such as the various types of land rights, a region's economic conditions, spatial planning, and zoning regulations;
- the available input and output channels for value capture, to ensure that value capture revenue provides returns to investors, but taking into account the limited means available for earmarking within the existing tax framework; and

- the most astute timing for the value capture (i.e., before or after the value is created, as appropriate).

(g) Conventional infrastructure planning already requires coordination among diverse stakeholders, notably led by the CMEA, CMMIA, and BAPPENAS. However, this review of the support for value capture offered by the existing regulatory and institutional framework finds that a whole-of-government approach could substantially increase the economic benefits and the ease infrastructure financing. Therefore, the authors have scoped out potential short-term actions to enhance the value capture framework for each of the relevant ministries and agencies, and these actions are listed in Table 6.1. The coordination of these activities should be the role of the **lead policy institution**.

(iii) **Selecting the lead implementing institution**. The lead implementing institution should be selected and assigned the responsibility for formalizing the value capture implementing guidelines. **BAPPENAS is considered the best fit for this role**. The responsibilities should include:

(a) selecting pilot project(s) for the development and testing of the value capture implementation guidelines;

(b) preparing national value capture implementation guidelines for city governments to apply consistently, with the guidelines covering the preparation of projects to recognize value creation opportunities, quantify the potential economic and commercial benefits to both users and broader beneficiaries, and to identify potential value capture mechanisms; and

(c) providing advice on improving tax assessment processes and assessing the effectiveness of tax and fee collection as a value capture mechanism through:

---

14 The lead implementing institution could be structured as a single powerful agency or as a joint coordination committee comprising various government stakeholders. It is important to ensure, however, that the institutional process for value capture is complementary to the existing business processes for conventional project development (e.g., for PPP projects), and that any duplication of processes be avoided.

Ministry/Agency	Potential Action
Ministry of Finance- (national)	• Directing policy development related to the taxation system and local levies to increase the potential fiscal revenue using value capture • Managing national tax revenue collection • Establishing policies and procedures for making multiyear budgetary provisions for long-term funding commitments, using value capture-based incremental tax revenue • Governing and exerting overall control over infrastructure financing • Establishing fiduciary mechanisms for channeling funds into repayments of up-front investments, and monitoring their effectiveness
Coordinating Ministry for Economic Affairs	• Coordinating the activities of the Ministry of Finance and the Ministry of Agrarian Affairs and Spatial Planning/National Land Agency regarding the development of value capture-related regulations, as part of the RPJMN and value capture guidelines • Monitoring and guiding the efforts of the Ministry of Finance and Ministry of Agrarian Affairs and Spatial Planning/National Land Agency to develop their own internal value capture policies
Coordinating Ministry of Maritime and Investment Affairs	• Coordinating the activities of the Ministry of Public Works and Housing, Ministry of Transportation, and the National Investment Agency regarding the development of value capture-related regulations, as part of their RPJMN and value capture guidelines • Monitoring and guiding the efforts of the Ministry of Public Works and Housing, Ministry of Transportation, and the National Investment Agency to develop their own internal value capture policies
Ministry of Agrarian Affairs and Spatial Planning/National Land Agency (national)	• Providing guidance to regional governments as they develop their regional spatial plans, detailed spatial plans, and zoning regulations—especially those aligned with the national government's economic master plan for transit corridors (meant to enable the densification of mixed-use urban developments) • Requiring that urban plans for value capture be incorporated into the economic master plan and economic cost-benefit assessments in city planning documents, which are to be signed off on • Developing a nationwide, digital market-based land value register, recorded in public digital cadastral mapping systems • Providing guidance on transit-oriented development relevant to value capture implementation
Ministry of National Development Planning/National Development Planning Agency (national)	• Facilitating the exploration of alternative infrastructure funding sources, both domestic and foreign • Coordinating and prioritizing infrastructure budget requirements for national and city transit projects (e.g., metro, light rail transit, bus rapid transit, highways, and inter-city rail) to provide connectivity between actual or potential nodes of economic activity and to enable economic uplift • Coordinating and prioritizing the allocation of shared funds from the national budget to the local governments
Ministry of Public Works and Housing	• Acting as the main developer of national and local infrastructure projects to enhance economic productivity that have the potential to increase land and property values in all regencies and cities in Indonesia • Developing the technical guidelines for the preparation of comprehensive business cases for all infrastructure projects, as inputs for economic master planning
Ministry of Transportation	• Formulating and determining all national and local transportation projects to enhance economic productivity that have the potential to increase land and property values in all regencies and cities in Indonesia • Developing the technical guidelines for the preparation of comprehensive business cases for all transportation projects, as inputs for economic master planning
Development Planning Agency at Sub-National Level (local)	• Leading and coordinating value capture preparatory work at the local level (i.e., setting up local regulatory and institutional frameworks) • Managing the budget requirements for citywide project pipelines
Treasury Agency	• Developing local regulations and policies related to local taxation and levy systems, to facilitate the implementation of the relevant value capture mechanisms • Managing local tax and levy revenue collection, especially the property tax and vehicle registration tax
Finance and Asset Agency	• Developing local regulations and policies regarding local asset management, to facilitate the implementation of the relevant value capture mechanisms • Managing the financing, including the revenue from value capture, especially the financing allocated to infrastructure development and local asset management
Transport Agency	• Identifying future budget requirements for transit infrastructure development
Public Works and Spatial Planning Agency	• Identifying future budget requirements for infrastructure development • Assessing business cases for all infrastructure projects and their relationships to the spatial plan and land values

Table 6.1: Summary of Potential Short-Term Actions to Enhance the Capacity for Value Capture

RPJMN = National Medium-Term Development Plan.
Source: Authors.

- regular reviews of the local governments' implementation of "low-hanging fruit" value capture opportunities (such as improvements in the collection of on-street and off-street parking fees, and the updating of the statutory base value for land and properties to reflect market values); and

- facilitation of interministerial discussions on reforming the property taxation regime, i.e., shifting away from using the sales value of a taxable object (NJOP) as the basis for property tax calculations, and toward the use of land-value zoning, which is more market-based (this reform has been initiated within the Ministry of

Land Use and will require support from other relevant government ministries and agencies).

(iv) **Selecting and implementing pilot project(s).** The lead implementing agency should select pilot project(s) for incorporating value capture mechanisms, potentially taken from the three cities' portfolios, to kick-start the initial adaptation and to learn lessons by means of the following steps:

(a) select the lead implementing agency to develop the screening tools and selection criteria for the pilot projects;

(b) have the lead implementing agency evaluate the political commitment to the pilot project(s) as a key criterion for the selection of the project(s), with the potential contribution from value capture as another key selection criterion; and

(c) establish value capture mechanisms for paying back the up-front investments in selected pilot project(s), using the current

taxation and fee collection regime (in particular, local governments would be able to implement value capture mechanisms more quickly for smaller infrastructure projects, whose mechanisms are based on the local government's *retribusi* system).

6.2. Medium-Term Action Plan

The medium-term action plan could commence immediately, and be fully implemented within 48 months, with a focus on:

- optimizing the tax framework to strengthen value capture tools;
- optimizing landownership laws and regulations to broaden value creation opportunities; and
- implementing large transformation programs for economic-development corridors, encompassing interrelated projects delivered within the new national value capture framework.

Thus, in the medium term, value capture efforts should be aimed at generating and capturing economic gains, taking a visionary approach to the commercially-oriented master planning of economic-development corridors. These commercially-oriented master plans should strive to create economically vibrant communities connected by economic infrastructure, while also striking a balance between guiding the direction of future developments and accommodating the different characteristics of each project.

The proposed medium-term action plan is illustrated in Figure 6.2.

An Example of a Pilot Project That Could Be Implemented in the Short Term

A local government repurposes several strategically located plots of land to create interchange hubs. Each hub will include a multistory parking facility (fee-based) on a park-and-ride basis, a bus interchange (government services), mixed small trader market (tenants), and a supermarket (tenant-based). Each hub project is valued at around $10 million–$30 million. The local government uses the *retribusi* framework to capture the revenue and value generated by the projects, and uses this income to pay back the up-front investments.

Figure 6.2: Medium-Term Action Plan

Regulatory changes in national tax framework → Changes in laws and regulations on landownership → Implementation of national LVC legal framework → Implementation of economic development corridor projects

LVC = land value capture.
Source: Authors.

The **lead policy institution** should drive and facilitate the following actions:

(i) **Regulatory changes in the national tax framework**. These would involve assessing the applicability of measures to improve the effectiveness of tax and fee collection, which will require more coordinated efforts, including:

   (a) conducting a legal analysis of the introduction of new mandatory fees—for instance, *biaya kawasan* (area fees) or *biaya pengembangan* (development fees)—and of the introduction of tax increment financing, in line with the amendment to Law 28/2009, which will enable pilot schemes to be fully implemented in Indonesia;

   (b) facilitating research on and policy-driven adjustments to the formulas for property-related taxes, such as the land value gains tax;

   (c) developing an integrated approach to the pricing of building permits and public utility-related fees, such as solid-waste and wastewater treatment fees, as a (dis)incentive for developers to align their planning with the government's; and

   (d) supporting research on and the policy-driven introduction of tax increment financing, to unlock further financing for infrastructure development.

(ii) **Regulatory changes in the landownership framework**. These would involve improving the landownership structure by:

   (a) strengthening the regulatory framework regarding the optimization of state assets and building ownership certificates (SKBGs) for apartment units constructed above state assets, to allow the mixed use of land (i.e., combining infrastructure assets and residential and commercial areas);

   (b) exploring the possibility of assigning contractual rights to utilize national and subnational government assets as security for the benefit of financiers;

   (c) considering the construction of station- and transit-oriented developments (e.g., apartments and offices) on privately owned land; and

   (d) facilitating research into, and the policy-driven introduction of, the concepts of air rights and underground rights, to allow the construction of infrastructure above or below private properties (thereby reducing the costs of land acquisition).

(iii) **Implementation of a national land value capture legal framework**. This should occur in the wake of regulatory changes to the taxation and landownership structure. The central government would also have to:

   (a) update the national guidelines on land value capture (LVC) implementation to reflect the regulatory changes; and

   (b) conduct training and capacity-building sessions for government officers, and for employees at state-owned enterprises (SOEs), if necessary.

(iv) **Continued support by the lead implementing institution to line ministries and local governments**. After the regulatory changes in the taxation and land ownership structure, the lead implementing institution should provide support for the implementation of **transformational economic-development corridor programs** by

   (a) developing screening tools and selection criteria for strategic transformation programs for economic-development corridors, and identifying the constituent projects;

   (b) evaluating the level of political commitment to strategic transformation programs for economic-development corridors as the main criterion for the selection of constituent project(s), and evaluating the potential contribution from value capture as another key selection criterion; and

   (c) applying the revised taxation and fee collection regime to the value capture mechanisms for paying back up-front investments in selected strategic transformation programs and constituent projects, also exploring novel private-sector financing based on new streams of revenue as options for financing up-front investments.

> **An Example of How Transformational Economic-Development Corridor Programs Could Be Financed in the Medium Term**
>
> The national government and local government select an area where economic growth could be stimulated through enhanced infrastructure connectivity. Constituent projects are identified and developed to create an economic corridor that will boost urban regeneration and transformation. The overall program of projects will be in excess of $1 billion. The national government exercises its authority in collecting future revenue from user fees, developer contributions, and incremental taxes to issue bonds to fund the up-front investment. The national government then allocates an appropriate portion of this revenue to the repayment of the up-front investment.

6.3. Creating a Set of National Value Capture Guidelines

Business Case Methodology

Private sector contributions in the form of cash or cash equivalents will be more easily accessible if the private sector is confident that it will receive a return on its infrastructure investments. Such confidence can only be won if the national government can transparently demonstrate the robust planning of projects that address tangible demand, a readiness for execution, and a viable strategy for revenue collection to pay back the up-front investments.

In the United Kingdom (UK), decisions on government spending proposals require documentary evidence of the thinking processes and readiness in the form of business cases. The business cases help decision-makers appraise the proposals objectively and ensure that the proposed projects bring the best public value for the money. Years of UK project-planning best practices have been chronicled for wider adoption

as the **"Better Business Case Guidance,"** issued by HM Treasury, and it covers the strategic, economic, commercial, financial, and management aspects of project planning. The Better Business Case Guidance is currently being adopted and adapted by the Ministry of National Development Planning/National Development Planning Agency (BAPPENAS) through the UK's Infrastructure and Projects Authority (IPA) Project Phase 2 for use in Indonesian infrastructure project planning. **This guidance can be readily applied and modified to support the development of national value capture guidelines**. A brief summary of how the Better Business Case model can be applied is provided below.

The Better Business Case model should be adopted to clarify to both the public and private sectors that the fiscal and commercial returns on infrastructure investments contribute to the government's infrastructure-development objectives.[15] This clarification could be done by the Business Case's component parts, as follows:

- The Strategic Case could show how the project is aligned with government objectives, and thus has regulatory support.
- The Economic Case could show that the maximization of public value for money is the main reason behind the choice of project scope, and that the private sector would be among the project beneficiaries.
- The Commercial Case could show that an assessment has been carried out to determine whether a project can best be carried out by the public sector, private sector, or a partnership of the two, and how risks could be properly allocated.
- The Financial Case could highlight the project's affordability and the government's strategy for project financing and funding. Recognizing that contributors to value capture mechanisms have varying levels of means, depending on their business characteristics,

---

15   This business model has been adapted by BAPPENAS to update BAPPENAS Regulation No. 4 of 2015 on the Procedure for Cooperation between Government and Business Entities in the Procurement of Infrastructure, through the Global Infrastructure Program.

regional economy, location, and timing, the guidelines should explore several value capture collection options, such as contributions in advance or upon project completion, in bulk or incrementally, and in cash or cash equivalents. This would ensure that the guidelines could apply to projects implemented under different conditions, and could maximize value capture collection.

- The Management Case could show that the practical execution strategy for a project has been considered from the early stages, to ensure that the project would be completed successfully. It should also show how value capture would be implemented and monitored to win confidence in the funding strategy.

This value capture mechanism was demonstrated in the UK by the Department for Transport and by Transport for London, which together fundraised over £500 million from London businesses (Appendix 4, Case Study 2), and obtained funding commitments from other government agencies. In Indonesia, designating the Better Business Case as the national model for project planning and value capture implementation would provide a legal and consistent approach that could achieve results more effectively than a B2B approach.

Every 5 years, the Indonesian government publishes a National Medium-Term Development Plan (RPJMN) and a Regional Medium-Term Development Plan (RPJMD), which stipulate the overall direction of national and regional development, including projects for infrastructure development and the associated funding and financing strategies. The 5-year cycle provides an opportunity to determine the use of the Better Business Case for project planning and for the funding or financing strategies at the national and regional levels.

A program for citywide urban development or an economic corridor initiative, for example, will require several different projects to accomplish its objectives. The strategic potential for value capture should be determined in the transport master plan. Hence, a strategic corridor business case can ensure that the project's efforts are focused on a common goal of maximizing public value, thereby bringing about a best practice value capture strategy for value creation. This strategy would include: a long-term land-use planning and regulatory framework, whole-of-government approach, economic master plan, and an integrated approach to urban and transport development. Project-level business cases or outline business cases can then be developed, not only to translate the program objectives into projects, but also to act as value capture tools.

Figure 6.3 illustrates the process of developing the business case for value capture. The Strategic Corridor Business Case aims to identify the potential beneficiaries of a project and the potential for value creation. Afterwards, the Outline Business Case determines the potential value capture and identifies a suitable value funding mechanism. Part of the analysis of value funding would include the formulation of "the best deal" structure, which would form the basis of the proposal to the beneficiaries. Further analysis should be carried out to develop sufficient guidelines for the preparation of value capture business cases.

6.4. Improved Tax Collection

Value creation has the potential to increase tax revenue. The efficiency of tax assessment and collection are therefore key mechanisms for value capture. Given the exact definitions of legal taxes and fees under Indonesian law, and the fact that tax reform is not a popular option, efforts to increase government revenue should focus on optimizing the collection of existing taxes and fees.

**Figure 6.3: Process of Developing a Business Case
to Justify a Value Capture Best Deal between the Government and Beneficiaries**

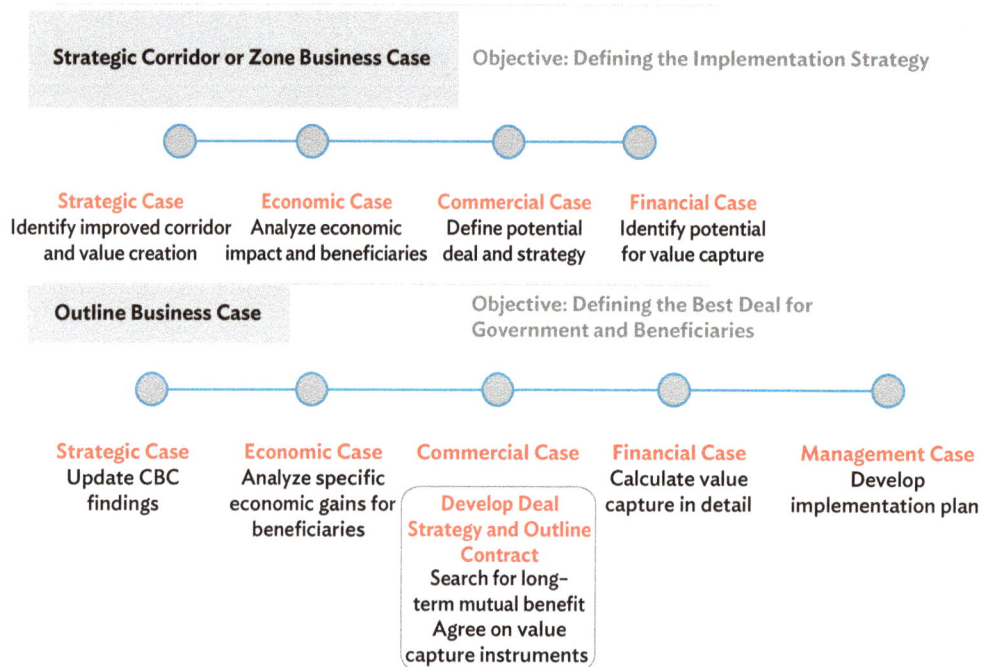

Strategic Corridor or Zone Business Case   Objective: Defining the Implementation Strategy

Strategic Case
Identify improved corridor and value creation

Economic Case
Analyze economic impact and beneficiaries

Commercial Case
Define potential deal and strategy

Financial Case
Identify potential for value capture

Outline Business Case   Objective: Defining the Best Deal for Government and Beneficiaries

Strategic Case
Update CBC findings

Economic Case
Analyze specific economic gains for beneficiaries

Commercial Case

Develop Deal Strategy and Outline Contract
Search for long–term mutual benefit
Agree on value capture instruments

Financial Case
Calculate value capture in detail

Management Case
Develop implementation plan

CBC = corridor business case.
Source: Authors.

There appear to be opportunities to optimize tax collection, as follows:

- Penalties for noncompliance with building and environmental permit regulations in the form of cash payments, cash equivalents, additional required public facilities, or transfers of development rights, could be made stricter and tailored to the needs of public infrastructure funding development.
- On-street parking fees in two of the three cities visited comprise an insignificant portion of total government revenue, despite the fact that on-street parking causes congestion in many Indonesian streets. This could indicate some scope for parking fee increases, apart from outright noncompliance by drivers or fraud by parking fee collectors.
- Similarly, property taxes on private parking lots could be raised to increase revenue.

- Unused public land could be provided under short-term leases to parking lot operators to generate additional revenue.

Parking fees have a high potential for use as a carrot-and-stick mechanism. In areas of heavy traffic, revenue and collection may be improved by applying on-demand pricing and installing electronic parking meters. In a designated park-and-ride lot, however, parking fees may be reduced as an incentive to use public transport, thereby increasing the revenue from public transport systems.

There also appear to be opportunities to optimize the assessment formula, as follows:

- When taxing land transactions, a tax formula that is based on capital gains will reach the target faster than a transaction tax based on a statutory base value. A capital gains tax rightly targets those who are converting their land into cash, while giving the buyer an incentive to report the land's statutory base value in accordance with actual market prices. This is also the preferred approach of the Ministry of Land and Spatial Planning.

- There is potential to embed a development impact fee into the formula for pricing building permits, particularly in the catchment areas of infrastructure projects. The development-impact fee is another reward-and-punishment instrument, in that high-density developments that potentially place a greater stress on public utilities are charged a higher impact fee, whereas developers who build their own local utilities and connections to the public utility grids are rewarded with a lower impact fee.

Appendix 1. Review of the Indonesian Regulatory Framework

Table A1.1: National Governance and Finance Laws and Regulations	
Law/Regulation **National Governance**	**Relevant Commentary**
Law No. 39 of 2008 on State Ministries (UU No. 39 Tahun 2008 tentang Kementerian Negara)	Specifies the different categories of ministries, and provides a scope of authority for each category. For instance, it mentions how a ministry that is categorized as dealing with "synchronisation of Government programmes" (e.g., Ministry of Public Works) is allowed to perform technical activities at the national level, while a ministry with a coordinating function (e.g., BAPPENAS) is not. Art. 4, 5, and 8.
Law No. 2 of 2018 on the Second Amendment of Law No. 17 of 2014 on the People's Consultative Assembly, House of Representatives, Regional Representative Council, and Regional House of Representatives (UU No. 2 Tahun 2018 tentang Perubahan Kedua Atas Undang-Undang No. 17 Tahun 2014 tentang Majelis Permusyawaratan Rakyat, Dewan Perwakilan Rakyat, Dewan Perwakilan Daerah, dan Dewan Perwakilan Rakyat Daerah)	Describes how the various houses of representatives play a role. For example, it notes that the Regional Representative Council can offer proposals to the National House of Representatives regarding the implementation of new tax regulations. Art. 249 (1).
Presidential Regulation No. 11 of 2015 on the Ministry of Home Affairs (Perpres No. 11 Tahun 2015 tentang Kementerian Dalam Negeri)	Describes, for instance, how the Regional Finance Directorate General of the Ministry of Home Affairs develops and implements policies regarding the management of regional taxes and fees. Art. 24.
National Finance	
Law No. 17 of 2003 on State Finance (UU No. 17 Tahun 2003 tentang Keuangan Negara)	Governs how the state finances at the national level are managed, and provides an indication of the key roles of the agencies involved. In relation to the implementation of potential value capture instruments, the following points are to be noted: • The national budget (*anggaran pendapatan dan belanja negara*) covers revenue, expenditure, and financing. Art. 11 (2). • The state revenue is comprised of the following: tax revenue, nontax revenue, and grants. Art. 11 (3). • The balance of funds from the central government is allocated to local governments according to Law No. 33 of 2004 on Fiscal Balance between the Central and Regional Governments (UU Nomor 33 Tahun 2004 tentang Perimbangan Keuangan antara Pemerintah Pusat dan Daerah). • The central government may give loans and/or grants to local governments, and vice versa (Art. 22 [2]), with the agreement of the Regional House of Representatives (Dewan Perwakilan Rakyat Daerah). Art. 22 (3). • Local governments are allowed to give/receive loans to/from each other. Art. 22 (4). • The central government may give loans/grants to, or receive the same from, foreign governments/entities, with the approval of the House of Representatives (Dewan Perwakilan Rakyat) (Art 23 [1]), and the same could be forwarded to the local governments/state-owned enterprises/regional-owned enterprises. While Law 17/2003 mainly governs state finances at the national level, it provides some references with regard to the roles and positioning of local governments, for example: • The local government (at either the provincial or city/regency level) is given the authority to manage local finances. Art. 6 (2) c. • The local government may collect local revenue in accordance with local regulations. Art. 10 (2) c. • The local government office/agency may collect nontax revenue. Art. 10 (3) d. • The local government manages local government assets Art. 10 (3) f. • The local budget (*anggaran pendapatan dan belanja daerah*) comprises revenue, expenditure, and financing. Art. 16 (2). • The local government revenue comprises local original government revenue (*pendapatan asli daerah*), balance fund (*dana perimbangan*), and other legitimate revenue sources. Art. 16 (3).
Law No. 1 of 2004 on the State Treasury (UU No. 1 Tahun 2004 tentang Perbendaharaan Negara)	Describes the state treasury institutional arrangements. For instance, the regional government's financial management entity collects the taxes (Art. 9 [2]), while the Ministry of Finance sets the exchange rates for tax payments originally in foreign currencies. Art. 7 (2).
Law No. 15 of 2004 on The State Financial Management and Accountability Audit (UU Nomor 15 Tahun 2004 tentang Pengelolaan Keuangan Negara dan Pemeriksaan Akuntabilitas)	The state auditor may carry out an investigative review in the case of any indication of national or local government financial loss and/or criminal offence. Art. 13.
Law No. 20 of 2019 on the State Budget Fiscal Year 2020 (UU No. 20 Tahun 2019 tentang APBN Tahun Anggaran 2020)	This law is updated annually to formalize specific budget requirements—for instance, that 25% of all general transfer funds be allocated to local government infrastructure (Art. 10 [22]); and that 10% of national government revenue from the land and buildings tax be allocated equally among the regions under the national budget, with the rest directly returned to the regions.
Law No. 9 of 2018 on Nontax State Revenues (UU No. 9 Tahun 2018 tentang Penerimaan Negara Bukan Pajak)	Provides a general guide on tariffs and types of nontax government revenue, which are regulated under the relevant ministry for the respective sector. Art. 10.
Government Regulation No. 24 of 2005 on Government Accounting Standards (PP No. 24 Tahun 2005 tentang Standar Akuntansi Pemerintahan)	Provides a general guide on how the regional government budget report should be structured.
Regulation No. 33 of 2019 on Guidelines for the Preparation of the 2020 Regional Budget (Permendagri No. 33 Tahun 2019 tentang Pedoman Penyusunan Anggaran Pendapatan dan Belanja Daerah Tahun Anggaran 2020)	Provides guidelines for the earmarking of taxes and fees, such as the following: • A minimum of 10% of the vehicle registration tax (including the Profit-Sharing Fund of the respective regency or city where the tax is collected) must be allocated to the development and the maintenance of roads, and to improvements in public transport modes and facilities. • A minimum of 50% of excise revenue from tobacco products must be allocated to the development of public health services and to law enforcement. The local governments may use up to 75% of the 50% sourced from their regions to finance the local operation of the national health insurance system. • The revenue from the street lighting tax must be partly allocated to provide more street lighting. • The revenue from traffic control (road tax) must be partly allocated to improvements in traffic control and public transport services.
Government Regulation No. 63 of 2019 on Government Investment (PP No. 63 Tahun 2019 tentang Investasi Pemerintah)	Provides a mechanism for circulating the money generated from the national revenue (e.g., taxes), profit-sharing funds, revenue from state-owned enterprises, grants, and other legitimate sources through government investments. Government investments can be made in three forms: • stocks that are listed and/or traded on a stock exchange; • bonds issued by national and regional governments, corporate entities, other nations, and international corporate entities, which can be channeled into the finance infrastructure; and • direct investment in regional loans for infrastructure development and investment partnerships.
Government Regulation No. 10 of 2011 on Procedures of Foreign Loans Procurement and Grants Receipt. (PP No. 10 Tahun 2011 tentang Tata Cara Pengadaan Pinjaman Luar Negeri dan Penerimaan Hibah)	Provides guidance for cases in which a local government wishes to *terus-pinjam* (forward-loan) or *terus-hibah* (forward-grant) to a regional government-owned company. The regulation states that the local government must send a proposal to the Ministry of Home Affairs (Art. 7 and 19), and the proposal must be reported in line with PP 24/2005.
Government Regulation No. 39 of 2007 on State/Regional Cash Management (PP No. 39 Tahun 2007 tentang Pengelolaan Uang Negara/Daerah)	Provides general guidance on the institutional arrangements for managing national and regional government funds, specifying their respective roles and responsibilities.

BAPPENAS = Ministry of National Development Planning/National Development Planning Agency, PP = Peraturan Pemerintah (Government Regulation), UU = Undang-Undang (Law).
Source: Authors.

Table A1.2: Local Governance and Finance Laws and Regulations	
Law/Regulation **Local Governance**	**Relevant commentary**

Law No. 23 of 2014 on Regional Government (as most recently amended by Law No. 9 of 2015 on the Second Amendment of Law No. 23 of 2014 on Regional Government (UU No. 23 Tahun 2014 tentang Pemerintahan Daerah, sebagaimana diubah oleh UU No. 9 Tahun 2015 tentang Perubahan Kedua atas UU No. 23 Tahun 2014 tentang Pemerintahan Daerah)	• Covers provincial and regional governance matters (including the provincial and regional budgets and budget changes, mid-term development plans, tax, fees, and land use), and must be reviewed by the minister of home affairs before it can be enacted. Art. 245 (1).
	• Provides an updated description of local government revenue nomenclature, introduced in Art. 285 (updating that specified in Law No. 17 of 2003 on State Finance, as described in Chapter 2), covering:
	  ◦ original local government revenue (*pendapatan asli daerah*), which includes:
	    ▪ local government taxes,
	    ▪ local government *retribusi* (fees);
	    ▪ local government asset-management revenue, and
	    ▪ other legitimate sources; and
	  ◦ transfers of funds, specifically:
	    ▪ central government transfers (balance funds, special autonomy funds, special region funds, and village funds), and
	    ▪ inter-local government transfers (profit-sharing revenue and financial assistance).
	• Other legitimate sources of revenue include: local government nontax revenue, local fees such as check services, and sales of local government assets. Art. 285.
	• Local government taxes and *retribusi* are governed by a local regulation. Art. 286 (1).
	• Local governments may not collect fees outside of those specified in the law. Art. 286 (2).
	• Transfers of funds from the national government are sourced from national tax revenues, which include the land and buildings tax and the income tax on individual citizens. Art. 288, Art. 289 (1) and (2).

Law No. 2 of 2018 on the Second Amendment of Law No. 17 of 2014 on the People's Consultative Assembly, House of Representatives, Regional Representative Council, and Regional House of Representatives (UU No. 2 Tahun 2018 tentang Perubahan Kedua atas UU No. 17 Tahun 2014 tentang Majelis Permusyawaratan Rakyat, Dewan Perwakilan Rakyat, Dewan Perwakilan Daerah, dan Dewan Perwakilan Rakyat Daerah)	Describes the roles of the various houses of representatives, for instance, how the Regional Representative Council can provide input to the national House of Representatives regarding proposals on the implementation of new tax regulations. Art. 249 (1).
Local Finance	
Law No. 33 of 2004 on Fiscal Balance between the Central and Regional Governments (UU No. 33 Tahun 2004 tentang Perimbangan Keuangan Antara Pemerintah Pusat dan Pemerintah Daerah)	Describes the structure of regional incomes. The regional income comes from regional revenues (taxes, levies, asset management, fiscal balancing transfers, and other sources) and regional finance (regional loans, bonds, budget surpluses, and other sources). The fiscal balancing transfer itself consists of profit-sharing funds, general allocation funds, and special allocation funds. The sources of profit-sharing funds are: • the property tax on plantations, mining, and forestry, of which 16.2% is allocated to the province where the tax is collected, 64.8% to the specific regency or city where the tax is collected, 9% to the payment of administration and collection fees, 6.5% to all regencies and cities, and 3.5% to regencies and cities that have achieved revenue realization; • land and buildings transfer tax on plantations, mining, and forestry, of which 16% is allocated to the province where the tax is collected, 64% to the regency or city where the tax is collected, and 20% to all regencies and cities; • business and individual income taxes, which of which 12% is allocated to the regency or city where the taxes are collected, 8% to the province or region where the taxes are collected, and 80% to the national government; • forestry business permit fees, of which 20% is allocated to the national government and 80% to the local government where the fees are collected; • reforestation fees, 60% of which are allocated to the national government and 40% to the local government where the fees are collected; • mining industry permit fees, 20% of which is allocated to the national government and 80% to the local government where the fees are collected; • revenue from the fishery industry, 20% of which is allocated to the national government and 80% to all local governments; • oil industry permit fees, 84.5% of which are allocated to the national government and 15.5% to the local government where the fees are collected; • natural gas industry permit fees, 69.5% of which are allocated to the national government and 30.5% to the local government where the fees are collected; and • geothermal industry permit fees, 20% of which are allocated to the national government and 80% to the local government where the fees are collected.
Law No. 28 of 2009 on Local Tax and Retribution (UU No. 28 Tahun 2009 tentang Pajak dan Retribusi Daerah)	• Provides a detailed description of each tax and fee that can be collected by the Indonesian government. • States that the city or regency is authorized to specify other types of taxes as long as it complies with the criteria set out in the law. • Prioritizes the utilization of the revenue from each type of *retribusi* for funding activities that directly relate to the services from which the revenue comes. Art. 161 (1). The terms regarding the allocation of the fee revenue are to be set by a *perda* (local regulation). Art. 161 (2).
Government Regulation No. 12 of 2019 on Regional Financial Management (PP No. 12 tahun 2019 tentang Pengelolaan Keuangan Daerah)	• Sets the local government budget annually. Art. 1 (4). • Allocates specific funds transferred from the national budget to the regions to fund specific regional requirements, physical and nonphysical. Art. 1 (9). • Takes into account the budget *sisa lebih perhitungan anggaran*, which is the remaining balance between revenue realization and budget expenditure for any one budget period. Art. 1 (48). • Provides a description of local government revenue nomenclature (similar to the one in Law 23/2014, Art. 285) in Art. 30 and 31, whereby Art 31. (3) allows for "other revenue" as long as it complies with the regulation. • Prohibits local governments from collecting fees other than those specified in the law (similar to Law 23/2014, Art. 286). The prohibition is set out in Art. 32, with an additional prohibition in Art. 32 (2) on collecting fees that could lead to a high-cost economy, hinder population mobilization, or obstruct the interregional flow of goods and services.
Government Regulation No. 39 of 2007 on State/Regional Cash Management (PP No. 39 Tahun 2007 tentang Pengelolaan Uang Negara/Daerah)	Provides the general guidance on the institutional arrangements for managing national and regional government funds, specifying their respective roles and responsibilities.

PP = Peraturan Pemerintah (Government Regulation), UU = Undang-Undang (Law).
Source: Authors.

Table A1.3: Transfer Mechanisms for Various Types of Land Rights				
Types of Land Rights	**Period of Ownership and Specifications regarding the Land**	**Those with Rights**	**Rights Transfer Mechanisms**	**Conditions for Abolition of Rights**
Ownership rights: right to fully own the land	• No limitation on the size of the land • No limitation on the length of time of ownership	• Indonesian citizens • Other legal entities, as determined by the national government	Rights can be transferred through a transaction, grant, inheritance, any transfer through a cultural inheritance, or by other transfers.	• The land was seized by the government due to a withdrawal of rights, voluntary surrender, or neglect of the land. • The land was lost due to a natural a disaster.
Right to cultivate: right to cultivate and otherwise utilize land for agriculture, fishery, and/or farming.	• Minimum of 5 hectares, with plots larger than 25 hectares required to comply with additional requirements under other regulations • Maximum of 25 years for ownership rights, which can be extended up to 35 years, depending on the type of business for which the land is used	• Indonesian citizens • Other national legal entities that were established under the law and are located in Indonesia	Rights must be granted by the government through a registration process, and the prospective rights owner needs to fulfill the requirements set by the government.	• The ownership period has ended. • The rights have been pending for an indefinite period and/or abolished due to a failure to meet requirements. • The owners abolished their own rights before the ownership period had ended. • The rights were abolished for the sake of public use or interest. • The land has been abandoned. • The land has been lost due to a natural disaster.
Right to build: right to construct and own buildings on a particular plot of land	• No limitations on the size of the land • Maximum of 30 years for ownership rights, which can be extended up to 20 years, depending on the owner's needs and the condition of the building(s)	• Indonesian citizens • Other national legal entities that have been established under the law, and are located in Indonesia	Rights must be granted by the government through a registration process, and the prospective rights owner must fulfill the requirements set by the government. However, the rights can also be transferred to another owner, in compliance with the regulations on land ownership.	• The ownership period has ended. • The rights have been pending for an indefinite period and/or abolished due to a failure to meet requirements. • The owners abolished their own rights before the ownership period ended. • The rights were abolished due to public use and/or interest. • The land was abandoned. • The land was lost due to a natural disaster.
Right to use: right to utilize a piece of land, but not under a lease agreement between the landowner and the user	• No limitation on the size of the land • During a set period, or as long as the land is utilized for a certain purpose, and can be granted without charge, in exchange with any kind of payment or services	• Indonesian citizens • Foreign citizens living in Indonesia. • Other national legal entities that are established under the law and are located in Indonesia • Other international legal entities with a representative office in Indonesia	Rights to land must be granted by the government and permitted by an authorized official, if the land is owned by the government. Rights must be transferred to other parties through an agreement, if the land is owned by individuals.	There are no procedures for the abolition of rights.
Leasehold right: right to use other parties' land by paying a lease or other charge	• No limitations on the size of the land • Valid as long as the rights owner pays the lease, whether through a one-time payment, regular payments, or payments before and after the land is used	• Indonesian citizens • Foreign citizens living in Indonesia • Other national legal entities that are established under the law and are located in Indonesia • Other international legal entities with a representative office in Indonesia	Land rights must be transferred to other parties through an agreement, without any extortion.	There are no procedures for the abolition of rights.
Other rights: rights to carry out land clearance, to collect forest products, to use water, to cultivate and catch fish, and to use airspace	• No limitations on the size of the land • The duration of land rights determined by the relevant government regulations	• Indonesian citizens • Other national legal entities established under law and located in Indonesia	The transfer of rights is provided for in the relevant government regulations.	The process for the abolition of rights is provided for under the relevant government regulations.

Source: Authors.

Table A1.4: List of Development Planning Documents		
Type of Planning Document	**Content**	**Guidelines**
City spatial plan	• City planning goals and objectives • City structures (roads, urban railways, and utilities) • Land use (development areas and protected zones) • Identification of key development areas • Policy direction for key development areas • Land use control instruments providing indicative principles for zoning regulation, principles for issuing development and building permits, development incentives and disincentives, and sanctions • Map scale of at least 1:50	• Minister of Agrarian Affairs and Spatial Planning/Head of National Land Agency Regulation No. 1 of 2018 on Guidelines for the Organization of Spatial Planning for Province, Regency, and City • Government Regulation No. 8 of 2013 on Spatial Mapping Accuracy

Detailed spatial plan	• Identification of the "partial planning area" (later to be called the "city subzone") and its objectives
	• City subzone structure planning (identification of city subcenter, utilities, transport network), covering:
	  • the transport network, including pedestrian pathways, bike lanes, public transport networks, public parking, and bus terminal locations; and
	  • utility networks, including electrical transmission, power substations, water transmission, telecom, and wastewater networks
	• City subzone land use planning, which covers green areas and protected areas, as well as areas slated for development, specifically:
	  • residential housing (R), including R-1 (high density), R-2 (dense), R-3 (medium density), R-4 (low density), and R-5 (very low density); and
	  • commercial (K), including K-1 (citywide commercial center), K-2 (city subzone commercial center), central business district, public service center, heavy industry area, medium industry area, mixed-use development, and other zones.
	• Zoning regulations, comprising the basic principles of land utilization, regulation of land use intensity, regulations on building blocks and skylines, regulations on basic infrastructure requirements, technical requirements for permits, and specific requirements (if any)
	• Policy suggestions for urban design guidelines
	• Map scale of at least 1:5,000
		Minister of Agrarian Affairs and Spatial Planning/Head of National Land Agency Decree No. 16 of 2018 on Detailed Spatial Plan and Zoning Regulation Guidelines regarding Map Accuracy for Planning Document.

Urban design guidelines on street block and neighborhood planning	• Building and neighborhood program • General-plan and urban-design guidelines Source: Authors. • Investment plan • Basic instruments for planning control • Guidelines for planning implementation and controls • Regulation of transferable development rights. In general, the maximum floor area ratio that can be transferred is equal to 10% of the specified GFA value.[a] A transfer of GFA values is possible when the GFA refers to a space that is in the same building and integrated into the overall planning areas. It is also possible when the building donors have utilized at least 60% of their GFA rights, as determined in the planning document.	Ministry of Public Work Decree No. 6 of 2007 on Building Blocks and Neighborhood Plan Guidelines.

GFA = gross floor area.

[a] The "floor area ratio" is the ratio of a building's total floor area to the size of the plot of land on which it is built.

Source: Authors.

Table A1.5: Facilities for Investment		
Arrangement for Investments	**Description**	**Mechanism**
Facilities for Investment		
Net and gross income reduction (Art. 18)	For new investments or new investment expansions, a private sector entity can utilize a government facility to officially reduce its net income, enabling it to pay lower income taxes.	The income tax generated by the private sector entity must strictly follow Government Regulation No. 45 of 2019 on the Calculation of Taxable Income and Redemption of Income Tax in the Current Tax Year. The income reduction applies to: • new pioneer industries, • labor-intensive industries, • human capital-related industries, and • research and development.
Property tax reduction (Art. 18)	For new investments or new investment expansions, the government provides facilities that will allow a private sector entity to pay a lower property tax.	The amount of property tax revenue generated by a private sector entity that has utilized a property may be reduced, depending on the type of business and on local regulations.
Easier Procedures for Obtaining Land Rights		
Easier procedures and services for obtaining the right to cultivate a plot of land (Art. 22)	For new investments or new investment expansions, the government can provide easier procedures and services to help a private sector entity obtain the right to cultivate a plot of land.	The period for which a private sector entity can obtain the rights in advance to a plot of land is 60 years, but it can be extended for another 35 years.
Easier procedures and services for obtaining the right to build on a plot of land (Art 22)	For new investments or new investment expansions, the government can provide easier procedures and services to help a private sector entity obtain the right to build on a plot of land.	The period for which a private sector entity can obtain these land rights in advance is 50 years, but it can be extended for another 30 years.
Ease of Obtaining Rights to Use Land (Art 22)	For new investment or new investment expansions, the government can provide easier procedures to help private sector entities obtain the rights to use a plot of land.	The period for which a private sector entity can obtain these rights in advance is 45 years, but it can be extended for another 25 years.

Source: Authors.

Appendix 2. City Profiles and Statistics

Background on Three Cities

Table A2.1: Macro Factors in the Case-Study Cities			
Macro Factors	**Jakarta**	**Makassar**	**Palembang**
Population in 2017—metro area	31,522,934	2,633,122	3,685,700
Population in 2017—core city[a]	10,374,235	1,489,011	1,623,099
Land—metro area (km^2)	6,213	4,245	33,923
Land—core city (km^2)[a]	622	176	401
Population density—metro area (per km^2)	5,073	620	109
Population density—core city (per km^2)	16,670	8.471	4.052
GDP per capita in 2017—core city, 2020 prices[b]	232,341,951	96,136,739	7,755,040
2012–2017 GDP growth—core city, 2020 prices (%)	76.01	46.54	71.98

GDP = gross domestic product, km^2 = square kilometer(s).

[a] Central Jakarta Administrative Statistics Agency. 2019. *Central Jakarta Municipality in Figures 2019*. Jakarta; Makassar City Central Bureau of Statistics. 2019. *Makassar Municipality in Figures*. Makassar; City of Palembang Central Bureau of Statistics. 2019. *Palembang City in Numbers 2019*. Palembang..

[b] Government of Indonesia. 2014. *Regional Medium-Term Development Plan, 2015–2019*. Jakarta.

Source: Authors.

Urban Features

The urban features of the three selected cities include spatial development patterns and major urban problems, especially problems caused by car-dependent urban development (e.g., congestion, pollution and shortages of affordable housing within a one-hour commute). They, along with national and local government urban-development strategies (particularly regarding the role of public transit in addressing the city's urban problems), were subjected to geographical information system (GIS) analysis, the results of which are presented below.

Jakarta

The most popular mode of transport in Jakarta is road travel in private or public cars and motorbikes. The city has an established network of roads, inner city toll roads, and outer ring roads, all of which

Figure A2.1: Jakarta Transport Infrastructure Plan

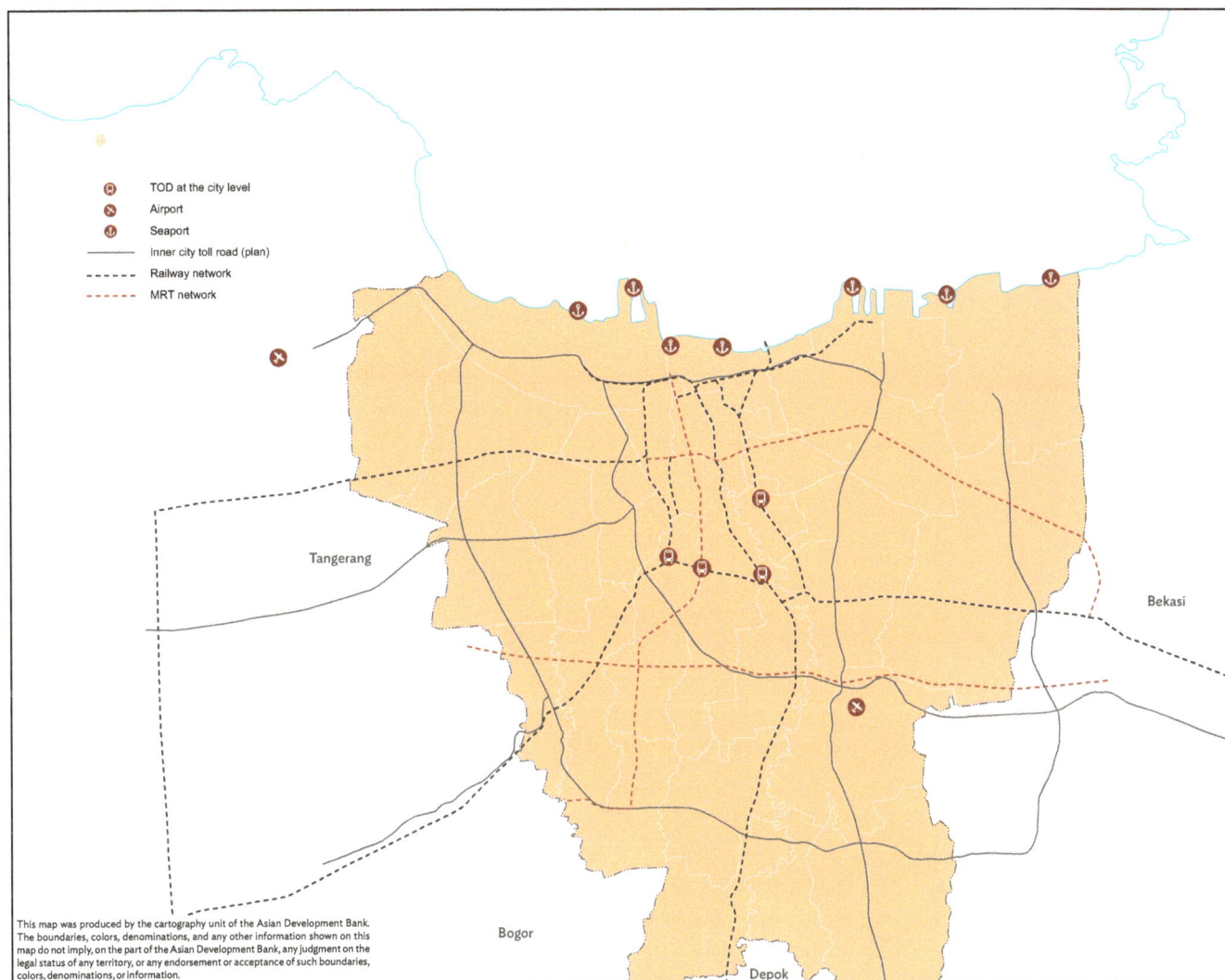

MRT = Mass Rapid Transit, TOD = transit-oriented development.
Sources: Regional Agency for Planning and Development (BAPPEDA), Special Capital Region of Jakarta; Authors.

are interconnected. The more affordable option for suburban commuters is an old commuter metro service that offers solid coverage of the Jakarta metropolitan area, including the new townships of Bumi Serpong Damai (BSD) City, Bintaro Jaya, Pantai Indah Kapuk (PIK), and Harapan Indah. Commuter train stations have been integrated into the TransJakarta bus rapid transit (BRT) system, which offers both dedicated-lane and shared-lane services. The bus service also has an interface with other light rail transit systems, such as Jakarta's Mass Rapid Transit (MRT) and Light Rail Transit (LRT), although Jakarta MRT and Jakarta

LRT each has only one corridor at the commercial operations stage.

Jakarta has plans to build a second layer outer ring road by 2030, as well as an extension of the existing MRT North–South Corridor, a new MRT East–West Corridor, a continuation of the inner-city loop line of Jakarta LRT, and a Greater Jakarta, or "Jabodebek," LRT line (for Jakarta–Bogor–Depok–Bekasi)—all to relieve some of the pressure on the old commuter line. This is because the population levels in the areas surrounding central Jakarta are higher than in the city center, but the city center is where the economic activity is concentrated. As a result, the development of connecting infrastructure between the peri-urban and urban areas, and within the central business district, is highly necessary, and thus inevitable.

Table A2.2 presents data on land use and land value in the vicinity of MRT stations before the Jakarta MRT was built, and shows that most of these plots have been used for housing. High demand for housing has led to high land prices and then to the gentrification of these areas, benefiting private landowners while driving people with lower incomes to find housing in more affordable areas, typically farther away from the city center. The challenge for the government is to provide services for all classes of the public despite these high

costs, for instance by providing affordable housing in the city center and capturing land value increases to contribute to the funding of these infrastructure development projects.

Table A2.2: Land Use and Land Values of Areas Surrounding Mass Rapid Transit Stations				
MRT Station	Green (%)	Housing (%)	Commercial (%)	ZNT Value in 50 m radius (Rp million/ m²)	ZNT Value in 700 m radius (Rp million/ m²)
Bundaran HI	1	68	31	130	54
Senayan	48	25	27	72.5	82
Cipete Raya	4	83	13	49	18
Fatmawati	2	86	12	32	21
Lebak Bulus Grab	7	76	17	14.7	19

HI = Hotel Indonesia, m = meter, m² = square meter, MRT = Mass Rapid Transit, Rp = Indonesian rupiah (national currency), ZNT = land value zoning, Source: Authors.

Figure A2.2: Population of the Jakarta Metropolitan Area

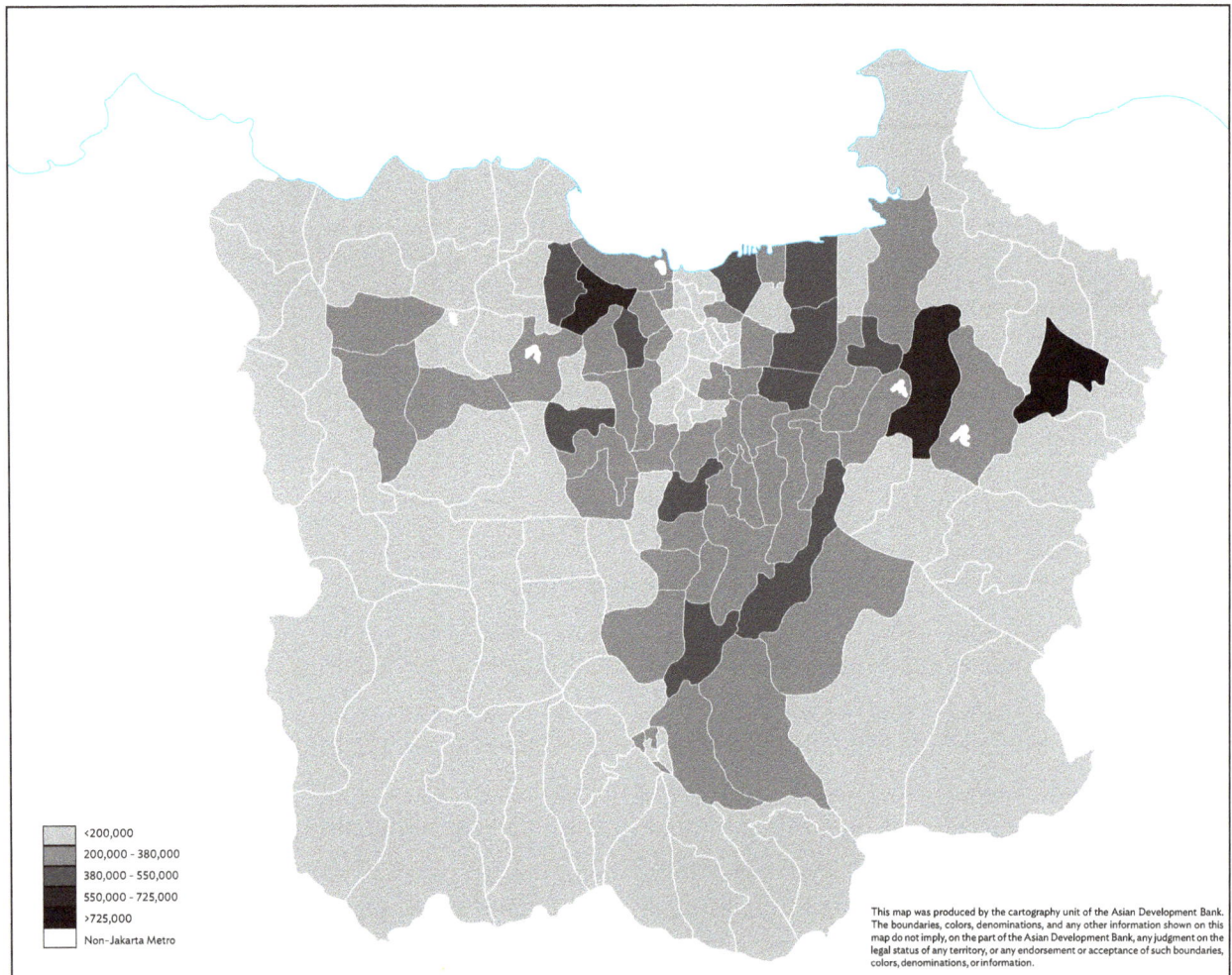

Legend:
- <200,000
- 200,000 - 380,000
- 380,000 - 550,000
- 550,000 - 725,000
- >725,000
- Non-Jakarta Metro

This map was produced by the cartography unit of the Asian Development Bank. The boundaries, colors, denominations, and any other information shown on this map do not imply, on the part of the Asian Development Bank, any judgment on the legal status of any territory, or any endorsement or acceptance of such boundaries, colors, denominations, or information.

Source: Authors.

A governor's decree in 2020 gave Jakarta MRT a mandate to effect transit-oriented development (TOD) in the areas around all MRT stations. Jakarta MRT has the authority to coordinate the land and building owners in the TOD areas (within a radius of 700 meters), and to encourage them to align their construction projects with the TOD urban-design guidelines developed by Jakarta MRT. However, unlike Hong Kong, China's Mass Transit Railway (MTR), which has the authority to allow various activities suitable for the catchment area and to create various revenue streams (see the international case studies section below), this new authority granted to the Jakarta MRT is likely to conflict with that of other government bodies. The governor's decree has less legal power than the provincial regulations delegating the responsibility for public works, housing, and spatial planning to various local agencies. This implies that Jakarta MRT, as a state-owned enterprise (SOE), has less power to coordinate the relevant agencies managing the catchment area. The conflicts of interest related to this TOD can be seen in Figure A2.3.

Palembang

The inner city of Palembang is interconnected by national and provincial roads, along which the TransMusi BRT operates as a shared-lane bus service. The only existing toll roads are the metropolitan roads connecting Palembang with Indralaya and with Kayu Agung. The city itself is split north and south by the Musi River, with four bridges across: the Ampera, Musi II, Musi IV, and Musi VI. To support the 2018 Asian Games, the national government built an LRT service from the airport, at the north end of the city, to the Jakabaring Sports Complex, at the south end of the city.

Palembang has big plans for thematic business-center TOD around its LRT stations, with housing developments at the terminus of each LRT line. The plan is expected to increase LRT ridership and enable Palembang residents to rent or purchase homes in more affordable areas, instead of in the city center. The government has further encouraged the growth of suburban commuter areas and towns by connecting Palembang's suburbs with a ring road and with the Trans-Sumatra Toll Road.

Makassar

The Port of Makassar is one of the main economic powerhouses in the region, not to mention Makassar New Port, a nearby facility that was reclaimed from the sea and has recently started commercial operations. A 6-kilometer toll road connects the ports to Makassar's inner-city roads, with an interchange connecting to the airport, northeast of the city. Makassar's suburbs are accessible from the city center only via provincial roads. There are no trains or light rail services operating between the city and the suburbs or within the city itself.

A public–private partnership project is building a train line that will link Parepare, Maros, and Makassar, but the line has not yet reached Makassar. There is a plan to build a Makassar ring road and BRT service within the city to improve accessibility. And some further reclamation work is still being done to expand the New Port.

Figure A2.3: Potential Conflicts of Interest in Jakarta's Mass Rapid Transit Station Areas Undergoing Transit-Oriented Development

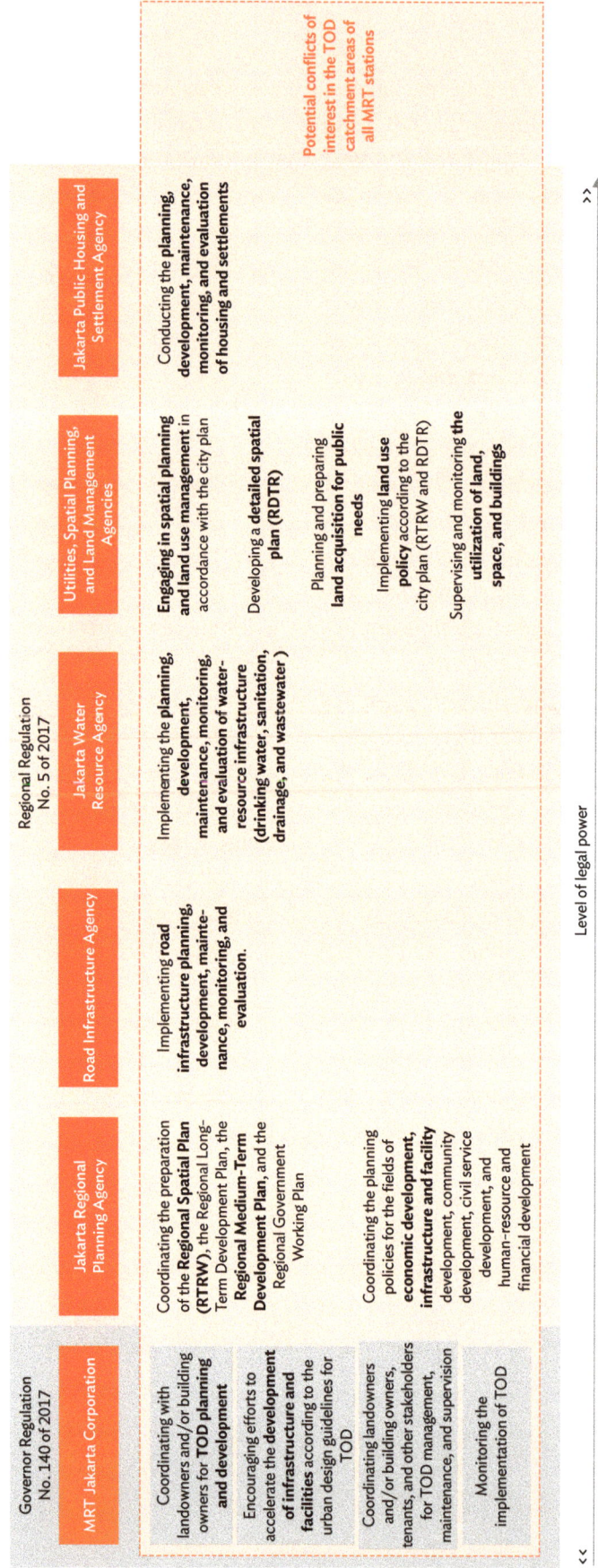

Governor Regulation No. 140 of 2017			Regional Regulation No. 5 of 2017		
MRT Jakarta Corporation	Jakarta Regional Planning Agency	Road Infrastructure Agency	Jakarta Water Resource Agency	Utilities, Spatial Planning, and Land Management Agencies	Jakarta Public Housing and Settlement Agency
Coordinating with landowners and/or building owners for **TOD planning and development** Encouraging efforts to accelerate the **development of infrastructure and facilities** according to the urban design guidelines for TOD Coordinating landowners and/or building owners, tenants, and other stakeholders for TOD management, maintenance, and supervision Monitoring the implementation of TOD	Coordinating the preparation of the **Regional Spatial Plan (RTRW)**, the Regional Long-Term Development Plan, the **Regional Medium-Term Development Plan**, and the Regional Government Working Plan Coordinating the planning policies for the fields of **economic development, infrastructure and facility** development, community development, civil service development, and human-resource and financial development	Implementing **road infrastructure planning, development, mainte-nance, monitoring, and evaluation.**	Implementing the planning, development, maintenance, monitoring, and evaluation of water-resource infrastructure **(drinking water, sanitation, drainage, and wastewater)**	**Engaging in spatial planning and land use management** in accordance with the city plan Developing a **detailed spatial plan (RDTR)** Planning and preparing **land acquisition for public needs** **Implementing land use policy** according to the city plan (RTRW and RDTR) Supervising and monitoring the **utilization of land, space, and buildings**	Conducting the **planning, development, maintenance, monitoring, and evaluation of housing and settlements**

Potential conflicts of interest in the TOD catchment areas of all MRT stations

Level of legal power

MRT = Mass Rapid Transit, RDTR = detailed spatial plan, RTRW = regional spatial plan, TOD = transit-oriented development.

Source: Authors.

Figure A2.4: Palembang Transport Infrastructure Plan

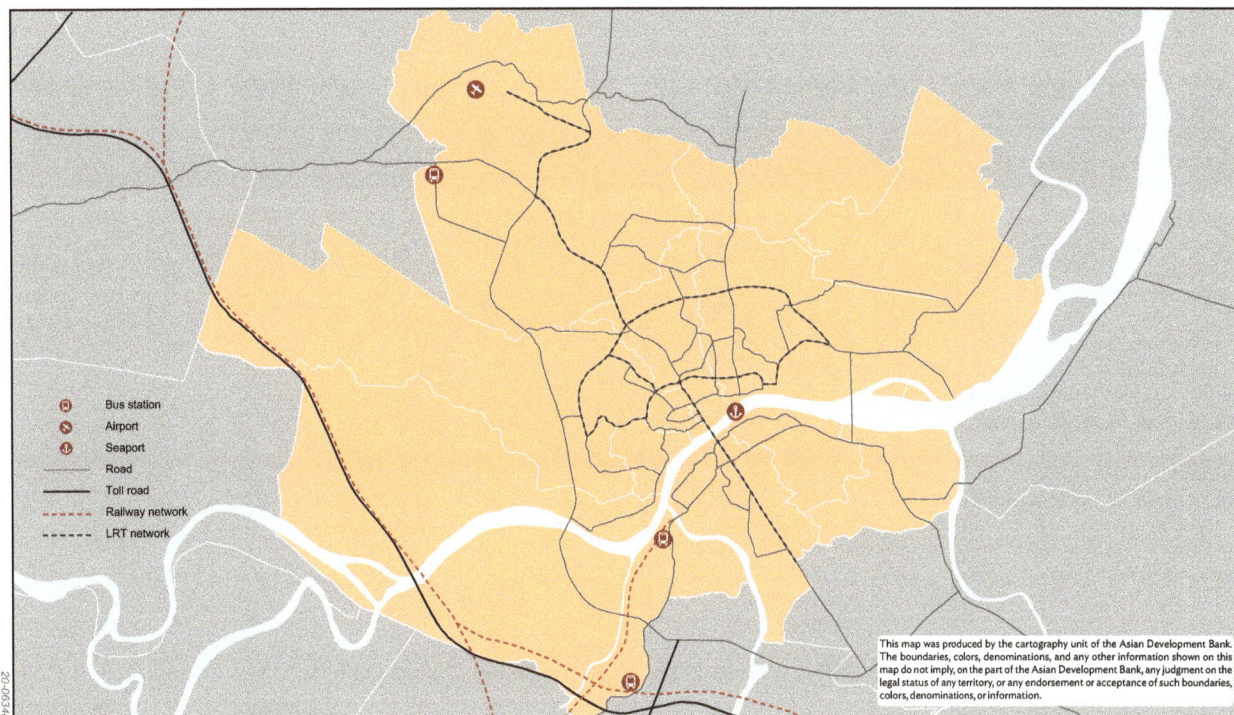

LRT = Light Rail Transit.
Sources: Regional Agency for Planning and Development (BAPPEDA) of South Sumatra; Authors.

Figure A2.5: Makassar Transport Infrastructure Plan

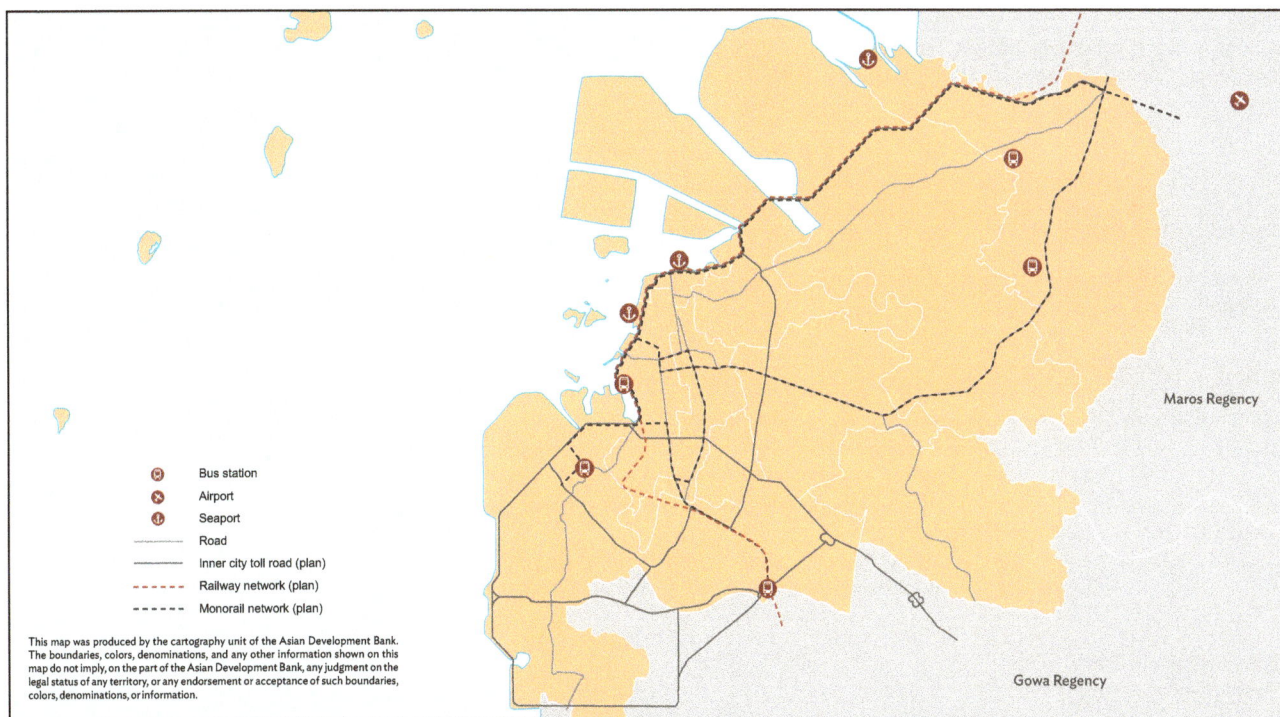

Sources: Regional Agency for Planning and Development (BAPPEDA) of Makassar; Authors.

Appendix 3. Review of Indonesian Economic and Spatial Planning

The tables below describe the readiness of government planning documents in terms of satisfying the minimum requirements for implementing value capture. The key requirements will be developed and scrutinized during the final study.

Table A3.1: Status of Planning Documents			
Status	**Jakarta**	**Makassar**	**Palembang**
Spatial planning document This document includes information on the planning vision, the future economic development vision, recognition of value capture mechanisms, etc.	Jakarta's spatial plan has been encapsulated in Regional Regulation No. 1 of 2012. Due to significant changes, the spatial planning document is currently being updated, and is still in the legislative process.		The Palembang spatial plan has been updated.
Detailed spatial planning document This document covers allowances for transfer development rights, links to land taxation, etc.	Jakarta has a detailed spatial plan that is registered as Regional Regulation No. 1 of 2014.		Palembang does not have a detailed spatial plan.

Note: A blank cell indicates that the column head does not apply.
Source: Authors.

Table A3.2: Other Identified Factors Affecting Value Capture Readiness			
Factors	**Jakarta**	**Makassar**	**Palembang**
Macro-fundamentals	n.a.	n.a.	n.a.
Technical capacity and administrative system	n.a.	n.a.	n.a.
Flexibility of zoning	Jakarta enforces zoning regulations. Transfers of development rights are done through a business-to-business mechanism, which should be determined at a high-level meeting with the governor.	n.a.	n.a.
Intergovernmental collaboration mechanism	n.a.	n.a.	n.a.
Entrepreneurship (reducing reliance on state funding)			
Clarity, fairness, and transparency of rules			
Availability and appropriateness of key value capture mechanisms	The governor of Jakarta levied charges for building rights to finance the new Semanggi flyover, constructed by Mori Building Co. Ltd., which requested additional gross floor area.		Palembang has recently increased the property taxes for areas surrounding Light Rail Transit stations.
Access to multiple funding sources			

Note: A blank cell indicates that the column head does not apply.
Source: Authors.

Table A3.3: Existing Value Capture Mechanisms		
Type of Mechanism	**Description**	**City**
Property taxes	The city government increased the property taxes for areas surrounding the Light Rail Transit stations, raising their tax object sales values by 120%.	Palembang
Exaction in exchange for density bonus	Mori Building Co., Ltd. erected the Semanggi flyover to obtain a building permit to engage in higher-density development.	Jakarta
Development rights	The Jakarta governor issued Governor Decree No. 60 of 2019, which assigned to Jakarta MRT the responsibility for managing transfers of development rights in areas surrounding MRT stations.	Jakarta

MRT = Mass Rapid Transit.
Source: Authors.

Appendix 4. International Case Studies

The following case studies showcase success stories and lessons learned from developed and developing countries that illustrate factors in successful value creation and value capture implementation.

Case Study 1—Value creation story of Marina Bay, enabled by dynamic urban governance grounded in sound institutions, effective legislation, and long-term planning, Singapore (Urban Redevelopment Authority).

Success story: Singapore's transformation from a colonial port city into a global financial center entailed years of urban redevelopment based at least partly on an integrated master planning and development paradigm enabled by a sound land administration and management system. Although a city-state lacking a hinterland and natural resources to support its economic growth, Singapore has transformed itself into the most livable city in Southeast Asia. Its success story is founded on what the Centre for Liveable Cities describes as "dynamic urban governance." Upon obtaining independence, Singapore gradually worked toward its goals by setting up sound institutions, creating effective legislative mechanisms, and formulating a long-term planning framework. Figure A4.1 shows milestones and timeline of the Marina Bay development.

Value Creation. Urban redevelopment is not only about the physical rebuilding of a city, it involves a wide range of socioeconomic elements vital to the overall life of a metropolis. Singapore's urban redevelopment process illustrates how social, economic, and environmental goals can be achieved within the constraints of a land-scarce, island city-state (Centre for Liveable Cities 2016).

Figure A4.1: The Marina Bay Story

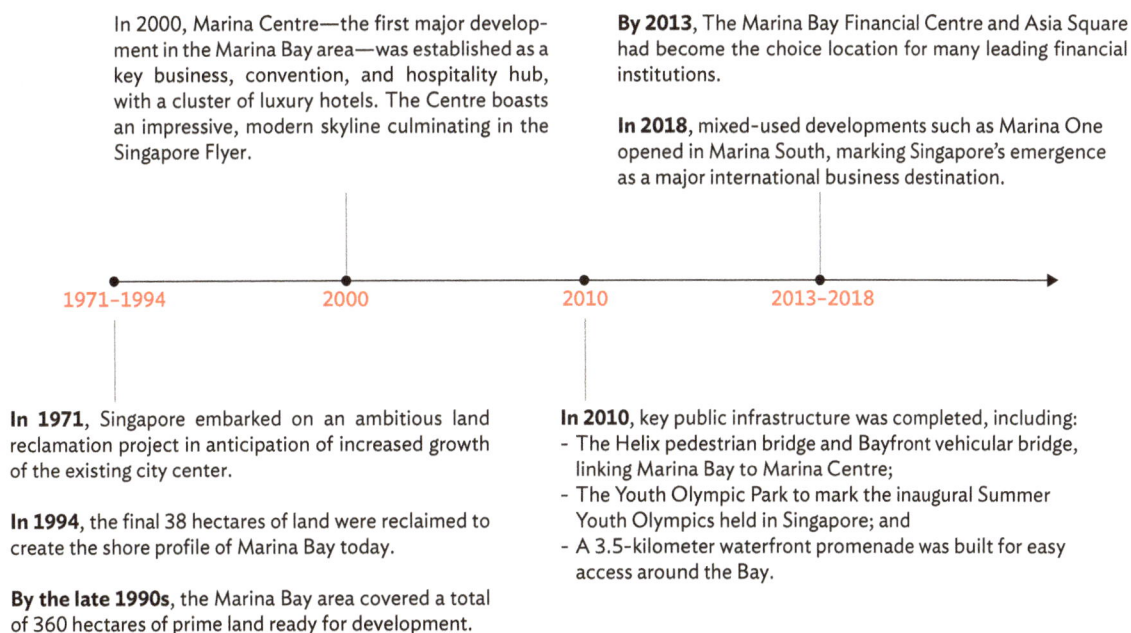

In 2000, Marina Centre—the first major development in the Marina Bay area—was established as a key business, convention, and hospitality hub, with a cluster of luxury hotels. The Centre boasts an impressive, modern skyline culminating in the Singapore Flyer.

By 2013, The Marina Bay Financial Centre and Asia Square had become the choice location for many leading financial institutions.

In 2018, mixed-used developments such as Marina One opened in Marina South, marking Singapore's emergence as a major international business destination.

1971–1994 — **2000** — **2010** — **2013–2018**

In 1971, Singapore embarked on an ambitious land reclamation project in anticipation of increased growth of the existing city center.

In 1994, the final 38 hectares of land were reclaimed to create the shore profile of Marina Bay today.

By the late 1990s, the Marina Bay area covered a total of 360 hectares of prime land ready for development.

In 2010, key public infrastructure was completed, including:
- The Helix pedestrian bridge and Bayfront vehicular bridge, linking Marina Bay to Marina Centre;
- The Youth Olympic Park to mark the inaugural Summer Youth Olympics held in Singapore; and
- A 3.5-kilometer waterfront promenade was built for easy access around the Bay.

Source: Urban Redevelopment Authority. The Marina Bay Story. https://www.ura.gov.sg/Corporate/Get-Involved/Shape-A-Distinctive-City/Explore-Our-City/Marina-Bay/The-Marina-Bay-Story.

Underlying success factors:

A robust and efficient land survey and registration system, and an equitable land taxation and pricing regime to facilitate the (re-)development of land. Singapore's land survey and registration system ensures the clarity of ownership and the availability of transparent and comprehensive land information, allowing property transactions to be carried out effectively and efficiently. This provides a basis for property tax and other land-based financing mechanisms and for facilitating the planning and development of land.

Reasons for confusion and chaos in the 1820s–1880s

- No proper land laws
- No proper system for the registration of land
- Poor land survey records
- No uniformity among the titles issued

Singapore's early days as a British colony—when there were no proper surveys and titles were issued without covenants— have been described as a time of "utter confusion and chaos." The lack of covenants, such as those regarding allowable use and maximum development intensity, meant that the use and development of land tended to be haphazard and uncoordinated.

Source: Centre for Liveable Cities. 2018. *Land Framework of Singapore: Building a Sound Land Administration and Management System*. Singapore. https://www.clc.gov.sg/docs/default-source/urban-systems-studies/uss-land-framework-of-singapore.pdf.

Singapore later developed a fair and efficient land-acquisition framework that allows private land to be assembled in a timely manner to facilitate the development of various public schemes that support national development. In the 1960s, substantial tracts of land were held by a relatively small group of private enterprises and individuals. Various pieces of legislation allowed the government to secure private land compulsorily for any public purpose, for public benefit and/or public utility, and for any residential, commercial and industrial purposes

without an excessive financial cost. This prevented landowners from raising the prices of their land in areas earmarked for such projects. Apart from this, the government's decision to acquire land was made undisputable. However, landowners were allowed to appeal the compensation paid, as the compensation was generally below market rates.

Key legislation that enabled affordable land acquisition by the government

- A 2-year rule that disregarded the value of improvements made by the owner to his property up to 2 years prior to the acquisition if they were made in anticipation of the acquisition
- A 7-year rule that disregarded any increase in the value that was attributable to infrastructure works in the surrounding estate carried out by the government up to 7 years prior to the acquisition

In 1964, the Foreshores Act was amended, allowing the government to acquire seafront land without having to compensate landowners excessively for their loss of seafront. This allowed the construction of large-scale public housing, such as Marine Parade, on prime reclaimed seafront land. It also laid the foundations for the future expansion of the central business district through the reclamation of Marina Bay, which started in the mid-1970s.

Source: Centre for Liveable Cities. 2018. *Land Framework of Singapore: Building a Sound Land Administration and Management System*. Singapore. https://www.clc.gov.sg/docs/default-source/urban-systems-studies/uss-land-framework-of-singapore.pdf.

Value creation. By compulsorily acquiring large parcels of land and redeveloping them comprehensively, the government also effectively kept housing and industrial infrastructure affordable, especially at a time when Singapore was still a young and developing nation. The Land Acquisition Act was undeniably the cornerstone of the vast low-cost housing programs in Singapore, and helped to address the nation's urban needs and support its social plans, transforming Singapore from a Third World country into a First World country within a generation (Centre for Liveable Cities 2018).

The Government of Singapore justifies its development decisions through a thorough and careful assessment of land value enhancements and public benefits to the surrounding land parcels. Instead of reclaiming land to add to Singapore's buildable area, the government made a strategic decision to create Marina Bay as a body of water, based on the economic potential of urban waterfronts (benchmarked against other waterfront developments around the world). The premiums for waterfront locations were estimated to make up for the loss of buildable area that could have otherwise been reclaimed in place of the bay. Apart from this, a reservoir was planned that would not only enhance Singapore's water security by boosting its water supply, but would also serve as a form of flood control for the central parts of Singapore.

Similarly, the decision to construct the 101-hectare Gardens by the Bay development in 2005 was made only after assessing that the payoffs would outweigh the opportunity cost of land that could otherwise have been developed.

Value creation. A flexible planning policy resulted in white-site zoning, which was introduced in Marina Bay in 1997 to give developers more room to decide on the use of their land parcels in response to changing market trends and demand. To ensure that development objectives were still achieved despite this flexibility, the Urban Redevelopment Authority prescribed urban design guidelines such as safeguards for public access to ensure accessible, people-friendly destinations.

"Marina Bay didn't come about as it is. ... Every sale site that goes out, [the Urban Redevelopment Authority] prepares urban design guidelines. Things don't just happen; they have to be planned and actually guided and steered."—Cheong Koon Hean, CEO of the Housing and Development Board and former CEO of the Urban Redevelopment Authority (Centre for Liveable Cities 2016).

The cultivation of trust through transparent, market-oriented and innovative policy making encourages private sector involvement. Before the current Master Plan system, Singapore's planning and regulatory framework was characterized by ad hoc rezoning, in which every case coming in was evaluated and, if granted, reflected in the Master Plan. Over the years, Singapore developed a rigorous long-term planning framework, enabling the government to manage its different development objectives effectively, allocating state land and properties for either interim or long-term uses to optimize the value of state assets. This has also offered a greater sense of certainty to the private sector, making businesses feel confident that they would be allowed to participate in the city-state's development efforts.

Key issues and challenges:

- Aggressive institutional and legislative reforms were required to orchestrate much of Singapore's value creation through urban governance.
- Long-term planning has made the development process transparent, providing greater certainty for stakeholders. However, it can be less flexible than a short-term development outlook, thus challenging the planners to become more innovative in setting planning policies.

References:

Centre for Liveable Cities. 2016. *Urban Redevelopment: From Urban Squalor to Global City*. Singapore: Centre for Liveable Cities. https://www.clc.gov.sg/docs/default-source/urban-systems-studies/uss-urbanredevelopment.pdf.

———. 2018. *Land Framework of Singapore: Building a Sound Land Administration and Management*

System. Singapore: Centre for Liveable Cities. https://www.clc.gov.sg/docs/default-source/urban-systems-studies/uss-land-framework-of-singapore.pdf.

Urban Redevelopment Authority. The Marina Bay Story. https://www.ura.gov.sg/Corporate/Get-Involved/Shape-A-Distinctive-City/Explore-Our-City/Marina-Bay/The-Marina-Bay-Story.

Case Study 2—Innovative funding, financing, and value capture mechanisms, contributing two-thirds of the project costs for Crossrail, United Kingdom (Buck 2017).

Success story: In 2001, Crossrail Limited was established to build the new Elizabeth Line through Central London. It is a wholly owned subsidiary of Transport for London, and is part of London's integrated transport network. Over 60% of Crossrail's funding requirement of £17.8 billion in 2019 (£14.8 billion in 2010) has been provided by identified beneficiaries, including other parts of the public sector, London residents, and London businesses. One of the biggest sources of revenue was the business rate supplement (BRS), which was paid by all the businesses in London. The BRS provided a secure revenue for Transport for London, which also raised £3.5 billion of debt with an initial repayment tenure of 15 years. See Table A4.1 for the shares of contributions between local and central governments.

Underlying success factors:

The Government of the United Kingdom clearly stated that the project could only be delivered through a beneficiary-pays model. At the outset, the government's preferred model for delivering the Elizabeth Line was a privately financed concession. However, this proved unachievable because of the sheer size and cost of the project. As a result, the government carried out an options analysis to select a more affordable solution, one that would reduce the cost and improve the value for money. Finally, the

Table A4.1: Key Contributors to Crossrail Limited

£14.8 billion: Cost to deliver the United Kingdom's largest transport project, the new Elizabeth Line east–west railway across London	£9.9 billion: Contribution from London businesses and future passenger revenue through an innovative funding, financing, and value capture mechanism
Local Government	**Central Government**
• £1.9 billion: Transport for London direct funding • £150 million: Transport for London additional funding	• £4.96 billion: Department for Transport direct funding • £2.05 billion: Department for Transport loan to the Greater London Authority • £290 million: Department for Transport additional funding to Network Rail • £150 million: Department for Transport additional funding
£5.25 billion: Fundraising for which Transport for London is responsible	£480 million: Fundraising for which the Department for Transport is responsible
• £4.1 billion: Business-rate supplemental borrowing and direct contributions • £300 million: Community infrastructure levy • £550 million: Sale of surplus land and properties • £300 million: Developer contributions	• £250 million: City of London-committed funding • £100 million: Contribution from the Greater London Authority • £70 million: Funding from Heathrow Airport Limited • £100 million: Voluntary funding from London businesses • £2.3 billion: Network Rail financing for work on the existing network • £220 million: Network Rail funding
£17.8 billion Overall funding in 2019 (£14.8 billion in 2010)	

Note: The funding increased from £17.6 billion to £17.8 billion as of July 2019. Source: Crossrail Limited. Funding. http://crossrail.co.uk/about-us/funding.

Treasury capped the government's contribution at a third of the overall costs, and required the remaining funding to be generated from the beneficiaries of the project.

While funding infrastructure through a combination of charges to direct users (i.e., fares) and through general taxation was commonplace, tapping the indirect beneficiaries on anything like the scale proposed had not been done before (Buck 2017).

The business case for Crossrail illustrated the productivity and development that would result from the Elizabeth Line, in order to justify beneficiary funding. It included a detailed economic cost–benefit analysis to explain the Crossrail project's transformative value to a wide range of beneficiaries, and to describe Crossrail's plan to implement an alternative funding mechanism, ensuring that those who benefit from the project would contribute substantially to its delivery. The identified beneficiaries, and their expected gains from the Crossrail project, are described in Table A4.2.

Figure A4.2: Crossrail Case Study, United Kingdom

In the case of Crossrail Limited, which built the new "Elizabeth Line" through central London, property developers stood to gain substantially from the proximity of their land and buildings to the rail line. Prominent among these was Canary Wharf Group, the owners of the Canary Wharf estate, in London's Docklands.

The Canary Wharf Group were early movers in this venture, lobbying strongly for the line to be built, agreeing to build the proposed station at Canary Wharf, and then agreeing to contribute £150 million toward the line's cost. In return, the government granted rights to the Canary Wharf Group to develop retail and leisure assets above the station.

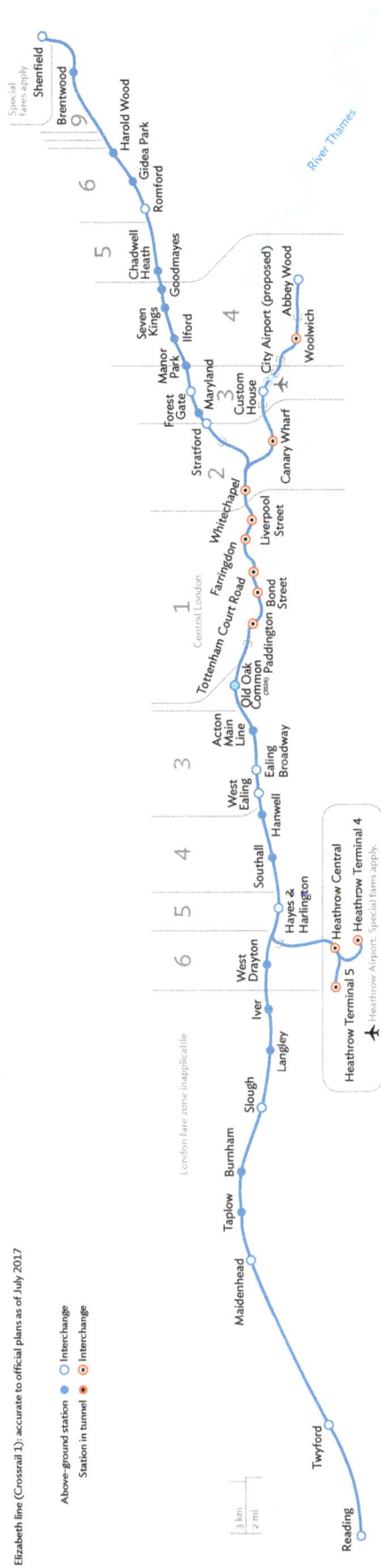

Elizabeth line (Crossrail 1): accurate to official plans as of July 2017

Source: M. Buck. 2017. Crossrail Project: Finance, Funding and Value Capture for London's Elizabeth Line. *Proceedings of the Institution of Civil Engineers* 170(CE6): 15–22. https://www.icevirtuallibrary.com/doi/pdf/10.1680/jcien.17.00005.

Table A4.2: Benefits and Beneficiaries of the Crossrail Project		
Type of Value	**Beneficiaries**	**Value Capture**
Improved access for current business employees, and access to an additional 1.5 million people, who will be brought within a 45-minute commute of central London	**Business community**—Ensuring that smaller businesses were exempt, and that the burden would fall on the larger businesses more able to absorb the cost, and most of which were located along the proposed route	**£225 million per year through a business rate supplement** levied by the mayor of London and the Greater London Authority, with which the Greater London Authority could support borrowing of around £3.5 billion. In April 2010, the mayor of London levied a £0.02 supplement to the business rates, which will be hypothecated to Crossrail, for properties with a ratable value over £55,000 per annum. The levy is expected to fall away once the bonds are fully repaid, which is forecast to occur in the 2030s.
	Organizations within the City of London	**£250 million total contributions** pledged to the Corporation of London by organizations within the City of London.
Substantial uplift in development potential as a result of the railway	**Property developers:** Canary Wharf Group	**The national government granted development rights for retail and leisure spaces above the station**, in return for building the proposed station at Canary Wharf and contributing of £150 million toward the cost.
	Property developers: Berkeley Group	**The national government granted development rights for residential spaces above the station**, in return for building a station box in a partially developed estate in Woolwich.
	Property developers: various commercial and residential	The mayor of London imposed a **Community Infrastructure Levy** on both commercial and residential developments, garnering **£100 million a year by 2015–2016**. Like the business rate supplement, the Community Infrastructure Levy was hypothecated to Crossrail. The applied rate is between £20/m^2 and £50/m^2, depending on the area of the development, and is set at the mayor's discretion. The levy for each location is agreed upon during the planning stage, but is only payable upon completion of the development.
Improved public transport access	**Heathrow Airport**	Heathrow Airport Holdings Limited contributed **£70 million**.

m^2 = square meter.
Source: M. Buck. 2017. Crossrail Project: Finance, Funding and Value Capture for London's Elizabeth Line. *Proceedings of the Institution of Civil Engineers* 170(CE6): 15–22.

The project sponsors championed collaboration with the business and property development communities in London to assemble a financial and funding package. Robust cost estimates and risk analysis enabled the sponsors to make political and financial commitments as necessary. Crossrail's investment model comprised simple Excel spreadsheets, and the risk model considered approximately 200 items, making the assessment robust.

To engage the business community, the Greater London Authority and Transport for London worked with London First to host a series of meetings and workshops to gauge the sentiment and rally support. Key at that stage was the strong government message that, without a significant contribution from London's businesses, the project would not happen. Early dialogue established the need for the contributions to be equitable and fair (Buck 2017).

The certainty of the funding provided to Crossrail generated a high level of financial stability, allowing it to raise debt for public infrastructure.

The Greater London Authority raised the funding against the projected income generated from the BRS and the Community Infrastructure Levy. The AA+ credit rating of Greater London Authority and Transport for London enabled funds to be secured at very attractive rates of interest, compared with the rates for tax increment financing or other project finance instruments, as the income was much more secure. Through a series of bond issues, Transport for London has raised £3.5 billion of debt with an initial repayment tenure of 15 years.

Key issues and challenges:

The BRS and Community Infrastructure Levy required primary legislation, and the Treasury had to agree to hypothecate the proceeds to the Crossrail project. Both mechanisms would be implemented by the mayor of London. Besides the attendant political risk of imposing a levy across the city, the mayor had to determine the rate to be applied, ensure the collection, and underwrite the subsequent bond-letting process, in order to meet the funding commitments to the project (Buck 2017).

References:

Buck, Martin. 2017. Crossrail Project: Finance, Funding and Value Capture for London's Elizabeth Line. *Proceedings of the Institution of Civil Engineers* 170(CE6): 15-22. https://learninglegacy.crossrail.co.uk/wp-content/uploads/2017/09/1C-002-Finance-Funding-and-Value-Capture.pdf.

Crossrail Limited. 2019. http://crossrail.co.uk/about-us/funding.

Case Study 3—Rail-based high-density development under the Rail + Property model, Hong Kong, China

Success story: Hong Kong, China Mass Transit Railway (MTR) pioneered the Rail + Property model (as illustrated in Figure A4.3) to create value capture opportunities in rail-based, high-density developments when funding the construction and operation of new lines, thereby providing seamless connections between MTR stations, and placing 75% of people and 84% of jobs in Hong Kong, China within 1 kilometer of a station. This model resulted in a large pool of skilled labor within easy commuting distance, high rates of public transport use, and low rates of car ownership. The increased transit ridership, bolstered by the layers of economic activity fostered by the Rail+ Property model, also created additional revenue sources for the municipal government (Salat and Ollivier 2017).

Land value capture takes time, and thus transit-oriented development (TOD) requires long-term property stewardship. Private railway companies in Tokyo and Hong Kong, China are committed to long-term property investment. They continue to improve the net profits arising from their commercial and retail real estate businesses along their transit lines, using the captured land value to cross-subsidize their railway operations (Ingram and Hong 2012).

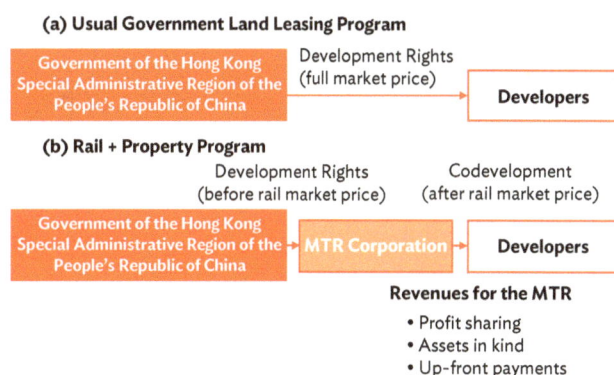

Figure A4.3: Rail + Property Model for Hong Kong, China Mass Transit Railway

MTR = Mass Transit Railway.
Source: Transport and ICT. 2017. Case Study: Hong Kong Mass Transit Rail Corporation. In *Railway Reform: Toolkit for Improving Rail Sector Performance.* Washington, DC: World Bank. https://ppiaf.org/ppiaf/sites/ppiaf.org/files/documents/toolkits/railways_toolkit/PDFs/RR%20Toolkit%20EN%20New%202017%2012%2027.pdf.

The core components of MTR's business model include:

- the Rail + Property model, which supports sustainable growth and secures demand; and
- the fare adjustment mechanism, which considers the factors affecting MTR's financial position, while balancing that against fairness to the customer.

Under the Rail +Property approach, MTR Corporation has been able to fund a large part of its transport system development by:

- creating land value through **integrated urban and transport planning**; and
- capturing such value by receiving **land development rights** from the government in "before rail" market prices, and codeveloping such land with private developers at "after-rail" market prices.

Figure A4.4 shows the MTR's revenue streams, which are primarily drawn from transport operations, and additionally from the station commercial businesses, property businesses, and international business.

Figure A4.4: Hong Kong, China Mass Transit Railway Earnings and Revenue Streams, 2011–2018

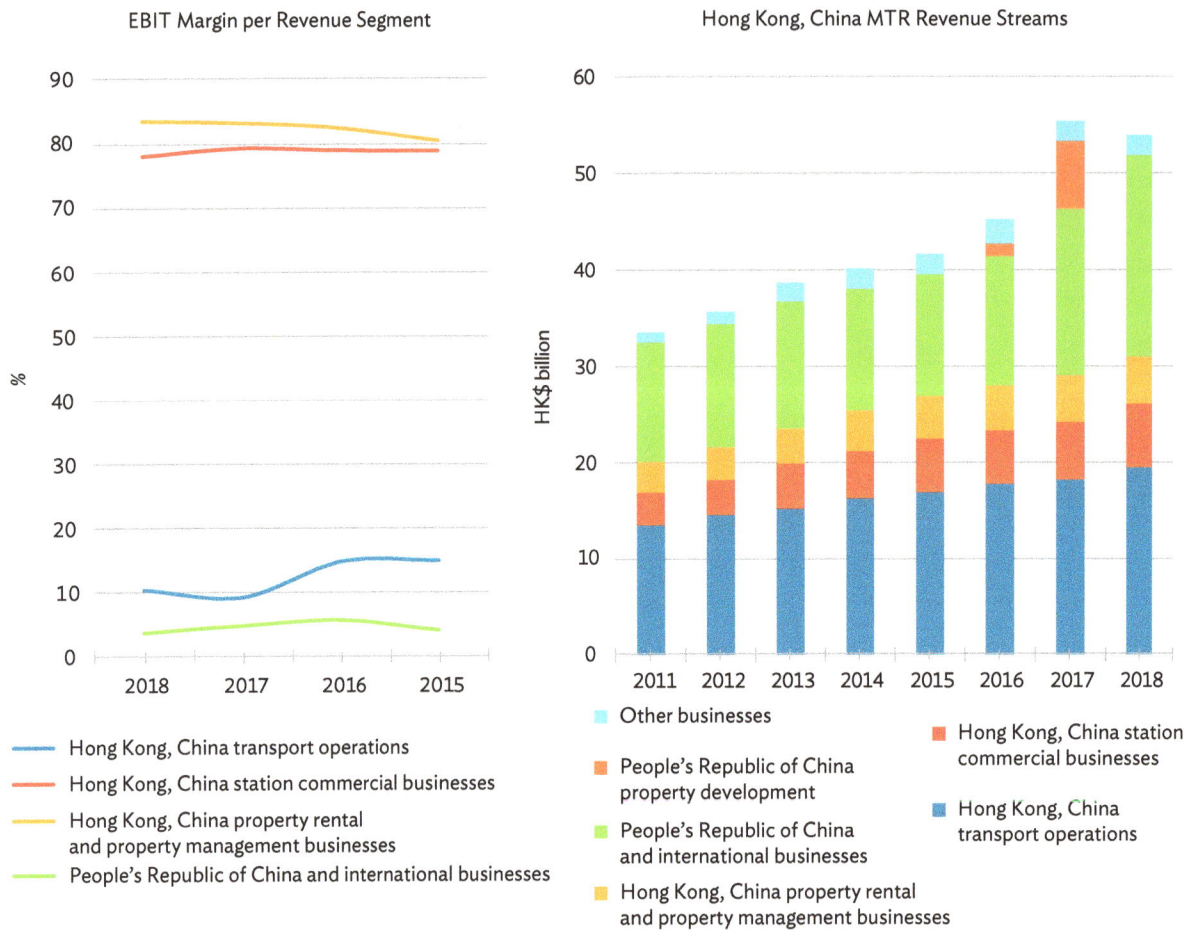

EBIT Margin per Revenue Segment

Hong Kong, China MTR Revenue Streams

Hong Kong, China transport operations

Hong Kong, China station commercial businesses

Hong Kong, China property rental and property management businesses

People's Republic of China and international businesses

Other businesses

People's Republic of China property development

People's Republic of China and international businesses

Hong Kong, China property rental and property management businesses

Hong Kong, China station commercial businesses

Hong Kong, China transport operations

EBIT = earnings before interest and taxes, MTR = Mass Transit Railway.
Source: Authors' analysis based on Hong Kong, China MTR annual reports.

Maximizing the benefits of investments through value creation and value capture

What is notable, from a purely operating revenue perspective, is that over time commercial businesses and property management have contributed more than 75% of the MTR's profits. This shows how the economic, social, and environmental benefits of public investment in infrastructure can be maximized through value creation and value capture. However, emphasis should be given to the MTR's status as a government-controlled corporation, and the indirect subsidies that it enjoys from the Government of the Hong Kong Special Administrative Region of the People's Republic of China.

The government fosters viability through two methods, underpinning MTR's financial strength and stability:

- the Rail +Property model, through the granting of development rights at "before-rail" prices; and
- cash when land is not available (e.g., one-off grants approved for the West Island line).

Source: World Bank and Imperial College London. 2017. *The Operator's Story: Hong Kong Case Study*. Washington, DC and London. http://www.transformcn.com/Topics_En/2017-12/19/c81f661ad3131ba2b9b401.pdf.

Underlying success factors:

The MTR is set up as a publicly listed, government-controlled company and the sole rail developer and operator in Hong Kong, China with an in-depth, whole-of-life approach. MTR Corporation has been sole rail developer and operator in Hong Kong, China since its merger with the Kowloon–Canton Railway Corporation in 2007. It is a publicly listed company that is 75% government-owned, established in 1975 as a government-owned enterprise to build, operate, and maintain a mass transit railway system in Hong Kong, China.

In 2000, the MTR's initial public offering (IPO) fundamentally changed the organization, insofar as its investment decisions needed to be financially viable in order to satisfy its shareholders, while maintaining reasonable fares for passengers. Owing to its organizational setup, the MTR is able to adhere to its Rail + Property model for the funding of a large part of its transport system by capturing land-based revenue to finance part of the construction and operating costs of new railway lines.

The Rail + Property model builds on government's commitment to developing its rail network. The Rail + Property model enjoys indirect government subsidies, with the government granting the MTR development rights to public land at before-rail prices, thus enabling the MTR to leverage the incremental value arising from rail development to enter into joint ventures with private developers. Where land is not available, the government has been granting monetary subsidies to the MTR to build rail infrastructure. Figure A4.4 illustrates the emphasis on rail development as a primary function and enabler of the Rail + Property model, and the critical importance of government commitment to the Rail + Property model's success.

The spatial strategy of TOD needs to be flexible in order to take into consideration changing economic and social conditions. For cities that are experiencing deindustrialization and an aging population, transit-oriented projects should focus on transportation connections to central business districts, satellite university campuses, and international airport terminals (Ingram and Hong 2012).

Concerted planning and integrated implementation allow station development to accommodate functions suitable to the catchment area, thereby creating various revenue streams. MTR station development encompasses residential, office, and retail spaces, diversifying the MTR's revenue streams. For example, a railway investment and housing development can be packaged together in order to capture land value increments resulting from the rapid economic and population growth along the railway corridors and around major stations in suburban areas (Ingram and Hong 2012).

Key issues and challenges:

The mixed-development approach may only work during rapid urbanization.

Timing is crucial. The mixed-development approach may work only during rapid urbanization and in a booming economy. During a period of rapid growth, private entities in Tokyo and Hong Kong, China embarked on railway extension projects, and were able to finance part of their undertakings with profits generated by their real estate investments. However, when the Japanese economy experienced a prolonged stagnation, public transportation companies were unable to self-finance similar projects (Ingram and Hong 2012).

Figure A4.5: Rail + Property Codevelopment—A Whole-of-Government Approach

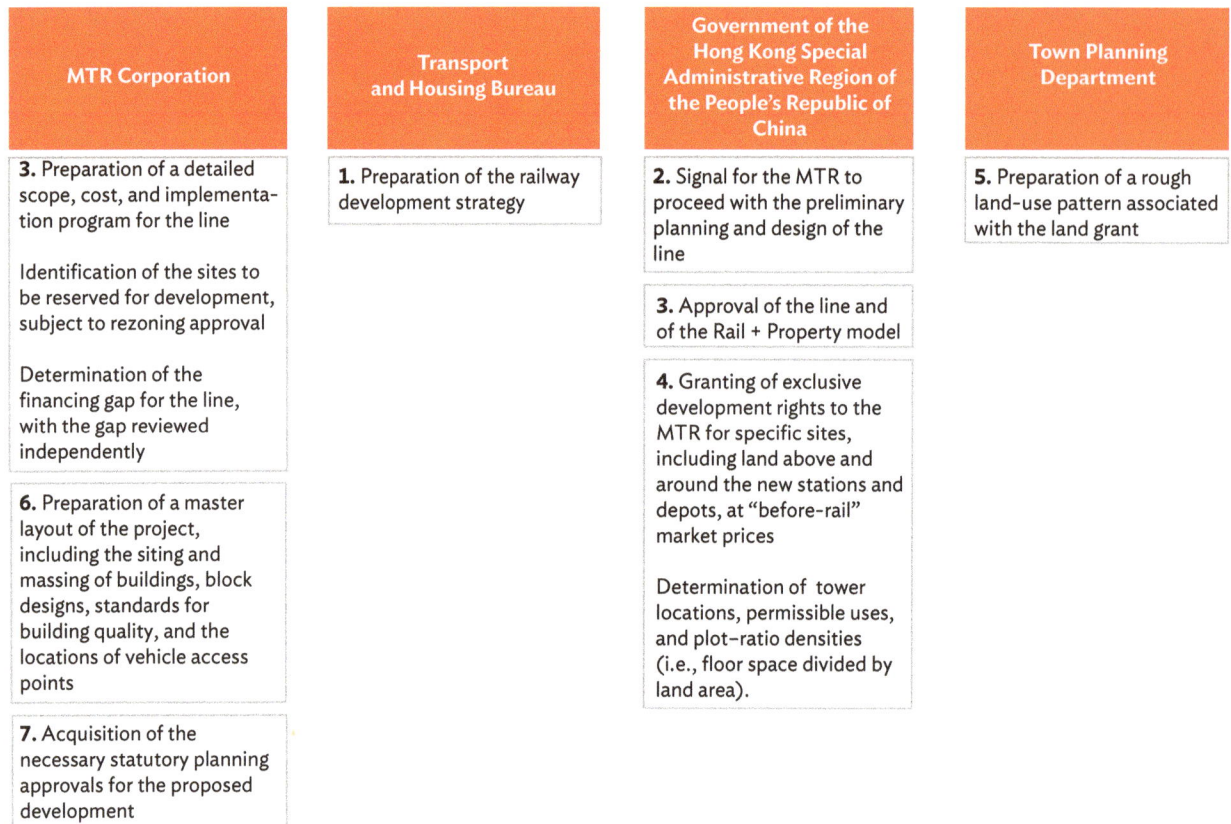

MTR Corporation	Transport and Housing Bureau	Government of the Hong Kong Special Administrative Region of the People's Republic of China	Town Planning Department
3. Preparation of a detailed scope, cost, and implementation program for the line Identification of the sites to be reserved for development, subject to rezoning approval Determination of the financing gap for the line, with the gap reviewed independently	**1.** Preparation of the railway development strategy	**2.** Signal for the MTR to proceed with the preliminary planning and design of the line	**5.** Preparation of a rough land-use pattern associated with the land grant
6. Preparation of a master layout of the project, including the siting and massing of buildings, block designs, standards for building quality, and the locations of vehicle access points		**3.** Approval of the line and of the Rail + Property model	
7. Acquisition of the necessary statutory planning approvals for the proposed development		**4.** Granting of exclusive development rights to the MTR for specific sites, including land above and around the new stations and depots, at "before-rail" market prices Determination of tower locations, permissible uses, and plot–ratio densities (i.e., floor space divided by land area).	

MTR = Mass Transit Railway.
Sources: Authors; Transport and ICT. 2017. Case Study: Hong Kong Mass Transit Rail Corporation. In *Railway Reform: Toolkit for Improving Rail Sector Performance*. Washington, DC: World Bank. https://ppiaf.org/ppiaf/sites/ppiaf.org/files/documents/toolkits/railways_toolkit/PDFs/RR%20Toolkit%20EN%20New%202017%2012%2027.pdf

References:

Ingram, Gregory K., and Yu-Hung Hong. 2012. *Value Capture and Land Policies.* Cambridge, Massachusetts, US: Lincoln Institute of Land Policy. https://www.lincolninst.edu/sites/default/files/pubfiles/value-capture-and-land-policies-chp.pdf.

Salat, Serge, and Gerald Ollivier. 2017. *Transforming the Urban Space through Transit-Oriented Development: The 3V Approach.* Washington, DC: World Bank Group. http://documents1.worldbank.org/curated/en/647351490648306084/pdf/113822-LOW-RES-MAIN-4-17-3Vapproach-orginal-reduced-Copy.pdf.

Transport and ICT. 2017. Case Study: Hong Kong Mass Transit Rail Corporation. In *Railway Reform: Toolkit for Improving Rail Sector Performance.* Washington, DC: World Bank. https://ppiaf.org/ppiaf/sites/ppiaf.org/files/documents/toolkits/railways_toolkit/PDFs/RR%20Toolkit%20EN%20New%202017%2012%2027.pdf.

World Bank and Imperial College London. 2017. *The Operator's Story: Hong Kong Case Study.* Washington, DC and London. http://www.transformcn.com/Topics_En/2017-12/19/c81f661ad3131ba2b9b401.pdf.

Case Study 4—Land Asset Management, Bases Conversion and Development Authority, Philippines (Peterson 2009).

Success story: In 1995, the Bases Conversion and Development Authority (BCDA) formed a joint venture with private sector partners to develop part of Fort Bonifacio, the last large remaining tract of undeveloped land in Metro Manila. BCDA sold 150 hectares of land for ₱30.4 billion (roughly $800 million at the time) to the Fort Bonifacio Development Corporation, the newly formed joint venture. BCDA has succeeded in converting a former US military compound within Metro Manila into an international business center, Bonifacio Global City.

Bonifacio Global City has experienced huge commercial growth, with the development of numerous high-rise condominiums, commercial buildings, housing, multinational corporations, educational institutions, and shopping centers. The proceeds from the initial sale of the land were allocated for infrastructure investment. Table A4.3 shows the share of the proceeds to each allocation.

Table A4.3: Allocations of the Proceeds from Bonifacio Global City

Allocations	Share (%)
Subic and Clark special economic zones	50.0
Modernization of the armed forces and military housing	32.5
Housing for the homeless	5.0
Local governments (Makati, Pateros, and Taguig)	2.5
National government	10.0

Source: Global Platform for Sustainable Cities. 2020. *Bonifacio Global City: A Public-Private Joint Venture - Case Study*. Washington, DC: World Bank.

Value creation. Approximately 240 hectares of Fort Bonifacio were turned over to BCDA to facilitate the conversion of former US military bases around Metro Manila for productive civilian use. By 2003, Ayala Land, Inc. and Evergreen Holdings, Inc. entered into a landmark partnership with BCDA to help shape and develop Bonifacio Global City—an area once synonymous with war and aggression—into the amiable, nurturing, world-class business and residential center it is today (Global Platform for Sustainable Cities 2020).

Underlying success factors:

Clear rules for the exercise of eminent domain. Republic Act No. 7227 was passed for the purpose of "accelerating conversion of military reservations into other productive uses." The act authorized the sale of land in military compounds in Metro Manila and created BCDA, which was given all the powers of an economic development and planning authority.

Well-prepared land asset management strategies. BCDA continues to plan the conversion of land on more urban military bases into more productive developments, while also planning for the relocation of the bases to equally suitable areas.

Key issues and challenges:

- The proceeds from the initial sale of the land were deposited into the government treasury, raising a dispute over the transparency of the allocations, as established by the BCDA Act of 1992.
- There was opposition from evicted military personnel and inadequate compensation for the military families that had to leave their housing in the military compounds.

Reference:

Global Platform for Sustainable Cities. 2020. *Bonifacio Global City: A Public-Private Joint Venture - Case Study*. Washington, DC: World Bank.

Peterson, George E. 2009. Unlocking Land Values to Finance Urban Infrastructure. *Trends and Policy Options* No. 7. Washington, DC: World Bank: http://documents1.worldbank.org/curated/en/723411468139800644/pdf/461290PUB0Box3101OFFICIAL0USE0ONLY1.pdf.

Case Study 5—Payment in Lieu of Taxes as an Innovative Financing Scheme for Hudson Yards, New York

Success story: The redevelopment of Hudson Yards is one of New York's most important responses to the demand for new office space to keep New York competitive with other global markets and to maintain agglomeration economies within the highly concentrated business districts in Manhattan. In 2005, the City Council approved the Hudson Yards' rezoning, transforming the low-density manufacturing area into a high-density, mixed-use district. By the end of 2006, $3 billion in Hudson Yards bonds had been sold, making the project fully financed, primarily through a scheme called "payment in lieu of taxes" (PILOT) as shown in Figure A4.6 (Salat and Ollivier 2017).

Underlying success factors:

A whole-of-government approach resulted in investor confidence in the bond issuance. The Hudson Yards Investment Corporation (HYIC), under the State of New York, financed the redevelopment of Hudson Yards, while the Hudson Yards Development Corporation, under the City of New York, implemented and managed the redevelopment. These two government-owned corporations had two separate financial statements, contributing to transparency in the financing and implementation of the project, support from the local and national levels of government, and improved investor confidence in the project (see Figure A4.7).

Figure A4.6: Payment in Lieu of Taxes Scheme for the Hudson Yards Redevelopment

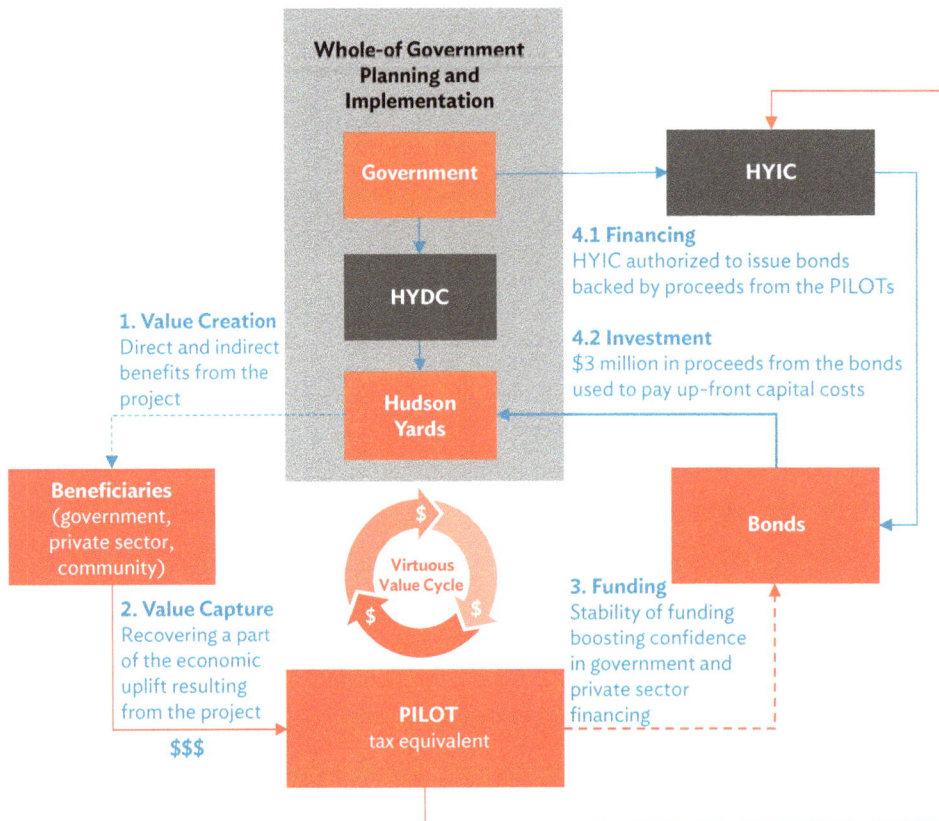

HYDC = Hudson Yards Development Corporation, HYIC = Hudson Yards Investment Corporation, PILOT = payment in lieu of taxes.
Sources: Authors; B. Fisher and F. Leite. 2018. The Cost of New York City's Hudson Yards Redevelopment Project. *Schwartz Center for Economic Policy Analysis (SCEPA) Working Paper Series* No. 2018-02. New York: SCEPA and Department of Economics, The New School for Social Research.

Figure A4.7: Institutional Approach of the Hudson Yards Development

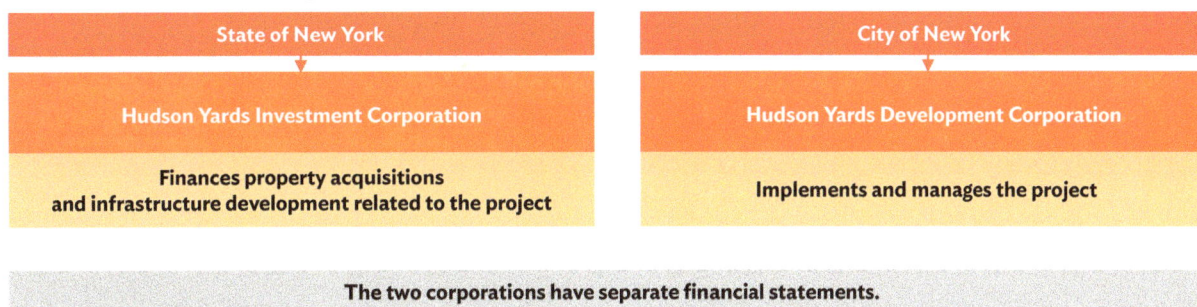

State of New York	City of New York
Hudson Yards Investment Corporation	Hudson Yards Development Corporation
Finances property acquisitions and infrastructure development related to the project	Implements and manages the project

The two corporations have separate financial statements.

Source: Authors.

The City of New York also backed the HYIC by committing to supporting its interest payments to cover the expected ramp-up period before revenues could materialize. The City agreed to cover HYIC's annual interest payments until it secured sufficient revenue, which relied on uptake in tenants within the district.

Value creation. The redevelopment of the Hudson Yards had a strong rationale, backed by the expected economic impacts. Hudson Yards, on the far west side of Manhattan, is just one of the three new or expanded central business districts that the public sector (the City of New York and State of New York) has planned in order to meet the future demand for office space. By 2024, when the project is completed, 125,000 people a day will work in, visit, or live in Hudson Yards. The following benefits were expected from the project:

- **1 million rentable square meters of new office space**—an amount greater than the total supply of office space in downtown Austin, Texas, or downtown San Diego, California, added to New York City's marketplace;
- **$19 billion** added annually to New York City's gross domestic product (GDP), accounting for 2.5% of the city's GDP;
- **$500 million** in annual taxes for New York City upon completion;
- **55,000 jobs** added for this new neighborhood on the west side of Manhattan; and

- **7,030 full-time jobs** during the estimated 13-year construction period, paying about **$761 million per year in wages.**

Value capture and value funding. The HYIC's $3 billion bond issuance was to be repaid primarily through property taxes from the Hudson Yards district. Specifically, property taxes from new commercial, residential, hotel, and other developments were allocated to the HYIC to support the repayment of the bonds.

But to attract tenants to the Hudson Yards district, tax breaks were found to be necessary. New York City implemented tax breaks for commercial developments in the form of PILOTs, which were paid by the developers directly to the HYIC. For new residential properties, hotels, and other developments, full property taxes were collected by the City and channeled into the HYIC in the form of tax equivalent payments (TEPs). See Table A4.4 for details.

Key issues and challenges:

Shortfalls in funding for repaying bondholders due to the 2008 financial crisis. While the proceeds from PILOTs and TEPs were expected to provide the bulk of the funding for the repayment of the bonds, the 2008 financial crisis delayed the pace of office development, which also delayed the first PILOT payments from 2012 to 2015. This resulted in a shortfall in the expected revenue for 2018. As shown in Table A4.5, of the various revenue streams for Hudson Yards, only the TEPs exceeded the projected revenue.

References:

Fisher, Bridget, and Flávia Leite. 2018. The Cost of New York City's Hudson Yards Redevelopment Project. *Schwartz Center for Economic Policy Analysis (SCEPA) Working Paper Series* No. 2018-02. New York: SCEPA and Department of Economics, The New School for Social Research.

Salat, Serge, and Gerald Ollivier. 2017. *Transforming the Urban Space through Transit-Oriented Development: The 3V Approach.* Washington, DC: World Bank Group. http://documents1.worldbank.org/curated/en/647351490648306084/pdf/113822-LOW-RES-MAIN-4-17-3Vapproach-orginal-reduced-Copy.pdf.

Table A4.4: Property Tax Schemes Implemented by the Hudson Yards Investment Corporation

Property Tax Scheme	Type of Property	Implementation
PILOT	New commercial developments	• Instead of paying property taxes to New York City, property developers pay a discounted amount directly to the HYIC. • The tax discount is up to 40%, as a way to convince developers to invest in Hudson Yards. • The tax break extends for 15 years, gradually returning to normal over the 5-year period after that. On the 20th year of residency, the owners pay full property taxes, which go to the HYIC for the remaining life of each PILOT agreement.
TEP	New residential properties, hotels, and other developments	• Property taxes collected by the City from hotels and residential developments in Hudson Yards are forwarded to the HYIC as TEPs, subject to annual appropriation through the city budget. • These properties do not receive a discount on their property taxes, even though they are located in the Hudson Yards district.

HYIC = Hudson Yards Investment Corporation, PILOT = payment in lieu of taxes, TEP = tax equivalent payment.
Sources: Authors; B. Fisher and F. Leite. 2018. The Cost of New York City's Hudson Yards Redevelopment Project. *Schwartz Center for Economic Policy Analysis (SCEPA) Working Paper Series.* No. 2018-02. New York: SCEPA and Department of Economics, The New School for Social Research.

Table A4.5: Hudson Yards Investment Corporation Revenue for Payments to Bondholders ($ million)

Tax-Based Revenue	Projected Revenue by 2018	Actual Revenue by 2018
PILOT	467.0	51.7
Tax equivalent payments	408.7	414.8
PILOT for mortgage recording taxes	128.6	96.6
One-Time Revenue		
District improvement bonuses	523.2	436.8
Transfer development rights	322.6	294.5
Total	**1,850.1**	**1,294.4**

PILOT = payment in lieu of taxes.
Source: B. Fisher and F. Leite. 2018. The Cost of New York City's Hudson Yards Redevelopment Project. *Schwartz Center for Economic Policy Analysis (SCEPA) Working Paper Series* No. 2018-02. New York: SCEPA and Department of Economics, The New School for Social Research.

Appendix 5. Detailed Regulatory Status and Updates

Table A5: The Status of Relevant Laws			
Abbreviation	**Legislation**	**Subject**	**Notes**
Law 39/2008	Law No. 39 of 2008 on State Ministries	Administration	Constitutional Court Decision No. 79/PUU-IX/2011 included the following changes: • In Article 10, the sentence, "In the event that there is a task that requires special handling, the President can appoint a deputy minister to a particular ministry" becomes invalid. • In the appendix to Article 10, the sentence, "What is meant by 'deputy minister' is a career official, and not a member of the cabinet" becomes invalid.
Law 2/2018	Law No. 2 of 2018 on the Second Amendment of Law No. 17 of 2014 on the People's Consultative Assembly, House of Representatives, Regional Representative Council, and Regional House of Representatives	Administration	Constitutional Court Decision No. 16/PUU-XVI/2018 included the following change: • In Article 73 paragraphs (3), (4), (5) and (6), Article 122 point I, and in Article 245 paragraph (1), the sentence, "Summons and requests for information from DPR Members in connection with the occurrence of a criminal act that is not related to the implementation of the duties referred to in Article 244 must obtain written approval from the President" becomes invalid.
Law 1/2004	Law No. 1 of 2004 on the State Treasury	Finance	Constitutional Court Decision No. 15/PUU-XIV/2016 included the following change: • In Article 40 paragraph (1), the sentence, "The right to collect on debts at the expense of the state/region expires 5 (five) years after the debt matures, unless otherwise stated by law" no longer has a binding effect when applied to pension arrangements concerning pension security.
Law 23/2014	Law No. 23 of 2014 on Local Government (as last amended by Law No. 9 of 2015 on the Second Amendment of Law No. 23 of 2014 on Local Government).	Administration	Constitutional Court Decision No. 56/PUU-XIV/2016 included the following change: • In Article 251 paragraphs (1), (4), (5), and (7), the phrase "Provincial regulations and" becomes invalid.
Law 28/2009	Law No. 28 of 2009 on Local Tax and Retribution	Taxation	Constitutional court decisions No. 52/PUU-IX/2011, No. 46/PUU-XII/2014, No. 15/PUU-XV/2017, and No. 80/PUU-XV/2017 included the following changes: • In Article 1 point 13, the phrase, "including heavy equipment and large tools that in operation use wheels and motors and are not permanently attached" becomes invalid. • In Article 1 point 28 and in Article 5 paragraph (2), the phrase "including heavy equipment and large equipment" becomes invalid. • In Article 6 paragraph (4), Article 12 paragraph (2), and Article 42 paragraph (2), the word "golf" becomes invalid. • Article 52 paragraphs (1) and (2), Article 55 paragraphs (2) and (3), and the appendix of Article 124 all become invalid.
Law 20/2011	Law No. 20 of 2011 on Strata Title Buildings	Land	Constitutional Court Decision No. 21/PUU-XIII/2015 included the following change: • In Article 75 paragraph (1), the phrase "Article 59 paragraph (2)" becomes invalid.

Source: The laws and Constitutional Court decisions listed in this table.

Appendix 6. Value Capture Readiness in Indonesia

Table A6.1: Tax-Based Value Capture Readiness Analysis				
Type of Tax	**Regulatory Readiness**	**Technical Readiness**	**Institutional Readiness**	**Potential Value Capture Channels**
Property tax	• Indonesia recognizes property-based taxes (on land and buildings), as well as the property transactions tax imposed by the local governments. • Indonesia's tax regime does not recognize "tax increment financing."	• The methodology for determining value, NJOP, is recognized, but may need improvement. • The Ministry of Agrarian Affairs and Spatial Planning/National Land Agency has been preparing a methodology to refine the NJOP, which is currently undervalued compared with the actual market values.	• The institutional framework for taxation is well established, but any changes may be difficult, as raising taxes and adding more tax instruments tend to be unpopular.	• Property taxes could be used for tax increment financing by updating the NJOPs affected by any property improvements, in order to fund up-front investments. An up-front tax increment is not possible, however, as the NJOP should be based on the current value. Hence, a robust NJOP value projection should be made when the government plans to refinance a project through this scheme.
Property transaction (rights transfer) tax	• The property transaction tax is recognized under Indonesian regulations, and managed by the local governments. • Law No. 28 of 2009 on Local Tax and Retribution sets out the general terms for revenue collection. • The detailed terms are set according to regional government regulations.	• The duty on the acquisition of land and building rights is calculated based on the NJOP, incentivizing both buyer and seller to understate the transaction value. • The property transaction tax is calculated based on the acquisition value. A table of acquisition values is provided, depending on the transfer mechanism (e.g., transfers via sales, grants, etc.). • If the acquisition value is unknown, the calculation is based on the NJOP. The tariff cap is set nationally.	• Not every local government is able to update the value of the NJOP every year.	• The capital gains tax can be increased by updating the formula used to calculate the value of property transactions.
Income tax	• The income tax is managed by the national government, whereas local governments have only a minimal capability to manage the tax; hence, local governments must negotiate the allocations of the proceeds.	• The income tax is normally deducted from the monthly salaries of workers in the formal economy.	• The institutional framework for taxation is well established. The funds are managed through a melting pot mechanism, instead of being earmarked, so it may be difficult to identify the tax revenues generated by the creation of jobs due to development in certain areas. • Local government has less control over this type of taxation, as the funds are mostly managed by the national government.	• The anticipated potential value capture channel for the income tax is still to be determined.
Transport tax	• Indonesia has three types of transport tax that apply to individuals: the vehicle ownership tax, vehicle stamp tax, and the fuel tax.	• These taxes are calculated based on a national table of NJKBs. • Vehicles are registered based on the address of the title holder.	• Transport taxes are managed jointly by the local tax office and traffic police.	• Vehicle title registration fees in value capture-target areas could be increased, with the increment allocated to value capture-related expenditures.

NJKB = motor vehicle sales value, NJOP = sales value of a taxable object.
Source: Authors.

Table A6.2: Fee-Based Value Capture Readiness Analysis			
Type of Fee	**Regulatory Readiness**	**Technical Readiness**	**Institutional Readiness**	**Potential Value Capture Channels**
Public Service Fees (*Retribusi Jasa Umum*)			
Solid-waste services fee	• Individuals and entities benefiting from solid-waste treatment services must pay this *retribusi* (fee). • Law No. 28 of 2009 on Local Tax and Retribution sets out the general terms for revenue collection. • The detailed terms are based on regional government regulations.	• The objects of this *retribusi* are the solid-waste treatment services provided by local governments. • A potential constraint concerns public areas, as they are exempt; if a private development is recategorized as a public area, there may be an argument for exemption (pending a legal analysis).	• The implementation of the solid-waste services *retribusi* usually requires a small committee to set up subscriptions for the users of these services.	• The solid waste services *retribusi* in value capture-target areas could be increased, with the increment allocated to value capture-related expenditures.
On-street parking fee	• Individuals and entities utilizing on-street parking must pay this *retribusi*. • Law 28/2009 sets out the general terms for revenue collection. • The detailed terms are based on regional government regulations.	• The objects of this *retribusi* are drivers parking in government-designated areas.	• The parking *retribusi* are managed by the local governments. • In some areas, implementation is undertaken by an SOE, and this function (pending legal specialist assessment) may provide more opportunities for creative revenue generation.	• On-street parking *retribusi* in value capture-target areas could be increased to improve accessibility to nearby public transport systems, with the incremental revenue allocated to value capture-related expenditures. • Meanwhile, parking rates at designated off-street facilities could be reduced to incentivize the use of these facilities as park-and-ride entry points to nearby public transport systems.
Market service fee	• Individuals and entities benefiting from market services must pay this *retribusi*. • Law 28/2009 sets out the general terms for revenue collection. • The detailed terms are based on regional government regulations.	• The objects of this *retribusi* are facilities for sellers in traditional markets, including stalls, yards, and stores. • Potential constraints include the markets operated by SOEs or private parties, as they are exempt from this *retribusi*.	• This *retribusi* seems to be imposed on individual sellers, while private companies are exempted, a policy that could be perceived as capitalistic and "not favoring the people." The result could be increased negative sentiment among the public (pending specialized legal analysis).	• The market service *retribusi* might not be suitable as a value capture channel, as it could be seen as harshly capitalistic. • However, public perceptions may alter if local governments provide evidence that they have reinvested the money collected in public infrastructure improvements.
Wastewater treatment fee	• Individuals and entities benefiting from wastewater treatment services must pay this *retribusi*. • Law 28/2009 sets out the general terms for revenue collection. • The detailed terms are based on regional government regulations.	• The objects of this *retribusi* are the wastewater treatment services for residential, office, or industrial buildings that use wastewater treatment facilities owned and/or operated by local governments. • The potential constraints are those who channel wastewater directly into rivers, sewerage systems, or other channels that are exempted.	• The wastewater-treatment *retribusi* might require training of building managers.	• The incentive and disincentive mechanism could be considered as a way to incentivize building operators to develop their own treatment plants, or to develop them jointly with adjacent building managers, and this would be compensated through extra floor space (in keeping with environmental limitations). • Based on careful and equitable calculations, funding from this *retribusi* could be allocated to improvements in wastewater treatment infrastructure and support services.

(continued on next page)

Table A6.2: Fee-Based Value Capture Readiness Analysis *(continued)*				
Type of Fee	**Regulatory Readiness**	**Technical Readiness**	**Institutional Readiness**	**Potential Value Capture Channels**
Telecom tower control fee	• Individuals and entities benefiting from telecom towers must pay this *retribusi*. • Law 28/2009 sets out the general terms for revenue collection. • The detailed terms are based on regional government regulations.	• The objects of this *retribusi* are the areas where telecom towers are constructed. • The parameter used as the basis for calculation is the space used to build each tower. This may not directly correlate with the benefits received by the users, as the company owning the tower owner can increase its revenue by accommodating more users without having to increase the use of space, given that the antennae are installed on the tower.	• The implementation of the telecom tower control *retribusi* may require coordination among several government agencies and ministries.	• The following policies could be considered: (i) imposing higher tower control rates for towers located in value capture-targeted areas; and (ii) modifying the base calculation of the fees, to consider not only the space to build the tower, but also the number of operators that will be using the tower.
Commercial Service Fees (*Retribusi Jasa Usaha*)				
Local asset-utilization fees (*retribusi pemakaian kekayaan daerah*)	• Individuals and entities utilizing local assets must pay this *retribusi*. • Law 28/2009 sets out the general terms for revenue collection. • The detailed terms (including tariff updates reflecting price indices and economic development) are based on regional government regulations.	• The objects of this *retribusi* are all local government assets. • A potential constraint is the fact that land assets that do not change their function are exempt (pending specialized legal assessment). • Issues may include the valuation of the utilized physical space under or over that of state-owned assets (e.g., when a private sector entity builds a structure under public land, or over a public road).	• This *retribusi* will require a project case institutional analysis, as it may involve many stakeholders with access to a public transport system, and will involve several agencies governing different parts of the structure and related utilities.	• The local asset-utilization *retribusi* has significant potential as a value capture channel because there is a growing precedent for this, but the regulatory framework has not kept up. For instance, there are still no clear regulations on development rights under and above a certain land areas.
Wholesale market or trading-complex fee (*retribusi pasar grosir dan/atau pertokoan*)	• Individuals and entities using wholesale-market or trading-complex facilities must pay this *retribusi*. • Law 28/2009 sets out the general terms for revenue collection. • The detailed terms are based on regional government regulations.	• The object of this *retribusi* is the wholesale market space provided by local governments (including via rental arrangements). • The potential constraints are those facilities owned and/or operated by SOEs or by private sector entities that are exempt from the *retribusi*.	• Some markets established by local governments are managed and/or operated by regional-owned enterprises and this is preventing the use of the *retribusi* as a value capture instrument.	• It may be possible to apply different tariff bands, based on the proximity of the wholesale market facility to the value capture-target areas.
Bus terminal fee (*retribusi terminal*)	• Individuals and entities using bus terminal facilities must pay this *retribusi*. • Law 28/2009 sets out the general terms for revenue collection. • The detailed terms are based on regional government regulations.	• The object of this *retribusi* is the space provided for vehicles and public buses, including for commercial activities, in a bus terminal area. • The *retribusi* is imposed on individual car or bus drivers (pending input from legal specialists). • The potential constraint is the exemption from the *retribusi* of certain bus terminals that are provided, owned, or operated by the national government, SOEs, or private parties.	• The type of entity operating a bus terminal is usually a technical unit under Jakarta's Transport Agency. Specifically, the Transport Agency is planning to shift the operations of bus terminals to a public service body that will be able to manage the cash flows more flexibly.	• Bus terminal *retribusi* could be developed as a value capture channel, through the imposition of higher tariffs on premium bus service operators serving high-density-demand areas. • Local governments must clearly demonstrate that they are using the money to improve access to the terminal, thus maintaining the overall sustainability of the bus service. • The provision of depot- or workshop-type services at bus terminals, when there is extra land available, could be a new channel for government revenue.
Dedicated parking fee (*retribusi tempat khusus parkir*)	• Individuals and entities using dedicated parking facilities must pay this *retribusi*. • Law 28/2009 sets out the general terms for revenue collection. • The detailed terms are based on regional government regulations.	• The objects of this *retribusi* are the dedicated parking spaces provided by local governments. • The potential constraints are the dedicated parking spaces provided, owned, or operated by the national government, SOEs, or private entities that are exempt from this *retribusi*.	• The collection of parking *retribusi* often coincides with informal "muscle man" activities, so it requires a delicate handling of the social aspects.	• The tendency of many citizens to park their cars on the street in front of their houses, often impacting the traffic capacity of the surrounding road network, provides an ample opportunity to impose parking *retribusi* on the car owners. This could be considered a supplement to the annual vehicle taxation mechanism.

(continued on next page)

Table A6.2: Fee-Based Value Capture Readiness Analysis *(continued)*				
Type of Fee	**Regulatory Readiness**	**Technical Readiness**	**Institutional Readiness**	**Potential Value Capture Channels**
Hotel/resort/ villa fee (*retribusi tempat penginapan/ pesanggrahan/ villa*)	• Individuals and entities staying at hotels, resorts, or villas must pay this *retribusi*. • Law 28/2009 sets out the general terms for revenue collection. • The detailed terms are based on regional government regulations.	• The objects of this *retribusi* are the lodging services provided by local governments. • The potential constraint is the lodging provided, owned, or operated by the national government, SOE, and private parties that are exempt from this *retribusi*.	• The *retribusi* is managed by the local governments. The local governments could adjust the calculation of their rates based on local needs and objectives.	• Based on careful and equitable calculation, the funding from this *retribusi* could be allocated to improvements in the infrastructure surrounding tourist areas.
Port and harbor service fee (*retribusi pelayanan kepelabuhanan*)	• Individuals and entities using port or harbor facilities must pay this *retribusi*. • Law 28/2009 sets out the general terms for revenue collection. • The detailed terms are based on regional government regulations.	• The objects of this *retribusi* are the port and harbor services provided by local governments. • The potential constraint is the exemption from this *retribusi* of certain port and harbor services or facilities that are provided, owned, or operated by the national government, SOEs, or private parties.	• This *retribusi* is usually managed by the local governments or by the port authorities.	• There are no significant value capture channeling opportunities.
Recreation and sports facility fee (*retribusi tempat rekreasi dan olahraga*)	• Individuals and entities using recreation or sports facilities must pay this *retribusi*. • Law 28/2009 sets out the general terms for revenue collection. • The detailed terms (including tariff updates reflecting price indices and economic development) are based on regional government regulations.	• The objects of this *retribusi* are the recreation and sports facilities by local governments. • The potential constraint is the exemption from this *retribusi* of certain recreation and sports facilities provided, owned, or operated by the national government, SOEs, or private entities.	• This *retribusi* is usually managed by the local government or by the local SOE that manages the facility.	• There are no significant value capture channeling opportunities. However, an affordable price may be charged to ensure operation cost recovery.
Specific Permit Fees				
Building permit fee (*izin mendirikan bangunan*)	• Individuals and entities requesting construction permits must pay this *retribusi*. • Law 28/2009 sets out the general terms for revenue collection. • The detailed terms (including tariff updates reflecting price indices and economic development) are based on regional government regulations.	• The objects of this *retribusi* are the permits granted by local governments to carry out construction. • The permit process involves a review of the design, construction, and delivery, to ensure compliance with building technical designs and land use plans, taking into account the building floor area ratio, building height coefficient, and building usage monitoring (including compliance with the safety requirements of the residents). • The potential constraint is the exemption from this *retribusi* of construction by the national and local governments.	• This *retribusi* is managed by the local governments, and could potentially be the most feasible value capture instrument, as the regulatory framework is widely understood by the market. • There is potential, and precedents, for allegations of fraudulent practices on various scales, whereby the authorities and users alike are taken to criminal court, mostly due to bribery or gratification.	• The function of a building permit fee could potentially be expanded to facilitate a development impact fee. • Pending specialized legal assessment, it may also be possible to set the rate based on the incremental increase in space, rather than just on the proposed construction (i.e., a *retribusi* for a permit to construct an additional 100 m² room will be different for a building that originally had 200 m² and a building that originally had 500 m²).
Route permit fee (*retribusi izin trayek*)	• Individuals and entities applying for route permits must pay this *retribusi*. • Law 28/2009 sets out the general terms for revenue collection. • The detailed terms (including tariff updates reflecting price indices and economic development) are based on regional government regulations.	• The objects of this *retribusi* are the permits to provide public passenger transport on one or more routes.	• There is a potential conflict with other regulations wherein public transport services may only be provided by a legal entity, and not by an individual, under the nation's public transport sector improvements as governed by Law No. 22 of 2009 on Traffic and Road Transport.	• An increase in the *retribusi* for route permits could be considered for high-demand or value capture-target areas. • Support for value capture-related infrastructure financing could be linked to the ease of route expansion and/or fleet development, to incentivize operators.

m² = square meters, SOE = state-owned enterprise.
Source: Authors.

Appendix 7. Payment-in-Lieu-of-Taxes Legal Mitigation Analysis

Development Rights

Kawasan permukiman (housing complexes) consist of individual houses, adjacent houses and/or condominiums. A housing complex may be mixed use, combining residential and commercial activities, and required to comply with the applicable spatial plans and zoning regulations.

Public infrastructure, facilities, and utilities within the housing complex may be constructed by the government or by private entities, provided that such public infrastructure, facilities, and utilities are delivered to the government after completion (Law No. 1 of 2011 on Housing and Settlement Areas, Art. 47). Regional governments have the authority to develop housing complexes or to establish or appoint another entity for that purpose (Law 1/2011, Art. 60).

The funding for the development of housing complexes may be sourced from the state government budget, regional budget, or other legitimate sources in accordance with the prevailing laws (Law 1/2011, Art. 119). This funding shall be used for the development of housing and housing complexes, and for subsidies for low-income housing (Law 1/2011, Art. 120).

Property owners within the housing complex are obliged to pay property taxes. The regional government has the authority to set the rates of property taxes and property-transaction taxes (including setting lower rates), subject to the maximum rate established by national legislation. Any state-owned enterprises (SOEs) or private infrastructure operators providing services in housing complexes are authorized to charge usage fees for the infrastructure under the user-pays principle. Law 1/2011 does not specifically authorize the imposition of additional fees (under the beneficiary-pays principle) by the developer on the property owners in the housing complex. **Accordingly, the introduction of payment in lieu of taxes (PILOT), which serves as a mandatory fee payable to an SOE, may require certain amendments to Law 1/2011.**

Property Rights

State and regional assets. All assets procured on the account of the state budget or a regional budget will become property of the state or region (BMM/D). The transfer, usage (use of assets for relevant government functions), utilization (use of assets other than for the relevant government function), and the removal of the BMN/D are subject to restrictive requirements under Government Regulation No. 27 of 2014 on the Management of State/Regional Property (BMN/D).

Infrastructure assets. The land required for infrastructure assets is typically owned by the national government or by a regional government, so these lands constitute BMN/D. The law is silent on whether or not the developer is allowed to retain the infrastructure (e.g., rail tracks and rail stations, public roads and toll roads) built over the land owned by the government. Approaches vary across infrastructure sectors.

In the toll road sector, roads must be owned by the government, even if they are constructed by a toll road concessionaire. This is specified in the standard toll-road concession agreement used by the Indonesia Toll Road Authority.

In the railway sector, particularly in the context of Jakarta's Mass Rapid Transit (MRT), the land is owned by the municipal government, but the infrastructure assets (signaling equipment, infrastructure, and rolling stock) are owned by PT MRT Jakarta, the developer and operator of the Jakarta MRT system.

Rights to property. There are two ways to establish a developer's rights over a parcel of land:

(i) This can happen through the creation of a property title, such as an ownership title or a right to cultivate (HGU), right to build (HGB), or *hak pakai* (right to use) title. Developers of housing complexes or private apartment complexes must typically procure an HGB title over the land. The HGB title can be granted for an initial period of 30 years, which can be extended for another 20 years, according to Government Regulation No. 40 of 1996 on the Right to Cultivate, Right to Build, and Right of Use over Land, Art. 25. Upon the expiration of the extended period, the HGB title can be renewed for another 30-year period, subject to compliance with the applicable requirements. The HGB title can be encumbered for the purpose of financing the development (Law No. 4 of 1996 on Encumbrance Right over Land and Land-Related Objects, Art. 4).

Developers of housing complexes and private apartment complexes are allowed to enter into a conditional sales and purchase agreement with the buyers of apartment units after, among other things, construction permits have been secured; construction has progressed to at least 20% completion; and assurance has been given regarding the availability of supporting infrastructure, facilities, and utilities (Law No. 20 of 2011 on Strata Title Buildings, Art. 44; and Minister of Public Works and Public Housing Regulation No. 11/PRT/M/2019 on the Preliminary House Purchase Agreement System).

The closing of the sale of an apartment unit (including the passing of the title) can be made upon the issuance of the functional worthiness certificate and the creation of an apartment ownership title (SHM Sarusun). The buyer shall then own a valid SHM Sarusun. The SHM Sarusun can be encumbered by the owners (Law 20/2011, Art. 47 [4]), however. Transactions involving an apartment with an SHM Sarusun, including the registration and encumbrance of the SHM Sarusun, is administered by the National Land Agency.

Table A7.1: Comparison of Utilization Schemes for Development					
Subject	Lease	Borrow-Use	Optimization Cooperation	BOT/BTO	Cooperation for Infrastructure Provision (KSPI)
Purpose	Utilization of assets for a certain period and the generation of revenue (**including the possibility of leasing air space or underground space adjacent to a BMN/D**)	Asset sharing among government agencies	Utilization of assets for a certain period and the generation of revenue	Construction and transfer of new assets by a private firm with the right to operate for a certain period	Infrastructure
Mechanism	Application for lease submitted to asset manager	Intergovernmental procedures	Tender	Tender	PPP tender
Period	Maximum of 5 years (may be extended for infrastructure purposes, projects that require a longer period, or as stipulated under the law)	Maximum of 5 years (may be extended one time)	Maximum 30 years (maximum of 50 years for infrastructure purposes)	Maximum of 30 years	Maximum of 50 years (extendable)
Consideration	Lease fee	No fee	Payment of fixed contributions and profit sharing: for infrastructure, the fixed contribution and profit sharing discounted by a maximum of 70% of the original estimate; a maximum of 10% of the fixed contribution and profit sharing possibly paid in-kind (in the form of physical assets)	Payment of fixed annual contribution	Possible application of clawback mechanisms (but may be waived)
Restrictions	BMN/D not allowed to be encumbered; the base construction of the assets not allowed to be changed	BMN/D not allowed to be encumbered or sublet	BMN/D not allowed to be encumbered; the developer not allowed to encumber the assets	BMN/D not allowed to be encumbered (under a BTO contract, the developer not allowed to transfer, assign, or encumber the assets developed or procured by the developer)	BMN/D not allowed to be encumbered

BMN/D = property of the state/region, BOT = Build–Operate–Transfer, BTO = Build–Transfer–Operate, KSPI = cooperation for infrastructure provision, PPP = public–private partnership.
Source: Authors.

The closing of sales of individual houses and adjacent houses can be made once construction is completed. The individual buyer will receive the HGB title for the house, and if the buyer is an Indonesian citizen, he or she can propose a change from HGB status to ownership rights.

(ii) Developers can also procure certain development rights over a BMN/D under a utilization scheme. There are five such schemes: lease, borrow-use, optimization cooperation, Build–Operate–Transfer (BOT)/Build–Transfer–Operate (BTO), and cooperation for infrastructure provision (KSPI). Table A7.1 compares them.

The development of mixed-use housing complexes or apartment complexes could potentially benefit from a BOT/BTO scheme (for new development) or from an optimization cooperation scheme (for the optimization and/or improvement of existing assets). The maximum period shall be 30 years. The developer is required to pay fixed contributions and offer profit sharing, depending on the scheme. Such proceeds shall constitute state revenue, and shall be deposited into the state account or regional account, as applicable.

Under Law 20/2011, the developers are allowed to sell the apartment units to buyers, and the buyers may own the apartment units by means of a building ownership certificate (SKBG). The SKBG has a different status from that of an SHM Sarusun. The detailed operating procedures for the administration of a SKBG have not been issued, and no SKBG is known to have been issued, but the SKBG should be considered as a support for PILOT initiatives.

Table A7.2 compares the HGB title with the right to utilize a BMN/D.

Financing through the Capital Market

The Indonesian capital market has provided a framework for the issuance of bonds and mutual funds to finance infrastructure projects.

Table A7.2: Comparison between a Right-to-Build Title and the Utilization of State or Regional Property		
Land Title	**HGB**	**Utilization of BMN/D**
Characteristic of title	Recognized as a property title, with the title holder protected by law	Protection subject to contractual agreements
Duration of title	Initial period: 30 years; may be extended for an additional 20 years; and then may be renewed for another 30 years; with a total of 80 years	Maximum 30 years; for optimization cooperation for infrastructure, up to 50 years
Encumbrance	HGB title allowed to be encumbered	BMN/D not allowed to be encumbered
		Possibility of assigning contractual rights for security purposes, subject to consent from the government
Title to space over apartment unit (air rights)	Clear procedure for the creation and registration of an SHM Sarusun	No clear procedures for the creation and registration of an SKBG, and no known precedents
Duration of title over apartment unit	Valid for the duration of the HGB title	Valid for the duration of the underlying contract
Administration	National Land Agency	Ministry of Finance and other relevant ministries (for state assets)
		Ministry of Home Affairs and the relevant regional governments (for regional assets)
Limitations	Difficult to combine with infrastructure assets	Possible to combine with infrastructure assets; for example, building a residential or commercial property over a rail station or public road
Potential development		Potential for SKBGs, if further developed, to unlock new property markets, which, in turn, could support the development of supporting infrastructure assets
		Possibility for the government to consider separating the development rights of infrastructure assets and adjacent apartment complexes, to allow different title durations (e.g., infrastructure assets transferred upon the expiry of 30 years, while the title over apartment units/SKBG lasts beyond 30 years)

BMN/D = property of the state/region, SKBG = building ownership certificate.
Notes:
1. "SHM Sarusun" means "apartment ownership title."
2. A blank cell indicates that the column head does not apply.
Source: Authors.

Debt securities issued by state-owned enterprises. Generally, an SOE or developer is allowed to issue debt instruments (e.g., bonds) through the capital markets, subject to compliance with certain requirements, including public offering requirements regulated by the Financial Services Authority (OJK) and the listing requirements regulated by the Indonesia Stock Exchange. Issuers have to submit a registration statement and supporting documents according to the OJK regulations on public offering registration procedures.

SOEs as bond issuers are fully responsible for the accuracy, adequacy, truthfulness, and fairness of all information contained in the registration statement and its supporting documents. Bond issuance may be implemented only after the submission of the complete registration statement to OJK.

Those who intend to issue bonds through the Indonesia Stock Exchange must fulfill certain requirements, for instance, being a legal entity that has operated for at least 3 years with a minimum equity of Rp20 billion. To be allowed to issue bonds, the entity must have also recorded a profit for the latest financial year, and must have been audited by an auditor recognized by OJK for each of the prior 3 years, with at least a qualified opinion. And the entity's credit rating must be at least BBB- (investment grade). Typically, bonds are issued without a security, as the prevailing laws and regulations do not specifically require a security to be granted for the bond's issuance. For the issuance of bonds by an SOE or regional-owned enterprise (ROE), there may be a limitation on the asset security provided the regional government, SOEs, or ROEs; and this must be analyzed on a case-by-case basis.

Investment funds for infrastructure assets. In 2017, OJK also introduced the "Infrastructure Investment Fund" (DINFRA), which is a collective investment fund for financing infrastructure development (OJK Regulation No. 52/POJK.04/2017 on Infrastructure Investment Funds in the Form of Collective Investment Contracts). DINFRA may (but is not obliged to) establish and use an SPC as a financing vehicle. At least 51% of the DINFRA funds must be invested in infrastructure assets (so only a maximum of 49% may be invested in money market instruments, domestic securities, and other financial instruments determined by OJK). DINFRA cash or cash equivalents must be set at 20% of the total net DINFRA funds. Investments in infrastructure assets can be made through direct investments (i.e., in infrastructure assets in Indonesia to support development programs and provide public benefits) and indirect investments (i.e., in equity or debt instruments issued by companies operating infrastructure assets, or in debt instruments for which payments originate from infrastructure assets).

The issuance of DINFRA funding may be made through a public offering or private placement, subject to certain registrations with OJK. Only infrastructure assets that have been generating revenue (or will generate revenue within 6 months) can be made available through public offerings. If the infrastructure assets have not been generating revenue, DINFRA funding can only be offered through private placement, subject to a thorough due diligence and the full disclosure of the characteristics of the assets.

DINFRA is allowed to borrow money for the financing of infrastructure assets that have been generating revenue, with the total debt valued at up to 45% of the infrastructure assets to be purchased. Such borrowing must be made through a special purpose company and must procure approval from the investors.

Mutual funds in limited collective investment contracts. There is an alternative form of investment, one that is made privately, rather than traded on the stock exchange, and is supervised by OJK: the limited participation mutual fund (RDPT). This is essentially a basket into which investors put their money to fund a certain company or project indirectly, and which is managed by an investment manager. The target of an RDPT is a company engaged in real-sector projects or businesses (e.g., infrastructure projects).

An RDPT may be in the form of equity securities issued by a nonpublic company, or in the form of debt securities not issued through a public offering. The RDPT portfolio must be used for the real sector. If the investment company makes nonreal-sector investments, it must disburse the funds to real-sector activities. Financial Services Authority Regulation No. 37/POJK.04/2014 on Private Funds does not clearly require a focus on the real sector, but it could be broadly interpreted to include investments in new shares issued by a company, or in the existing shares of shareholders in the infrastructure sector. The procedures for establishing an RDPT are set out in Figure A7.

The initial net asset value of an RDPT amounts to Rp1,000 or, if in foreign currency, $1 or €1. The minimum investment of each RDPT holder is five million units, with an initial total investment of Rp5 billion. In managing a RDPT, the investment manager is restricted to:

- purchasing offshore securities;
- purchasing securities issued by an affiliated party of the investment manager, to another party taking the role due to government capital injections;
- purchasing debt securities or capital securities; and/or
- taking out any types of loans.

Municipal bonds. Regional governments are allowed to issue municipal bonds to finance infrastructure assets or investments that generate revenue, upon consultation with the Ministry of Home Affairs and upon the approval of the Ministry of Finance. The local government may obtain *pinjaman daerah* (regional loans) as an alternative to financing in cases of: (i) local budget deficiency, (ii) expenses, and/or (iii) cash flow deficiency. Sources of regional loans may vary; for instance, they may originate from the issuance of *obligasi daerah* (local bonds) through the domestic capital market and in Indonesian rupiah. The issuance of bonds by local governments is limited to the investment activities related to public services that might generate local revenue, subject to the latest local financial audit. Only local governments with *wajar dengan pengecualian* (qualified) or *wajar tanpa pengecualian* (unqualified) opinions regarding the prior financial year may issue local bonds (Minister of Finance Regulation. No. 111/PMK.07/2012 on Procedures for the Issuance and Accountability of Municipal Bonds, as amended by Minister of Finance Regulation No. 180/PMK.07/2015).

In general, local governments are prohibited from providing locally owned assets as security. However, there is an exemption from these restrictions specifically for regional bonds, as local governments may provide the project and the locally owned assets related thereto as security. All risks associated with the issuance of local bonds are borne by the local government, as the national government is prohibited from acting as a guarantor for local bonds.

Figure A7: Procedures for Establishing a Limited Participation Mutual Fund

Participation by Investors Investors are offered an RDPT unit.

Due Diligence Due diligence is done on the companies and real-sector industries to be targeted by the RDPT.

Collective Investment Contract This contract is a notarial deed between the investment manager and custodian bank.

Registration The investment manager submits the registration application to OJK, along with the executed collective investment contract and other supporting documents.

Investment The RDPT invests in the target companies and real-sector industries.

OJK = Financial Services Authority, RDPT = limited participation mutual fund.
Source: Authors.

Please note that local governments must satisfy certain requirements before obtaining local loans, among others (Government Regulation No. 30 of 2011 on Regional Loans, Art. 15.1):

- the total existing local loans plus the total proposed drawdown not exceeding 75% of the total local revenue during the previous financial year;
- the debt service coverage ratio (DSCR) of 2.5 times; and
- other requirements, as may be required by the financier(s).

In addition to the above, the local government must submit a plan for the issuance of local bonds to the Ministry of Finance and the local parliamentary house for their approval. The approval of the local parliamentary house must be obtained first, as its approval in principle is a prerequisite for obtaining the approval of the Ministry of Finance. The issuance of local bonds must be stipulated through local regulation, and the repayment of bonds, including the principal and interest, must be stipulated in the annual local budget until the bonds have been fully repaid.

The issuance of local bonds is set out under a trustee agreement executed by the governor, regent, or mayor and a trustee representing the bondholder. A trustee agreement must contain the following information:

- nominal value,
- due date,
- interest payment date,
- interest rate (coupon),
- interest payment frequency,
- the method of interest-payment calculation,
- provisions on the right to repurchase local bonds, and
- provisions regarding the transfer of ownership.

Asset collateral. Regionally owned assets may not be used as collateral (Law No. 23 of 2014 on Regional Government, Art. 307 [4]), with the exception of projects or assets financed and/or purchased through the issuance of municipal bonds (Law No. 33 of 2004 on Fiscal Balance between the Central and Regional Governments, Art. 55 [3]). Regions are also not allowed to guarantee or agree to their assets being encumbered as security for third parties' indebtedness, including the indebtedness of SOEs and ROEs.

In infrastructure development, the underlying assets are typically owned by the national government or regional government. The regional government will typically own the underlying land and immovable infrastructure assets. Where bonds are to be issued by SOEs or SPCs, the underlying land or immovable assets are typically injected as an in-kind equity contribution by the regional government to the relevant bond issuer, to allow the issuer to encumber the infrastructure assets. Project revenue could also be secured by an SOE or ROE.

Alternatively, the issuer may procure contractual rights to utilize the assets under the lease, borrow-use, BOT/BTO, optimization cooperation, or cooperation for infrastructure provision/KSPI schemes. In such cases, the issuer will procure usage rights (but no ownership title) to the infrastructure assets during the given period. However, this is arguably less favorable than the HGB title. The issuer is also subject to certain restrictions and limitations, such as the obligation to pay rent or share revenue and limitations on the transfer of rights. There is also some uncertainty as to whether or not these contractual rights may be assigned for security purposes; a further review is required.

Industrial estates. Industrial estates provide fiscal incentives and work to boost efficiency as part of the national government's effort to accelerate economic development. Government Regulation No. 142 of 2015 on Industrial Estates holds that the development of industrial estates must be done by an Indonesian legal entity in the form of SOEs or locally owned enterprises, cooperation between enterprises, or a limited liability company. In order to open in an industrial estate, a company must hold an Industrial Estate Business Permit (IUKI), as required by the national, provincial, regional, regency, and municipal spatial planning agencies. Further, a company located in an industrial estate must provide a minimum amount of infrastructure there, as follows:

- raw water installation system,
- wastewater installation system,
- drainage system,
- street lighting installation, and
- roads.

An IUKI holder is entitled to obtain an HGB title to the land that is slated for development. The land covered by the permit may be divided by the IUKI holder into numerous plots. A *hak pengelolaan* (right-to-manage) title may be granted if the IUKI holder is either an SOE or a locally owned enterprise.

An industrial estate company and an industrial enterprise seeking to locate in the estate are both entitled to local incentives. Article 43 paragraph (1) of GR 142/2015 specifies the incentives that may be provided to them, for instance: a reduction of, or relief or exemption from, local taxes and/or local *retribusi*—such as the duty on the acquisition of land and building rights (BPHTB), the original *pajak bumi dan bangunan* (property tax), and the *pajak penerangan jalan* (street lighting tax) for roads within industrial estates—as well as other permissible incentives under

the prevailing laws and regulations. Set out below are the applicable tax facilities based on the classification of an industrial estate as an "industrial development area."

- Advanced Industrial Development Area,
- Developing Industrial Development Area,
- Potential Industrial Development Area I, and
- Potential Industrial Development Area II.

Industrial estate companies must have a set of industrial estate regulations that, at the very least, includes the following:

- rights and obligations of the industrial estate company and industrial enterprise,
- a provision on the management and monitoring of the environment,
- related prevailing laws and regulations, and
- other provisions as further determined by the industrial estate company.

In addition to the above, the right to land utilization by an industrial enterprise is set out under written agreements that must include: (i) the duration of land utilization; (ii) the land utilization fee; and (iii) any other relevant provisions as may be agreed upon between the industrial estate company and the industrial enterprise seeking to move to the estate (GR 142/2015, Art. 49).

Table A7.3: Applicable Tax Facilities Based on the Classifications of Industrial Development Areas				
Tax and Customs Facility	WPIM	WPIB	WPIP I	WPIP II
CIT reduction of 10%–100% for 5–15 years from the start of commercial production	√	x	x	√
Income tax facilities similar to tax allowance under income tax concessions	√	√	√	x
VAT exemption on imports and purchases of machines and equipment (excluding spare parts) directly used to produce VAT-eligible goods	√	√	√	√
Import duty exemption on imports of machines or materials that are used to produce goods and/or services	√	√	√	√

CIT = corporate income tax, VAT = value-added tax, WPIB = Developing Industrial Development Area, WPIM = Advanced Industrial Development Area, WPIP I = Potential Industrial Development Area I, WPIP II = Potential Industrial Development Area II.
Note: √ = yes, x = no.
Source: Authors.

Glossary

Value capture principles and tools have been well studied and documented in several publications and case studies. This glossary contains useful terms from various sources to help readers understand the framework set out in this report, and to enrich their understanding of value creation and value capture.

The main external sources for these definitions are:
- ADB. 2017. *Guidelines for the Economic Analysis of Projects*. Manila.
- APMG International. Glossary. https://ppp-certification.com/ppp-certification-guide/glossary.
- R. Amirtahmasebi, M. Orloff, S. Wahba, and A. Altman. 2016. *Regenerating Urban Land: A Practitioner's Guide to Leveraging Private Investment*. Washington, DC: World Bank.
- S. Salat and G. Ollivier. 2017. *Transforming the Urban Space through Transit-Oriented Development: The 3V Approach*. Washington, DC: World Bank.

Agglomeration economies	Benefits from the concentration of economic activity
Affordability	The ability of a project to be realistically accommodated within the periodic budget constraints of the government.
Betterment levy	A form of tax or a fee levied on land that has gained in value because of public infrastructure investment. It tries to capture part of the infrastructure investment already made by the government.
Business case	A document that articulates the rationale for undertaking an investment.
Cadastral map	A map that shows the boundaries and ownership of land parcels.
Capital expenditure (CAPEX)	The initial construction costs of the infrastructure plus any expenditure on the constructed assets that is not an operating expense.
Capital markets	Markets concerned with raising capital by buying and selling debt and equity, and by dealing in shares, bonds, and other long-term investments.
Central business district (CBD)	An area where a city's major businesses (financial institutions, stores, convention and sport facilities, hotels, etc.) are concentrated. These areas produce agglomeration economies.
Compact city	An urban planning and urban design concept that promotes cities with short travel distances within them. Compact cities are usually based on high-density residential areas; mixed land use; an efficient public transit system; and a layout that encourages walking and cycling, low energy consumption, and reduced pollution. A compact city provides opportunities for social interaction, as well as a feeling of safety. It is more sustainable than urban sprawl because it is less dependent on cars and requires lower (and cheaper per capita) infrastructure provision.

Concession A grant of economic rights to a public asset in an administrative law jurisdiction to a private party by the government, including the legal title to the land. It may also refer to a public–private partnership (PPP) contract, though these are generally contracts under which most of the revenue will come from the users.

Cost–benefit analysis (CBA) A type of economic analysis that compares estimated economic costs and benefits associated with an investment project. It is primarily used to assess the economic viability of a project. An economically viable project generates an economic surplus above its opportunity cost.

Developer exaction A mechanism whereby the government obliges the developer either to build infrastructure or pay for public investment in infrastructure.

Development charges In exchange for development rights (or tenure rights over land, or rights of approval of land use changes), a developer's obligation to compensate in cash (or provide in-kind) the cost of certain items of public infrastructure benefiting a larger area.

Development rights transfer A developer's ability to buy and sell air rights—within the limits of the floor area ratio (FAR) allotment or the unused development rights that remain when a building does not use up its FAR allotment. Typically, these apply only to certain land parcels, and often can only be transferred to specific "receiving" parcels.

Economic uplift Externality effects, also sometimes referred to as "spillover effects," "network effects" and/or "indirect effects." They are defined as socioeconomic benefits that accrue outside the specific target area of the infrastructure activity and its direct service provision, due to the creation of a network of physical assets, functions, and stakeholders.

Economic infrastructure Infrastructure that makes business activity possible, such as communications and transportation infrastructure, as well as power, water, and sanitation.

Employment density Number of jobs in a geographic area.

Floor area ratio (FAR) Ratio of a building's total floor area to the size of the plot of land on which it is built: the higher the FAR, the higher the density. It is also referred to as the "floor space ratio" (FSR) or "floor space index" (FSI).

Financing	The source of money required up front to meet the costs of building infrastructure. Financing is typically sourced by the government through surpluses or borrowing (traditional infrastructure procurement), or by the private sector through debt or equity finance.
Funding	The money required to meet payment obligations. In a PPP context, the term refers to money sourced over the long term to pay the PPP private partner for the investments and the operating and maintenance costs of the project. Funding is typically sourced from taxes (in government-pays PPPs) or from user charges (in user-pays PPPs).
Gentrification	The transformation of a neighborhood due to an influx of affluent residents and businesses. Gentrification does not always result in worse outcomes for the original dwellers in terms of affordable housing, accessibility and mobility, but in a cultural sense, gentrification can erode the social fabric (Capps 2019).
Hypothecation of tax	Earmarking of tax revenue for a specific purpose.
Impact fee	A one-time, up-front fee charged as a precondition for public approval to develop land, levied by governments to cover the cost of the additional public infrastructure and services when the new development leads to increased demand for expansion in infrastructure capacity (such as for roads, water supplies, and public spaces).
Infrastructure	The basic physical and organizational structures and facilities, such as buildings, roads, and power supplies, needed for the operation of a society or enterprise.
Intensification area	Built-up area with good existing or potential public transit links that can support redevelopment at higher than existing densities.
Land administration and management	Land administration: the way in which the rules of land tenure are applied and operationalized; land management: the way in which the use and development of land resources is managed.
Land pooling or readjustment	A process in which landowners or occupants voluntarily contribute part of their land for infrastructure development or offer it for sale. In return, each landowner receives a serviced plot that is smaller, but with a higher value within the same neighborhood.
Land value capture (LVC)	A promising community infrastructure financing method that recovers part or all of the value (e.g., increases in land prices) generated by developing and/or upgrading neighboring public infrastructure or, more generally, public goods and services. It is based on a common perception

or general recognition that infrastructure, especially transport and public-amenity infrastructure, creates economic benefits that exceed the costs of their development (i.e., positive economic externalities), and that the beneficiaries (usually landowners, householders, or developers) would be willing to pay a premium for well-serviced commercial and residential properties, as well as some of the costs of implementing such infrastructure or offsetting any negative impacts.

Leveraging public real assets

Disposition (sale or lease) of excess or underutilized public assets (land, property) for cash to be reinvested in local infrastructure.

Mixed-use development

Pattern of development characterized by diversified land use, typically including housing, retail premises, and private businesses, either within the same building space (vertical mixing) or in close proximity (horizontal mixing).

Operational expenditure (OPEX)

The costs of operating infrastructure assets after construction delivery.

Population density

Number of people living in an urban area, divided by the land area.

Place value

Determinants of the attractiveness of a place, including the amenities; schools; health-care facilities; types of urban development; accessibility of local amenities by walking and cycling; quality of the urban fabric around the station, in particular its pedestrian accessibility; the small size of urban blocks and fine mesh of connected streets, which create vibrant neighborhoods; and the mixed patterns of land use. Place value is measured based on a composite index.

Public commons (or "public realm")

Publicly owned streets, pathways, rights-of-way, parks, publicly accessible open spaces, and any public and civic buildings and facilities.

Public–private partnership (PPP)

Formal partnership between a public sector entity and a private firm, often used to construct and operate infrastructure facilities or to develop certain urban areas.

Redevelopment (or regeneration)

Type of development that seeks to reinvest in already developed areas, typically targeting parcels that are underutilized, such as vacant or abandoned properties.

Retribution

A term that is used conventionally by Indonesian English speakers to refer to local government charges or fees, not always related to a "punishment" or disincentive.

Risk	An uncertain event that may cause the actual project outcomes to differ from the expected outcomes.
Risk assessment	The evaluation of the likelihood of the identified risks materializing, and the magnitude of their consequences if they do materialize.
Social infrastructure	Infrastructure that accommodates social services: hospitals, schools and universities, prisons, housing, courts, and so on.
Tax increment financing (TIF)	A financing approach that allows local governments to invest in public infrastructure and other improvements up front, and to pay for those investments by capturing the future anticipated increase in tax revenue generated by the project. TIF is possible when a new development is of a sufficiently large scale, and when its completion is expected to result in a sufficient increase in the value of the surrounding real estate, such that the resulting increases in local tax revenue could support a bond issuance.
Transit-oriented development (TOD)	Planning and design strategy to ensure compact, mixed-use, pedestrian- and bicycle-friendly, and suitably dense urban development, organized around transit stations. TOD embraces the idea that locating amenities, jobs, shops, and housing around transit hubs promotes transit use and nonmotorized travel.
Urban sprawl	The unrestricted expansion of existing cities, often characterized by low-density residential housing, single-use zoning, and increased reliance on private automobiles for transportation. Urban sprawl creates new demand for infrastructure, which is often costly to build and maintain.
User charges	Payments made by users of the infrastructure, such as road tolls.
Value capture	A policy-based approach that enables communities to recover and reinvest land-based value increases and increases in economic productivity that result from public investment and other government actions. Also known as "value sharing," it is rooted in the notion that public action should generate public benefits.
Value sharing	See "Value capture."
Zoning	The division of land into zones within which certain uses are permitted. Zoning aims to promote orderly development and to separate incompatible land uses, such as industrial and residential, to ensure a more pleasant environment.

References

ADB. 2017a. *Guidelines for the Economic Analysis of Projects*. Manila.

———. 2017b. *Meeting Asia's Infrastructure Needs*. Manila.

———. 2019a. *Asian Development Outlook 2019 Update: Fostering Growth and Inclusion in Asia's Cities*. Manila

———. 2019b. *Sustaining Transit Investment in Asia's Cities: A Beneficiary-Funding and Land Value Capture Perspective*. Manila.

Buck, Martin. 2017. Crossrail Project: Finance, Funding and Value Capture for London's Elizabeth Line. *Proceedings of the Institution of Civil Engineers* 170 (CE6): 15–22.

Buensuceso, Haraya and Cesar Purisima. 2018. *Funding Transport Infrastructure Development in the Philippines: A Roadmap Toward Land Value Capture*. Santa Monica, CA: Milken Institute.

C40 Cities. 2014. Super Blocks: Small-Scale Solutions to City Challenges. 19 September.

Capps, Kriston. 2019. The Hidden Winners in Neighborhood Gentrification. *Citylab*. 17 July.

Centre for Liveable Cities (CLC). 2016. *Urban Redevelopment: From Urban Squalor to Global City*. Singapore: CLC.

———. 2018. *Land Framework of Singapore: Building a Sound Land Administration and Management System*. Singapore: CLC.

Clarke, Edward, Nada Nohrová, and Elli Thomas. 2014. Milton Keynes Tariff: Funding Infrastructure Upfront. *Centre for Cities*. 31 October.

Germán, Lourdes and Allison Ehrich Bernstein. 2020. *Land Value Return: Tools to Finance our Urban Future*. Policy Brief. Cambridge, MA: Lincoln Institute of Land Policy.

Government of Australia, Department of Infrastructure, Transport, Regional Development and Communications. Australian Government Response to the House of Representatives Standing Committee on Infrastructure, Transport and Cities: Harnessing Value, Delivering Infrastructure.

Government of Indonesia, Ministry of National Development Planning/National Development Planning Agency (BAPPENAS). 2019. "Technocratic Design Draft RPJMN 2020–2024: Energy and Electricity Sector." Presentation prepared for a meeting at the Directorate of Energy, Telecommunications and Informatics. Jakarta. 17 October.

Government of the Philippines, Bases Conversion and Development Authority. https://www.bcda.gov.ph/.

Government of the Philippines, Philippine News Agency. 2019. PCC Approves New Clark City Power Distribution Deal. 3 July.

Government of the State of Victoria, Australia. 2017. *Victoria's Value Creation and Capture Framework: Maximising Social, Economic and Environmental Value from Infrastructure Investment*. Melbourne: Government of the State of Victoria.

Hong, Yu-Hung and Barrie Needham, eds. 2007. *Analyzing Land Adjustment: Economics, Law, and Collective Action*. Cambridge, MA: Lincoln Institute of Land Policy.

Institute for Government. 2018. Funding Infrastructure. 22 November.

Ochoa, Oscar Borrero. 2011. Betterment Levy in Colombia: Relevance, Procedures, and Social Acceptability. *Land Lines*. 14–19 April.

Peterson, George E., 2009. Unlocking Land Values to Finance Urban Infrastructure. *Trends and Policy Options* No. 7. Washington, DC: World Bank.

PricewaterhouseCoopers (PwC) Australia. Investing in the Future: Using Value Creation and Value Capture to Fund the Infrastructure Our Cities Need. https://www.pwc.com.au/infrastructure/investing-future.html.

RAC Foundation. 2018. Council Parking Revenue in England 2017–2018. https://www.racfoundation.org/research/mobility/council-parking-revenue-in-england-2017-18.

Salat, Serge and Gerald Ollivier. 2017. *Transforming the Urban Space through Transit-Oriented Development: The 3V Approach*. Washington, DC: World Bank.

SASEC: South Asia Subregional Economic Cooperation. Economic Corridor Development. https://www.sasec.asia/index.php?page=economic-corridors in.

Singapore Land Authority. https://www1.sla.gov.sg/property-boundary-n-ownership/property-boundaries/survey-maps-and-plans.

Singapore Land Authority, Integrated Land Information Service. https://www.sla.gov.sg/inlis/.

UN ESCAP. 2014. *Regional Connectivity for Shared Prosperity*. Bangkok.

_____ 2019. Infrastructure Financing for Sustainable Development in Asia and the Pacific. *ESCAP Financing for Development Series* No. 3. Bangkok: United Nations.

Urban Land Institute. 2019. *Value Capture Finance*. London.

Urban Redevelopment Authority. Concept Plan 2011 and MND Land Use Plan. https://www.ura.gov.sg/Corporate/Planning/Concept-Plan/Land-Use-Plan.

Winarso, Haryo. 2016. "Pro-Poor Land and Housing Development." Lecture given at the Institut Teknologi Bandung, Bandung, Indonesia, 30 September.

World Bank. 2017. Case Study: Hong Kong Mass Transit Rail Corporation. In *Railway Reform: Toolkit for Improving Rail Sector Performance*, 415–25. 2nd ed. Washington, DC: World Bank.

World Bank. Decision Tool Kit for City Planners. Urban Regeneration. https://urban-regeneration.worldbank.org/.

World Bank, City Resilience Program. n.d. *Land Value Capture: Investment in Infrastructure*. Washington, DC: World Bank.

Yoshino, Naoyuki. 2019. "Sustainable Development in Asia." Presentation prepared for a meeting at the Asian Development Bank Institute. Tokyo. May.

Yoshino, Naoyuki, Matthias Helble, and Umid Abidhadjaev, eds. 2018. *Financing Infrastructure in Asia and the Pacific: Capturing Impacts and New Sources*. Tokyo: Asian Development Bank Institute.

Yoshino, Naoyuki, Masaki Nakahigashi, and Victor Pontines. 2017. Attract Private Financing to Infrastructure Investment by Injection of Spillover Tax Revenues. *Nomura Journal of Asian Capital Markets* 1(2): 4–9.

Yoshino, Naoyuki and Victor Pontines. 2015. The "Highway Effect" on Public Finance: Case of the STAR Highway in the Philippines. *ADBI Working Paper Series* No. 549. Tokyo: Asian Development Bank Institute.

www.ingramcontent.com/pod-product-compliance
Lightning Source LLC
Chambersburg PA
CBHW050044220326
41599CB00045B/7273